BIBLICAL THEOLOGY
in the
LIFE OF THE EARLY CHURCH

BIBLICAL THEOLOGY
in the
LIFE OF THE EARLY CHURCH

RECOVERING AN ANCIENT VISION

STEPHEN O. PRESLEY

© 2025 by Stephen O. Presley

Published by Baker Academic
a division of Baker Publishing Group
Grand Rapids, Michigan
BakerAcademic.com

Printed in the United States of America

All rights reserved. No part of this publication may be reproduced, stored in a retrieval system, or transmitted in any form or by any means—for example, electronic, photocopy, recording—without the prior written permission of the publisher. The only exception is brief quotations in printed reviews.

Library of Congress Cataloging-in-Publication Data

Names: Presley, Stephen O., author.
Title: Biblical theology in the life of the early church : recovering an ancient vision / Stephen O. Presley.
Description: Grand Rapids, Michigan : Baker Academic, a division of Baker Publishing Group, [2025] | Includes bibliographical references and index.
Identifiers: LCCN 2024038996 | ISBN 9781540966414 (paperback) | ISBN 9781540968371 (casebound) | ISBN 9781493447756 (ebook) | ISBN 9781493447763 (pdf)
Subjects: LCSH: Bible—Theology. | Bible—Criticism, interpretation, etc.—History—Early church, ca. 30–600. | Church history—Primitive and early church, ca. 30–600.
Classification: LCC BS543 .P74 2025 | DDC 230/.04109015—dc23/eng/20240928
LC record available at https://lccn.loc.gov/2024038996

Unless otherwise indicated, Scripture quotations are from The Holy Bible, English Standard Version® (ESV®), copyright © 2001 by Crossway, a publishing ministry of Good News Publishers. Used by permission. All rights reserved. ESV Text Edition: 2016.

Cover design by Peter Gloege
Cover art: *Adoration of the Magi* by Jean-Hippolyte Flandrin, Alamy

Baker Publishing Group publications use paper produced from sustainable forestry practices and postconsumer waste whenever possible.

25 26 27 28 29 30 31   7 6 5 4 3 2 1

To my love, Haley,
who is walking this journey with me

CONTENTS

Preface   ix

Introduction   1

1 ◆ Ecclesial Biblical Theology   15

2 ◆ Signs of God   35

3 ◆ Narratives of Scripture   65

4 ◆ Christ in All Things   93

5 ◆ The Good Life   121

6 ◆ The Community of Faith   147

Conclusion   169

Abbreviations   177
Bibliography   179
Index of Authors   191
*Index of Scripture and Other Ancient
    Writings*   193
Index of Subjects   199

PREFACE

Last year I published a book on cultural engagement in the early church entitled *Cultural Sanctification: Engaging the World like the Early Church*. That book examined the similarities between ancient paganism and the secularizing world today. What we are experiencing, I argued, is a new form of "modern paganism," to borrow the description of T. S. Eliot. I explained how the early church fathers engaged the pagan world and considered how their cultural engagement could encourage us as we journey down similar roads. I termed their approach "cultural sanctification": a way of life that did not retreat or encourage a combative posture but walked the line between an indigenizing principle and pilgrim principle. The early Christians were embedded in the world and sought to live faithfully in it, while at the same time always reminding themselves that they were pilgrims living in hope of the full realization of the kingdom of God.

After finishing that book, I recognized that there were some fundamental assumptions guiding their spiritual lives. For the early Christians, the spiritual life was not just a matter of practical application. Cultural engagement was not a program that needed to be implemented; it demanded an entirely different view of reality. This book explores that view of reality, or what Charles Taylor calls a "social imaginary"—that is, the way ordinary people perceive the social world. I try to get underneath the hood, as the saying goes, of their spiritual lives and examine the fundamental assumptions—assumptions derived from the revelation of Scripture—that informed all aspects of their social imaginary.

This book, then, is necessary prereading for *Cultural Sanctification*. Before we can talk about how to live Christianly in this world, we should take a step back and see the world through a scriptural vision. That vision, which

I term an "ecclesial biblical theology," recenters biblical interpretation in the church. This book also, like *Cultural Sanctification*, attempts a *ressourcement*, recovering the best of the Christian tradition to help the church navigate the world we inhabit—a world, I will add, that increasingly looks like the world of the early church.

I have been interested in the recent developments in biblical theology and biblical studies for many years. These disciplines naturally influence the way pastors and Christian leaders read and interpret Scripture. For far too long a Christian way of reading exemplified in the fathers has been maligned in our cultural institutions and slowly sidelined in preference for the critical assumptions of modern hermeneutics. In recent days, these trends continue to evolve as hermeneutics becomes more complex and diversified in a postmodern world. At the same time the church in the West is hemorrhaging members, and along with it many Christian institutions of higher education, seminaries, and other religious organizations or parachurch ministries.

As the people of God experience these cultural changes, we do not need to fret or fear. We need to return to the hallowed halls of the church and focus on discipleship and a theological vision that shapes our own social imaginary. I believe that recovering a truly Christian way of reading Scripture can help us navigate this pagan world. The early church fathers embody this, and I hope that we can too.

The path toward writing this book was not a solitary journey; many people helped shape the contents and my thinking. First, I want to thank Anna Gissing. I have been discussing this project with her for many years, and I am indebted to her patience, encouragement, and wisdom through the writing process. I also want to thank James Korsmo, as well as many others on the Baker Academic editorial team, who helped guide this book through the editing process. The project is better because of their diligent work.

I also want to thank the leadership at First Liberty Institute, who have given me the opportunity to research, write, and teach on issues at the intersection of religion and culture. Through the vision of my good friend Trey Dimsdale, First Liberty launched an educational think tank called the Center for Religion, Culture, and Democracy (CRCD), and I am grateful to be part of this important work. We live in contentious days, when the Christian faith is increasingly viewed with suspicion, if not outright derision. First Liberty and CRCD are helping preserve the cultural space for religious people and people of goodwill to live out their religious convictions. My regular conversations with CRCD staff, including Trey, Jillian Barr, Jordan Ballor, and Drew McGinnis, always challenged me to think through the important implications of this work for the local church.

What I argue in this book is the culmination of researching, writing, and teaching patristics for close to two decades. My mentor and friend Jeff Bingham inspired my love for the fathers many years ago in several church history classes at Dallas Theological Seminary. He has similarly inspired a generation of evangelical patristic scholars, and I am grateful to be counted among them. Alongside a love for the early church, my doctoral supervisor at the University of St. Andrews, Mark Elliott, taught me to love biblical theology. It was at St. Andrews that I began to appreciate the contributions that biblical theology and the theological interpretation of Scripture have made to biblical studies.

I also want to thank the administration, faculty, and students at The Southern Baptist Theological Seminary. I have discussed the ideas of this book with numerous students and colleagues, especially John Wilsey, who has entertained these ideas over too many cups of coffee. I also have some of the best and brightest doctoral students at Southern Seminary. We have discussed and debated these topics in seminars, on Zoom, and over good meals. Many of them are actively researching and writing on the topics I discuss here, and, in countless ways, they helped me refine the contents of this book.

Finally, I want to thank my family: my wife, Haley, and my four kids, Isla, Emma, Luke, and Andrew. They are my greatest source of joy and encouragement, and in them I experience the blessings the Lord promises in Psalm 128.

INTRODUCTION

Walking into the Church of Saint-Germain-des-Prés, I discovered a living biblical theology. I was in Paris for the summer, studying French as part of my postgraduate program. On one sunny afternoon, while walking back to my flat, I took a detour and stumbled upon a stunning church nestled on a picturesque city square. Out of curiosity, I stepped inside. The sanctuary was generously sized, filled with a modest number of worshipers and tourists.

The church was long and narrow with stately columns on both sides, bracing the colorful nave walls that rose upward, blending into intricate vaulted ceilings. I could see the transept crossing the church and the choir and central chapel in the distance in front of me. I walked slowly through the nave, soaking in the architectural beauty. The church contained a variety of ecclesial ornamentation—altars, chapels, chairs, lecterns, statues, and paintings, all the sights and smells that tickled the senses.

As I was strolling through the church, admiring these features, something gave me pause. Spanning the upper wall of the entire nave, from left to right, was a series of frescoes depicting the story of salvation—a visual illustration of biblical theology. During the French Revolution, this church suffered serious damage, and over the years, several restoration campaigns worked to restore it to its original glory. During one of these campaigns, the artist Hippolyte Flandrin (1809–64) was commissioned to paint this mural. From 1856 to 1861, he worked carefully on each piece, composing twenty-four frescoes framed in twelve diptychs, or pieces of art consisting of two images placed side by side. The first scene in each panel was taken from the life of Christ, and they were all chronologically arranged, beginning with his birth narrative and ending with his ascension. These scenes were coupled with stories from the Old Testament, creating a visual theological connection between them.

Flandrin clearly intended the viewer to interpret these biblical scenes together, visualizing Christ as the fulfillment of God's work in the history of salvation.

I slowly analyzed each image. The first picture on the upper left side depicted the Annunciation, the angelic announcement to Mary that she would give birth to the Christ child. Alongside this image was God's self-revelation to Moses at the burning bush. Just as God revealed to Moses in the burning bush that he would lead the people out of bondage to slavery, so, too, was it revealed to Mary that God incarnate in her womb would lead the people out of bondage to sin. Christ is the greater Moses, in whom the words of the prophet are fulfilled: "Out of Egypt I called my son" (Hosea 11:1; Matt. 2:15; cf. Acts 3:22–23).

Similar parallels between Christ and the Old Testament continued in each panel. Christ's birth was laid alongside the fall of Adam and Eve. Christ is the second Adam, the one through whom comes life and righteousness (Rom. 5:12–17). The scene of the magi adoring the Christ child was positioned next to an image of the prophet Balaam, whose predicted star led the magi to the child (Num. 24:17; Matt. 2:1–2), suggesting, among other things, that gentiles would be included in salvation. The baptism of Jesus was likened to Israel's passage through the Red Sea. In the same way that the people of God were baptized into Moses, so, too, are they baptized into Christ and thus salvation (1 Cor. 10:1–2; Gal. 3:26–27). Finally, Jesus at the Last Supper was paired with Melchizedek offering bread and wine to Abraham, indicating that the gift of salvation comes only through Christ offering up his body and blood—signified by bread and wine in both Old and New Testament accounts (Gen. 14:18; Luke 22:19–20).

Then I turned to the right side of the nave for the rest of the story. A second set of six diptychs continued coordinating the life of Christ with the Old Testament. Judas's betrayal (Matt. 26:47–50) was set alongside the account of Joseph, who was sold by his brothers (Gen. 37:23–28). Jesus, just like Joseph, was betrayed by those closest to him. After this, the crucifixion of Christ was portrayed with the sacrifice of Isaac (Heb. 11:17–19), followed by Christ's resurrection coupled with Jonah emerging from the water (Matt. 12:38–41). Finally, the second-to-last panel compared Christ's commissioning of the apostles with the dispersion of the people of Babel (Gen. 11:1–8; Matt. 28:18–20), and the last panel united Christ's ascension with Elijah's translation into glory (2 Kings 2:11; Luke 24:51).

The theological sophistication of these intertextual linkages captivated me for some time. I sat in quiet contemplation, beholding the cosmic drama of salvation wrought in Christ. The colors, figures, postures, facial expressions—the whole environment of each image—visually depicted the beauty of biblical

Introduction

theology. Each moment of Christ's life revealed how the whole story of salvation, the whole story of human history, centers on him. He is truly "before all things, and in him all things hold together" (Col. 1:17).

In that moment of wonder and adoration, I found myself worshiping God, which reminded me that the drama continues even now in the church. The words of Hebrews 11:39–40 came to mind: "All these, though commended through their faith, did not receive what was promised," the author writes, "since God had provided something better for us, that apart from us they should not be made perfect." The author of Hebrews draws the reader, the church, into the drama of salvation. We find ourselves among a great cloud of witnesses who have gone before us participating in the narrative of salvation.

There, in the Church of Saint-Germain-des-Prés, I remembered that I am living this narrative too; the story continues even today as the people of God wait for Christ to return in glory to judge the living and the dead and establish a kingdom that has no end. In that quiet moment I worshiped God, celebrated the glorious work of Christ, and thanked God that I was found within his story.

But these images were not the only features of the church that caught my attention. After an extended reflection on the biblical narrative, I continued strolling around the sanctuary to see what other treasures the church contained. I meandered through the tourists toward the front, nearing the central chapel, and I noticed something out of place—a different kind of image from those I had just observed.

In a dimly lit side chapel, I found myself standing before a dark plaque bearing the name René Descartes (1596–1650), the father of modern philosophy. Descartes died in Sweden and was initially interred at St. Olof's Chapel for several years. French officials eventually brought his remains back and buried him in the Church of Saint-Germain-des-Prés.

The contrast between the frescoes and this grave was not lost on me. Descartes stands at the fountainhead of a philosophical tradition that began slowly undermining religious faith, which led to the collapse of traditional ecclesiastical authority. There, in the shadow of the biblical narrative that proclaims the divine work of salvation for the people of God, lay the philosopher who planted the seeds of an inward turn or an "expressive individualism" that has reshaped the Western world.[1] This church is a living symbol of the struggle facing our world today—the old premodern vision of biblical theology, which

---

1. Quote from Bellah et al., *Habits of the Heart*, 80; see also Taylor, *Sources of the Self*, 143; Trueman, *Rise and Triumph*, 94; Watkin, *Biblical Critical Theory*, 75.

gathers up the individual in a unified drama of salvation, set in sharp relief with Descartes's legacy, which repels this vision.

The discipline of biblical theology in the last three centuries has tried to recover some features of that old-world vision, but now cultural and institutional changes are posing new problems, revealing that the only way forward is a greater appreciation for what lies behind us. If biblical theology is going to offer anything in the coming years, it needs to recapture the ancient vision that I experienced in the nave of Saint-Germain-des-Prés—a vision that conceives culture through the lens of the story of Scripture and the church, a vision that is as old as the church itself.

The theologians of the early church understood that the Scriptures provide the best framework for understanding reality. If we can recapture this vision, and tether biblical theology to the life of the ancient Christian community, we can emerge out of the tragic world of Descartes's modernity and reacclimate ourselves to the true world where God reigns and the church lives the story of salvation.

The End of Biblical Theology?

The tension between the frescoes and Descartes's grave in Saint-Germain-des-Prés helps us visualize why biblical theology is at an impasse. Johann Philipp Gabler (1753–1826) famously conceived of biblical theology as a discipline distinct from dogmatic theology, and ever since, the discipline has struggled to find a sense of identity.[2] Scholars and pastors often talk about biblical theology, call themselves biblical theologians, and hope that their theology is biblical. But what is biblical theology?

Most who use the term today intend to say something meaningful about the unity of Scripture. Brevard Childs, a lion in the field, argues that biblical theology is "theological reflection on both the Old and New Testament," assuming that "the Christian Bible consists of a theological unity formed by the canonical union of the two testaments."[3] The canon is the field on which biblical theology plays, always aiming for some kind of unified reading. Old Testament scholar Craig Bartholomew agrees. Biblical theology is an attempt to discern "the inner unity of the Bible."[4] Finally, Hans Frei, prominent theologian of the Yale school, explains that biblical theologians

2. Gabler, "Oration on the Proper Distinction."
3. Childs, *Biblical Theology*, 55. His brief discussion of the history of biblical theology as a discipline also helps situate this conversation. Childs, *Biblical Theology*, 3–9.
4. Bartholomew, "Biblical Theology," 86.

Introduction 5

have worked against the grain of critical biblical scholarship in hopes "to establish the unity of religious meaning across the gap of historical and cultural differences."[5]

Despite this attempt to say something meaningful about the unity of Scripture, the term *biblical theology* (or its modern cousin, *theological interpretation of Scripture*) can mean many different things. In their book, *Understanding Biblical Theology*, Edward Klink and Darian Lockett provide a taxonomy that situates the current conversation. They identify no less than five rival versions: "Historical Description," "History of Redemption," "Worldview-Story," "Canonical Approach," and "Theological Construction."[6] These types are staged among a historical-theological spectrum, with history on one end and theology on the other. The initial categories tend to view biblical theology as a historical project, a way to recover some feature of the text's history. On the other end, biblical theology is more of a theological enterprise, an attempt to grasp the text's doctrinal message.

Klink and Lockett use a "nexus of issues" to differentiate these categories. Such issues include the knotty problem of linking the Old Testament and the New Testament, Scripture's historical diversity versus its theological unity, the scope and source of any perceived unity, the proper subject matter of biblical theology, and the appropriate setting for biblical theology as a churchly or academic discipline. The way any interpreter answers these questions will position them along the spectrum mentioned above. Take the relationship between the Old and New Testaments. The history side of the spectrum tends to privilege the unique contributions of each testament, book, and section, whereas the theology side tends to be more constructive, observing more continuity. The same kinds of divisions shape how biblical theologians navigate the other issues too.

While scholars disagree about the purposes, methods, and goals of biblical theology, the situation is even more complicated in the broader field of biblical studies. The advent of postmodern readings, advances in our analysis of material culture, and increase in evaluation of social location in readings have all served to produce a wider array of interpretive possibilities. These competing readings, mixed with an assortment of "multiplied methodologies," have concocted a discipline that is "increasingly incoherent."[7] The landscape of biblical studies exhibits "methodological disarray, lack of consensus on key questions, the triviality of a great deal of historical scholarship, and a

5. Frei, *Eclipse of Biblical Narrative*, 8.
6. Klink and Lockett, *Understanding Biblical Theology*, 22–25. See also Bartholomew and Thomas, *Manifesto for Theological Interpretation*.
7. Legaspi, *Death of Scripture*, 6.

problematic relation to the Bible's readership."[8] Today, even the definitions of *history* and *theology* are evolving in our academic climate, while debates about proper methods and procedures continue unabated. The future looks only more diverse, with a wider array of competing methodologies and more conflict between various religious and moral identities. We are standing before a hermeneutical buffet that never ceases to serve up new dishes.

Within this malaise, the methodological diversity in biblical interpretation raises serious questions about the possibility of any unified readings of Scripture. The next step is not to organize more seminars and debate definitions; instead, we need to think about assumptions, to look beneath the diverse methodological symptoms and diagnose the underlying causes. When we do this, when we ask about assumptions, we move the conversation into a different realm, the realm of metaphysics. We are forced to ask not just *How* do I interpret the Bible? but *Why* do I interpret the Bible? When we ask this question, it exposes the simple irony that many biblical scholars do not appreciate what the Bible is for.[9] The Bible might provide some interesting insights about ancient Near Eastern communities or religious life in ancient Rome. It may help reinforce some philosophical or moral agenda or provide self-help wisdom. But the Bible, as the Bible, often performs no normative function for the academic community.

In the church, things are different. The Bible is the center of a worshiping community that gathers around its pages, embraces its contents, and lives its narrative. The church absorbs the theological and moral commitments in Scripture, and then, drawing from the Scriptures, crafts liturgical rhythms that reinforce these assumptions, creating an environment that nurtures good interpretation. In the church, biblical theology is not a discipline but a way of life that reads the Bible as a culture-shaping text. The Bible shapes our vision of life, not the other way around. The earliest Christian communities model this kind of biblical theology. Looking at the way they lived biblical theology, I hope to help reframe the conversation and, at last, return the Scriptures to their rightful place within the community of faith.

For too long, biblical interpretation has been performed by those who theorize about the Scriptures, not those practicing them. The historian Jaroslav Pelikan puts this observation in perspective. "During the years 100 to 600," Pelikan writes, "most theologians were bishops; from 600 to 1500 in the West, they were monks; since 1500, they have been university professors." "Each of these life styles," he continues, "has left its mark on the job description of the

---

8. Legaspi, *Death of Scripture*, 167.
9. Legaspi, *Death of Scripture*, 169.

Introduction

theologian, but also on the way doctrine has continued to develop back and forth between believing, teaching, and confessing."[10] Academics have certainly left their mark on the study of Scripture. The expansion of universities and the proliferation of biblical studies programs relegated the serious, critical study of Scripture to the university. Untethered from the church and without any shared theological and moral commitments, scholars are free to roam, creating meaning as their desires lead them. Without a worshiping community that embraces a way of life, or a rule of faith, the study of the Bible will remain stuck in an endless cycle of legitimization.

To break this cycle, I hope to recover an appreciation for what I call an "ecclesial biblical theology"—a living biblical theology that was practiced in the early church. I argue that the basis for biblical theology is a Christian culture crafted through the Scriptures. Sound biblical interpretation is not about mastering methods but about careful catechesis in the patterns of faith and practice within a Christian community. Getting the setting right is the first step through the haze of competing methodologies and helps set the Christian on the right path, guiding the people of God through the current cultural moment and leading the faithful safely home to the kingdom of God that is to come. Like a good soldier who does not get "entangled in civilian pursuits, since his aim is to please the one who enlisted him" (2 Tim. 2:4), our discussion of biblical theology need not get lost in the discussion of proper procedures without first beckoning Bible readers back to the church to discover a biblical theology that is worthy of God.

The Ecclesial Shaping of Biblical Theology

What I propose now is the recovery of premodern interpretation in ways that revive and revitalize the ecclesial shaping of biblical theology. Hermeneutics is not really about procedures anyway but rather is about essential questions of reality. The modern world has been furiously trying to untie the Gordian knot of methodology, without concern for the metaphysical assumptions that various methodologies harbor. But now, biblical interpretation must learn to think holistically, to walk outside the room and see how the whole project of biblical theology participates in a Christian culture.

Our dialogue partner for this journey is the early Christian community that models an ecclesial biblical theology. I recognize that the church fathers do not use the term *biblical theology*, but they do say meaningful things about the unity of Scripture. I continue to use the term to capture how their reading

10. Pelikan, *Emergence of the Catholic Tradition*, 5.

of Scripture unifies their ecclesial culture, and I bring their voice to bear on the current conversation. The fathers show us that the unity of Scripture makes sense only to those who participate in it. Ancient Christians do not merely theorize; they practice their biblical theology. They read Scripture as a sacramental guide on the journey of salvation.[11] The Scriptures guide their attunements and perceptions, refracting all things through the telos of the storyline of Scripture, demonstrating "the inseparability of theology, exegesis of Scripture and spirituality, an integration by no means apparent in the modern world."[12] Their liturgies, readings, postures, and prayers are filtered through the Scriptures, creating patterns of life from the culture-forming nature of the church's biblical interpretation.

Understanding how the fathers approach Scripture is like entering a different world. The early church works with a different view of reality, or what philosopher Charles Taylor has called a "social imaginary," which explains the ways people "imagine their social existence."[13] As we will see, the early church was born into a world that did not share its first principles. They had to learn—and learn quickly—how to live their faith and reimagine their social existence in light of it.

By way of illustration, my first teaching position was in a seminary degree program in a Texas prison. I was slated to teach a regular diet of Bible courses covering both the Old and New Testaments. Entering the world of incarceration was like stepping into a foreign land, with its own governance, bartering system, and natural hierarchies. As I began teaching, I realized quickly that all my lectures and illustrations were framed for people living in the "free world," a world these offenders left far behind. By contrast, they were embedded in a different world with its own mores and patterns. I knew that if I was going to connect with them, I needed to see things from their vantage point. So I sat down with one of them and asked him to walk me through their daily lives. For a long time, he explained the process of arrest and conviction, followed by sentencing and the slow, steady acclimation to prison life. We discussed living conditions, meals, free time, and cellmates. I came to understand the rhythms of the day, the small joys, and the many struggles.

Understanding ecclesial biblical theology requires something similar. We must step into the early Christian social imaginary and conceive of the world from that vantage point. "It is senseless," theologian Fred Sanders argues,

---

11. Boersma, *Scripture as Real Presence*, xii. R. R. Reno, too, argues for an "ecclesiological reading" that draws from the well of premodern interpretation. Reno, *End of Interpretation*.

12. Young, *Biblical Exegesis*, 265.

13. Taylor, *Secular Age*, 171.

"to try to retain the result of the early church's holistic interpretation of Scripture—the perception of the biblical doctrine of the Trinity—without cultivating, in a way appropriate for our own time, the interpretive practice that produced that result."[14] We need to think about the whole culture of theology, the ways and patterns that unite Scripture in a drama of salvation under the provision and direction of the one true God. This does not happen by picking up the scattered procedures of exegesis used here or there; rather, it happens by conceiving of the whole.

The early church is a good case study for our age, because the religious and philosophical diversity of their age demanded that they debate first principles. Planted in a Greco-Roman world with all its mores and rituals, these premodern readers knew that they could not come to the Bible with their inherited cultural assumptions—Greek and Roman assumptions that were frequently at odds with basic theological claims in the Bible. They recognized implicitly that "biblical texts can only be interpreted in relation to something else: a concept, a question, a belief, a historical reality."[15] So they had to read the Bible in a way that shaped their culture, not the other way around. Through their totalizing reading of Scripture, the early church called for "a radical revision of the first principles," which challenged the very foundations of classical culture.[16] Their reading involved a different conception of reality, with unique metaphysical, epistemological, and ethical assumptions that expressed themselves in different patterns of religious life and social mores. The church forged a vision of salvation history that brought them into constant struggle with their intellectual and social environment. Christians never fully felt at home in the Roman world, and ultimately, the two could not coexist in peace.[17] Eventually, by the fourth century, the church gained enough ground to influence the institutions of the ancient world and begin to build Christendom. At that point, the synergy between the Bible and culture took on a more intimate relationship that began shaping the culture in new ways.

But now in the modern world, Christian cultural hegemony is vanishing at a rapid pace, and a new kind of secular age is emerging—a society in which, as Taylor describes, belief in God is "one option among others, and frequently not the easiest to embrace."[18] The competition of social imaginaries today mirrors the ancient world and makes a patristic ecclesial biblical theology as relevant as ever. Like the ancient Christians, I pray that we run to the church,

14. Sanders, *Triune God*, 177.
15. Legaspi, *Death of Scripture*, 164.
16. Cochrane, *Christianity and Classical Culture*, vi.
17. S. Smith, *Pagans and Christians in the City*, 14.
18. Taylor, *Secular Age*, 3.

forming a community that never forgets that we are "a chosen race, a royal priesthood, a holy nation, a people for his own possession" (1 Pet. 2:9), united like a great cloud of witnesses and living the story of God.

Summary of Chapters

Crafting an ecclesial biblical theology begins by exploring the performance of Scripture in the early church. While we can learn much from the whole premodern tradition, I have chosen to focus on some of the main theologians in the Latin- and Greek-speaking churches up through the fifth century, from the apostolic fathers to Augustine (354–430). Occasionally a few later figures wander into the conversation, because they help us to understand the thinking in the early church. Many nuances and differences exist among these patristic writers, and this book runs the risk of generalization. But I think it's a risk worth taking, for while they might disagree over particular readings, they are generally united against the assumptions of other ages. "Every age has its own outlook," C. S. Lewis writes, and people involved in the controversies of earlier ages "thought that they were as completely opposed as two sides could be, but in fact they were all the time secretly united—united with each other and against earlier and later ages—by a great mass of common assumptions."[19] In spite of its diversity, the early church exhibited a mass of common assumptions embedded in an interpretive community that rivals our age, and it is these assumptions that I want to explore.

The chapters all work together, each one laying a new tile in the mosaic of early Christian interpretation. In chapter 1, I begin with first principles, the backdrop for any good Bible-reading performance. I argue that three things work together to frame the fathers' ecclesial biblical theology: Scripture, the rule of faith, and liturgy. When forged together, this cord of three interpretive strands is not easily broken. The rule of faith emerges out of Scripture and guides sound interpretation, while the liturgy attunes and refines interpreters' assumptions and sensibilities, conforming their lives to Scripture's teachings. Nestled within this triumvirate, the biblical theologian is free to explore, contemplate, and enjoy the blessings that Scripture proclaims. In other words, the fathers are less concerned about learning the right methods and more concerned about nurturing the right culture, which guides the theologian. They teach us that the basis for biblical theology is not canon, historical context, or even salvation history; rather, it is a Christian culture formed through the intertwining threads of Scripture, theology, and worship that frames their

19. Lewis, preface to *On the Incarnation*, 12–13.

Introduction

whole exegetical project. I hope we can recover these assumptions today, learning once again the importance of forging this synergy.

In chapter 2, I show how early Christian theologians come to the text assuming some first principles that flow from the discussion in the previous chapter. They argue that any interpreter must confess a basic understanding of the nature of God and God's relationship with the world. This understanding, moreover, extends to several interpretive postures that frame the exegete's perspective on Scripture. What the fathers teach us is that no good exegesis exists apart from a holy conception of God. Coming to Scripture without a true conception of God is like taking a wrong turn at the beginning of a journey; we have little hope of ever arriving at the right destination. For some modern interpreters, this approach may seem backward, but the fathers believe it is necessary to put first things first. They show us that we should not rid ourselves of God and then try to read the Bible; we understand Scripture only if we begin by confessing God.

In chapter 3, I move from a discussion of the transcendent God to the immanent creation and argue that for the fathers, the basic literal sense comprises the very words of Scripture, or the words "according to the letter." The literal sense pays special attention to "the way the words go," the arrangement of the words in their immediate literary context. However, this immediate context, in their minds, is never divorced from the larger narrative storyline of the Bible. For them, the literal sense provides the framework for uniting the words, stories, and books of Scripture into a narrative of salvation history. As such, it is a complex unity, a cohesion based on the very wording of Scripture, but working to unite the immediate setting and characters with the larger story of Scripture. There is an ideal narrative that threads the Scriptures in an archetypal form, moving from creation to the kingdom of God. Any description of this narrative relies on the actual wording of Scripture and the unity of the books of the Bible. The fathers see themselves as part of this narrative, living the story of Scripture through their spiritual lives and liturgies. At the same time, they construct summary narratives through thematic or covenantal arrangements that are like SparkNotes summaries of the larger narrative and even assume a larger ideal narrative that threads through Scripture. The literal sense, or what I am calling the narrative substructure, enables ancient Christian thinkers to link texts through all kinds of intertextual reading strategies. These other kinds of intertextual links are like tributaries that feed into the metanarrative stream of theological history.

This discussion of narrative is where our modern conversation about biblical theology intersects with the fathers' assumptions, though they do not ask the same kind of "historical" questions that we ask today. The fathers exhibit a different theological understanding of history, framed with different first principles. While they might not answer all our historical questions, they can help us reimagine the literal sense and help us recognize that we are participating in the drama of Scripture.

Chapter 4 picks up the conversation of the spiritual sense begun in chapter 2; only in this case, the focus is not the nature of God but the Son of God, who unites the narrative in a variety of ways. I describe these christological reading strategies under three headings: personal, prophetic, and partitive. These categories reflect my attempt to classify the diverse ways that the fathers find Christ in Scripture like a treasure hidden in a field. They remind us that reading Christ in the text is about not merely seeing the way he fulfilled prophecy but recognizing his preexistence in the text and interpreting Scripture in ways that respect both natures that concur in his person. The fathers can help us cast off our interpretive inhibitions and teach us to find theology *embedded in Scripture*, draw it out, and behold the work of Christ.

In recent years, scholars have been moving away from the categories of typology and allegory, trying to describe the fathers' interpretive strategies more precisely. My descriptions of "personal," "prophetic," and "partitive" are an attempt to frame their interpretive strategies in general categories that capture their hermeneutical posture toward a spiritual sense in Scripture. In each category I provide ways of reading the spiritual sense that discerns the person and work of Christ. For example, I describe a key reading strategy of a "two-advent hermeneutic." Certain passages point directly to the person and work of Christ and anticipate his coming, both in his first advent and in his second. Early Christian writers are motivated to link scriptural texts based on the way they directly coordinate with specific moments or episodes of the Christ event, including passages recounting his birth, life, death, resurrection, ascension, and second coming. The Christ event offers waypoints marking the web of interconnections between the Old and New Testaments. These interpretive strategies reinforce the metaphysical framing that guides the fathers' interpretation and, therefore, reinforce the culture that flows from their readings.

Chapter 5 transitions the discussion to the human person as the interpreter of Scripture. I show that biblical theology, in the fathers' vision, is an interpretive life lived through virtue and journeying toward beatitude. Virtue is not merely the application of Scripture—though it is certainly that—rather, it is required from the beginning and is part of the whole process of reading. The fathers do not assume that the interpreter will be perfect, only that they will be simply further down the road of virtue and committed to holy living.

Introduction 13

I also argue in this chapter that three key portions of Scripture help frame a virtuous reader: the life of Christ, the Wisdom literature (including Proverbs, Song of Songs, Ecclesiastes, and Job) and the book of Psalms, and models of the spiritual life in Scripture. Naturally, the life of Christ is the supreme example of virtue. Christ is the embodiment of all the virtues, the paradigm of the good life. The Wisdom literature provides guidelines for godly living, directing the interpreter in the practice of virtue. Finally, the examples of virtue in the lives of the patriarchs, the prophets, and the apostles—faithful travelers on the journey of salvation—can help us envision the beauty of the virtuous life. Ironically, modern conceptions of biblical theology struggle to find a place for the Wisdom literature, which is often seen as an anomaly and an outlier. The fathers see things differently. The Wisdom literature has pride of place as it guides the spiritual life.

There is also no illusion among the fathers that we come to Scripture as a tabula rasa, with no prior assumptions, nor any desire to suspend assumptions and evaluate Scripture from a value-free perspective. Instead, virtue was part of the whole process, and it must be so for us as well. While we acknowledge that we are justified before God, we are not yet fully sanctified; we remain in pursuit of virtue, hoping, little by little, to be conformed to the likeness of Christ.

In chapter 6, all things come together in the church. In this chapter, I argue that premodern biblical theology is an ecclesial biblical theology. The proper arena for reading the Bible is the church, where the church's faith and liturgy cast a vision of the good life lived in community—a community of worshipers gathered to find themselves in Scripture and remind each other that they are on a journey toward the kingdom of God. Because biblical theology is ecclesial, it entails proclamation for the sake of edification. Within the worship setting, preaching was an important way the fathers guided God's people toward the right appointed end. The purpose of gathering around the Scriptures is to learn how to live holy lives and make incremental progress in conformity to the likeness of Christ. This final chapter is the capstone for an ecclesial biblical theology—a communal life committed and devoted to following Christ, seeking virtue, and hoping for the coming of the kingdom of God. This is the kind of biblical theology that we need to recover today.

In the conclusion, I make a final plea for recovering an ecclesial biblical theology. The Scriptures are the church's text: the living community reads them, prays them, and reveres them. They are the authoritative, life-giving Word of God for the people of God. When biblical theology is once again ecclesial, I believe we will find a worshiping community gathered around the Scriptures, building a culture imbued with the love of God and love of neighbor.

It is this vision of the Scriptures that I long for, which is why I did not linger long at Descartes's grave in the Church of Saint-Germain-des-Prés. The side chapel where he rests is small, and there was not much to see except a dark plaque memorializing him. Instead, I quickly returned to the nave, reclaiming my seat among the worshipers. I sat for some time reflecting again on the beauty of salvation history. I hoped then, as I do now, that we can embrace the best of patristic exegesis and finally reacclimate to the world where God dwells and the people of God gather to be transformed by the truth of the gospel.

ECCLESIAL BIBLICAL THEOLOGY

Augustine of Hippo's (354–430) journey to Christianity followed a circuitous path. While his influential Christian mother, Monica (ca. 332–87), never gave up hope, for many years it looked like Augustine was lost to the church. When he was a young intellectual studying rhetoric, he relished the bubbling cauldron of sin in the city of Carthage. He meandered his way through various philosophical streams, eventually landing as a "hearer," or one who was pursuing membership, in a religious group known as the Manicheans. But ultimately, Manichean doctrines left him unsatisfied. Then, through a providential series of events, Augustine found himself sitting under the preaching of Ambrose (ca. 339–97), who revealed to him the beauty of the Scriptures. When compared with the literary works of renowned philosophers and rhetoricians, the Scriptures had always seemed to Augustine to be crude and juvenile.

As Augustine recounts the story of his conversion in his autobiography, aptly titled *Confessions*, he is simply undone through Ambrose's preaching. The Scriptures are the rock he crashes himself against. His intellectual crisis leads him to a garden where he bares his heart before God. Broken and contrite, Augustine experiences a "vast storm" in his soul that leads to a "massive downpour of tears."[1] I have always found this contrast staggering. In this garden scene, we find one of the most influential intellectuals in the history of Western thought broken and weeping like a child. Deep conviction about his depravity overwhelms him; he longs for forgiveness and cries out to God, petitioning him to forgive his iniquities.[2]

In his anguish, Augustine hears the words of a child chanting, "Pick up and read; pick up and read." He interprets the words as a sign, takes a copy of the Scriptures, and immediately opens it at random and reads the first passage that his eyes fall upon. There, he reads the words of Romans 13:13–14: "Not in riots and drunken parties, not in eroticism and indecencies, not in strife and rivalry, but put on the Lord Jesus Christ and make no provision for the flesh in its lusts." By reading Scripture, he is transformed. He perceives "a light as it were of serenity" in his heart, and "all the darkness of doubt vanishe[s] away."[3] Arrogance and achievements fade into the background, as the words of Scripture convict and guide. God alone, not a philosophy, satisfies the soul. At long last, Augustine is home.

Augustine's intellectual journey has traversed through the thorns and thistles of various religious and philosophical systems, leading, at last, to the doorstep of the church. When he opens the door, his soul embraces God and the teachings of the Scriptures. From that point, Augustine begins his spiritual journey toward God. In his writing, he frequently expresses a longing to see God "face to face" (1 Cor. 13:12)—a euphoric image of endless satisfaction, love, and praise often called the beatific vision, which simply means the beholding of the glory of God.[4] The opening lines of his *Confessions* provide a good example. He begins declaring the glory and magnificence of God in a prayerful posture: "'You are great, Lord, and highly to be praised (Ps. 47:2): great is your power and your wisdom is immeasurable' (Ps. 146:5)." Humans have been created for God, and without God, they have no hope or purpose. But being a part of God's creation, humanity longs to adore God. "You have made us for yourself," Augustine writes, "and our heart is restless until it rests in you."[5] The last clause, "our heart is restless until it rests in you," threads together Augustine's spiritual journey. Whether we know it or not, we crave the divine, and we are unable to find peace until we find God. We have been created *homo liturgicus*—"embodied, practicing creatures whose love/desire is

---

1. Augustine, *Confessions* 8.12.28.
2. Augustine, *Confessions* 8.12.28.
3. Augustine, *Confessions* 8.12.29.
4. Passages such as Rom. 8:30 and Phil. 3:21 point to the beauty of this end. See the discussion in Jamieson and Wittman, *Biblical Reasoning*, 6–11.
5. Augustine, *Confessions* 1.1.1.

aimed at something ultimate."[6] Try as we might to amuse or educate ourselves, only God "satisfies the longing soul, and the hungry soul he fills with good things" (Ps. 107:9). Early church thinkers, such as Augustine, understand that this basic assumption guides their exegesis. "Beholding God in the face of Christ in the new creation, we will enjoy life eternal, perpetual peace, joy, and rest."[7] Without this true telos, we are aimless travelers spinning philosophical tales and charting myths to nowhere.

For too long, discussions of biblical interpretation have fixated on method—treating Bible reading like a step-by-step assembly process, very much like the way one might put together a piece of IKEA furniture. We rarely stop to contemplate who created the furniture and what the ultimate purpose of the furniture is. There is nothing wrong with contemplating methods; they are just secondary to more-fundamental metaphysical concerns that transcend methods.

To understand anything about patristic interpretation, we must begin with the end in mind. With respect to hermeneutics, exegesis, biblical theology, theological interpretation—whatever these terms mean—Augustine reminds us that our destination sets us on the right course, orienting our plan of action. Without the right orientation of our hearts, we have little hope of offering good interpretations. We will be like a boat without a sail, floating untethered and tossed amid the waves of competing methodologies.[8] Setting our sights on God is the first step in understanding early Christian biblical theology. Knowing the telos orients us; it guides us safely to the right destination. It does not mean that the journey will be easy or painless. In this life, we will experience many ditches and dangers along the homeward path. But we will also experience beauty, mystery, joy, and hope. When we at last arrive home and behold God, then, Augustine writes, "we shall rest and see, see and love, love and praise."[9]

This first chapter casts the general architecture of the fathers' ecclesial biblical theology. I try to step back and take in the whole as we look at the synergy between Scripture, the rule of faith, and the spiritual life that forms the culture in which biblical theology incubates. First, I argue that all biblical reflection in the early church involved perceiving the Scriptures through the lens of what is known as the rule of faith. The rule of faith exists in close relationship with the Scriptures, emerging from and containing the language and concepts of the Bible's teaching; in turn, it becomes a theological framework for making

6. J. Smith, *Desiring the Kingdom*, 40.
7. Jamieson and Wittman, *Biblical Reasoning*, 11.
8. Billings, *Word of God*, xii.
9. Augustine, *City of God* 22.30.

sense of Scripture. Much has been written about the rule of faith, but I hope what I say here is something fresh. I argue that the rule frames reality. It is more than merely summarizing the essential commitments of the church's faith, though it is that. In the early church, the rule of faith portrays what Charles Taylor calls a "social imaginary," which explains how the world is perceived through the lens of a community and how that perception is often at odds with other social imaginaries embedded within the fabric of any culture.[10]

Second, the church also married Scripture and the rule to its liturgical practices and spiritual lives, viewing all things through its trinitarian confession. Every prayer, every sacramental act, every sermon—not to mention every political and social activity—was beheld through a vision of the divine, articulated in the rule. In the modern age, academic theologians disconnected from any ecclesial setting are often ill equipped for the task of biblical theology; they are simply not catechized or actively liturgized in patterns of life and belief emanating from Scripture. True biblical theology is found among the faithful, who are discipled in the faith and embedded within their liturgical contexts, contemplating the Scriptures while seeking to behold God.

Together, this triumvirate—Scripture, the rule of faith, and liturgy—provides the general framework for an ecclesial biblical theology.

Scripture and the Rule of Faith

The fathers recognize that any study of Scripture must begin with theology and, specifically, a trinitarian view of reality. What we believe about God influences the way we read Scripture, because the "theologian is exegete; the exegete is theologian."[11] In other words, "metaphysics and biblical interpretation [are] closely connected," so that "the way we think about the relationship between God and the world is immediately tied up with the way we read Scripture."[12] Everything is downstream of a theological vision of life.

Before I can talk about interpretive methods or structures in the early church, before I can talk about the differences between typology and allegory—if there are any differences—I need to discuss the object of exegesis, the one to whom we should direct all our attention, love, and adoration. Metaphysics, or what Aristotle called the "science which studies Being *qua*

---

10. Taylor, *Secular Age*, 171–72.
11. Young, *Biblical Exegesis*, 282.
12. Boersma, *Scripture as Real Presence*, 5.

Being, and the properties inherent in it in virtue of its own nature," is the theoretical basis for early Christian biblical theology.[13] Put simply, "Good metaphysics leads to good hermeneutics,"[14] as Hans Boersma writes, and, conversely, I would add that bad metaphysics leads to bad hermeneutics.

Early Christian believers implicitly understood the importance of a worldview, or the "constellation of beliefs that, even if not reflected upon, govern and control our being and our doing."[15] We all interpret Scripture from the vantage points of some view of reality. As we have already seen, Taylor calls this a "social imaginary." A social imaginary, as Taylor defines it, is much more than an intellectual scheme of life; it is "the ways in which [people] imagine their social existence, how they fit together with others, how things go on between them and their fellows, the expectations which are normally met, and the deeper normative notions and images which underlie these expectations."[16] A social imaginary is complex; it ties together all the threads that make up our relations in this world—the kinds of common assumptions that make up the expectations and integrations of our lives.

The early church's social imaginary was framed in the rule of faith. It was a theological vision that imagined the relations between God, creation, and humanity. The fathers began with metaphysics, and that vision put every other intellectual inquiry (epistemology, ethics, aesthetics) in its proper place. Craig Carter explains how a vision of "theological metaphysics" emerges from the Scriptures. Theological metaphysics is "the account of the ontological nature of reality," Carter writes, "that emerges from the theological descriptions of God and the world found in the Bible."[17] Scott Swain highlights the proper theological ordering. "Theological interpretation of Scripture," Swain writes, "rests on the conviction that the Trinity precedes, not just biblical interpretation, but the Bible itself. The Bible and its interpretation are downstream, not upstream, from the Trinity, products of the Triune God's willingness to make himself the object of creaturely knowledge, love, and beatitude."[18] For the

13. Aristotle, *Metaphysics* 4.1.

14. Boersma, *Scripture as Real Presence*, 5. For early Christians, "God was the starting point, and Christ the icon that displays the face of God" (Wilken, *Spirit of Early Christian Thought*, 15). The apostles begin with an appeal to God as well. Cf., e.g., Gen. 1:1; Exod. 3:14–15; Isa. 45:5; and Acts 17:24–25. In these passages, there is no qualification or equivocation; there is only the metaphysical assumption that only one true God exists, who created all things and reigns providentially over creation.

15. J. Smith, *Desiring the Kingdom*, 23–24.

16. Taylor, *Secular Age*, 171.

17. Carter, *Interpreting Scripture with the Great Tradition*, 63 (italics omitted).

18. Swain, *Trinity and the Bible*, 121.

20   Biblical Theology in the Life of the Early Church

early church, nothing else in this world ultimately mattered except seeking the face of God. So with them, "let us enter together on the path of charity in search of Him of whom it is said: 'Seek his face evermore' [Ps. 105:4]."[19]

One way to see the importance of metaphysics and Scripture in the early church is to consider the fathers' constant polemic against false conceptions of God. In the Scriptures, Paul provides a good example of this. When he engages the philosophers of Mars Hill, he critiques their pantheon of gods and proclaims to them that "the God who made the world and everything in it is the Lord of heaven and earth and does not live in temples built by human hands" (Acts 17:24 NIV). Paul begins his statement of first principles with monotheism, the primary assumption that there is only one God, not many gods. With that assumption in place, Paul continues to instruct in other points of doctrine.

Like Paul, the patristic writers frequently critique bad theology. These theological perspectives, often developed through the ingenuity of human reason, not revelation, took on various forms of monism and dualism. These include forms of deism, Monarchianism, atheism, Arianism, tritheism, pantheism, polytheism, and other theological perspectives that misconstrue either the unity or the diversity of the divine nature. In conversation with these and other conceptions of God, the fathers argue that one cannot interpret Scripture well without assuming that "God, though without beginning, is the absolute beginning of all, and the maker of the beginning"; God is the first and efficient cause of all things.[20] Adherents of the aforementioned bad theologies, Basil of Caesarea (ca. 330–79) argues, have discovered all but one thing, the most important thing—"the fact that God is the Creator of the universe, and the just Judge who rewards all the actions of life according to their merit."[21]

The problem with much of the discussion of biblical interpretation today is that metaphysics is ignored. Modern theorists often encourage interpreters to lay aside their assumptions and come as objective observers to the Scriptures. The problem is not that they come with assumptions; rather, it is that they come with unexamined and unacknowledged assumptions. This is why in modern biblical studies "the operative theology in reading Scripture is Deistic rather than Trinitarian."[22] Maybe an interpreter believes in God in some generic sense, but that conviction has no conscious bearing on the actual practice of interpretation. They strive for neutral, value-free, unbiased interpretation. Postmodern theories of hermeneutics have headed in a different

19. Augustine, *Trinity* 1.3.5.
20. Clement of Alexandria, *Stromata* 4.25.
21. Basil, *Hexameron* 1.4.
22. Billings, *Word of God*, 86.

direction, rejecting objectivity and embracing personal ideological assumptions. These ideologies most often derive from internal sources of authority that must be expressed regardless of theological or historical norms. Postmodern hermeneutical streams of interpretation, such as postcolonial, feminist, queer, or ethnic perspectives, impose ideologies on the text, conforming it to fit personal tastes. But the fathers challenge us to chart a different course. Just as Joshua exhorts the people of God before they enter the promised land, the fathers challenge us to "choose this day whom [we] will serve," whether the triune God of Scripture or the god(s) of deism, pantheism, polytheism, and the like. But may we say with Joshua, "As for me and my house, we will serve the Lord" (Josh. 24:15).

The Rule of Faith

When the early church catechized new converts, it framed its spiritual formation through instruction in the rule of faith (sometimes in polemical contexts called the "rule of truth").[23] The language of "rule" (Greek *kanōn*) likely conjures up images of boundary marking or regulating, and in a certain sense, that was exactly what was happening. The fathers did not assume that interpretation was unbounded exploration, like a feral animal wandering the streets wildly unencumbered. Modern interpreters often characterize the fathers in these ways and assume that they themselves are much more bounded. I have often discussed the notion of the rule of faith in seminary classes. Students understand the concept but always seem to be nervous about the apparent lack of interpretive controls and the lack of a normative and officially sanctioned summary of the rule. But the irony is that patristic exegesis is often much more controlled than modern exegesis. Without an explicit rule of faith, modern exegetes are free to find in the text whatever they desire. Not so for the ancients. With their social imaginary, their rule of faith, the text cannot mean anything; it must comport with the proper revealed theological reality expressed in the rule.

From the earliest days of the church to the time of Augustine, the term *rule of faith* was used to describe, in the words of J. N. D. Kelly, "a condensed summary, fluid in its wording but fixed in content, setting out the key-points of the Christian revelation in the form of a rule."[24] In Kelly's summary, the

---

23. In Irenaeus's catechetical manual, it is called the rule of faith, and in his polemical work, *Against Heresies*, it is called the rule of truth.

24. Kelly, *Early Christian Doctrines*, 37. Another way to think about the rule of faith is to cite a related concept called the Scripture's hypothesis. The term *hypothesis* was common in Greco-Roman circles and typically meant "the presentation (sometimes in a summary) of a

rule is both "fluid" and "fixed," which means some features of the rule are stable, while others are flexible. The fixed parts of the rule are the structural features, such as the triadic order and the key persons organizing each section: Father, Son, and Spirit. The fluid features include the terms and words that populate the rule. For example, theologians can include several different attributes of God or ways of describing Christ's two natures in the rule. The language of the rule always works in concert with Scripture. In both structure and content, the rule exists in a dialogical relationship with Scripture and develops in response to changing cultural circumstances.[25]

As the church encountered different cultural contexts with alternative theological and philosophical perspectives, the rule provided a way for it to summarize the faith and hold in tension several key paradoxes: the unity of God and the diversity of divine persons, dogmatic and narrative structures of theology, immanent and economic descriptions of God, and the deity and the humanity of Christ. Time and time again, when the fathers debated heretical views of God, they appealed to the rule of faith, not method. We find this in Irenaeus's engagement with the Gnostics and Tertullian's refutation of Marcion and Praxeas. Their dissenters misunderstand the Scriptures because they misunderstand God. In this way, the rule of faith is like a wise docent that guides the faithful in virtuous interpretation, providing general theological guidelines that set the interpreter on the right path.

One way to help explain the rule of faith is to cite the traditional distinction between two conceptions of faith. When it comes to the notion of faith, theologians have conventionally distinguished between "the faith that is believed" (*fides quae creditur*) and "the faith that believes" (*fides qua creditur*), and in the early church, there was a close association between these senses. Early-church historian Robert Wilken captures these sentiments when he describes how early Christian thinkers "went about the task of giving conceptual form to their faith, that is, reasoned about what was believed."[26] The former sense, the faith that is believed, frames the objective sense of *faith*, such as a creed or confessional statement. Faith is not blind assent. The fathers understand that faith must have an object and that Christians can, with intellectual tools and sources, describe that object in some way. In other words, there is a substance (*res*) to faith that transcends any verbal (*verba*) expression, but statements of faith capture some measure of transcendent truth.

---

plot or structure intended by an author such as Homer." The rule captures this summary of Scripture or its primary thrust. Grant, *Irenaeus of Lyons*, 47.

25. James Andrews argues that the rule of faith in Augustine arises out of Scripture itself. Andrews, *Hermeneutics and the Church*, 103.

26. Wilken, *Spirit of Early Christian Thought*, 84–85.

On the other hand, the faith that believes is the subjective or personal faith that moves one to confess or believe the summary of faith. Faith is not mere mental assent to a set of propositions. Christians, either ancient or modern, are not justified by mere acquiescence to some set of propositions. They must confess with their mouth and believe in their heart that Christ was raised from the dead. But without some object, faith becomes purely emotive and subjective, lacking an ontological grounding. Christians must have some sense of what they are confessing; they must give some account of the object of their belief.

I like to compare these notions of faith to wedding vows. At a wedding, a husband and a wife stand before each other, reciting words that express heartfelt commitments, but their vows do not say everything. Instead, they capture, in a few lines, essential commitments that express the essence of their personal devotion. In a similar way, the rule of faith provides the words (*verba*) of the faith, but the rule does not say everything. The substance (*res*) of the faith transcends those words. Together, faith in God and the aim to express that faith work together to articulate the ontology of God and God's relationship with humanity and creation in the form of the rule of faith.

Augustine provides a good example of the union between these senses of faith. He argues that faith is something unseen that happens in and to a person, involving the heart rather than an outward expression of the body. Because faith is a matter of the heart, it can be "feigned by pretense, and thought to be in him in whom it does not exist," Augustine writes. But faith is also common, he continues, citing John: "But to as many as received him, he gave the power of becoming sons of God; to those who believe in his name" (John 1:12). Describing the unity of both the faith that is believed (*fides quae creditur*) and the faith that believes (*fides qua creditur*), Augustine writes that "the faith is indeed impressed from one doctrine on the heart of the faithful who believe this same thing." He distinguishes these senses because the objective sense of faith is external, observable, and common, typically found in confessions like the rule of faith, but the subjective sense is internal, private, and personal; it is a matter of the heart. Summarizing these points, Augustine writes, "those things that are believed are one thing, but the faith by which they are believed is another thing. For the former are in the things of which it is said that they either are, or have been, or shall be, but the latter is in the mind of the believer, and is visible to him only of whom it is."[27]

These two senses are not isolated from one another but compose the whole notion of faith in God. The rule lives at the hermeneutical center of the

27. Augustine, *Trinity* 13.2.5.

church's life, expressing what the faithful believe and guiding them to confess and live within the contours of the truth it reveals. The rule of faith, codified in a set of assertions, is more than mere propositions; it describes a perception of reality, of God, world, and salvation as they are rightly understood and truly known.[28] While the truth of God supersedes and precedes the rule, truth is expressed in the rule, for "truth brings about faith," as Irenaeus (ca. 130–ca. 202) states.[29] Because "faith is established upon things truly real," he continues, "that we may believe what really is, as it is, and <believing> what really is, as it is, we may always keep our conviction of it firm."[30] When we confess the faith, we believe what "really is," and what "really is" is God and God's work in us and our world. We participate in these realities, see the world through them. "Christian biblical exegesis, in accord with the Christian and biblical understanding of reality," Matthew Levering writes, "should envision history not only as a linear unfolding of individual moments, but also as an ongoing participation in God's active providence, both metaphysically and Christologically-pneumatologically."[31] We live and move and have our being in these metaphysical and theological structures, and they guide all our hermeneutical endeavors. Without the rule of faith, the church has no hope for proper scriptural interpretation.

The Rule of Faith as Dogmatic and Narrative

What I have described above is the basic confession of faith that guides the church's biblical interpretation. Now I want to focus on the content of the rule of faith. In the early church, there was no single summary of the rule that was universally recognized, but there were many different versions that all shared a family resemblance. In a similar way that children born of the same parents are all unique, but undoubtedly share some physical traits, there are several different articulations of the rule of faith among communities. Two traits transcend all summaries of the rule: First, they include a basic dogmatic summary of God, with a simple set of attributes and theological language that characterize the nature of God. Second, the dogmatic summary of God is always framed through the narrative of God's work in salvation history. I could describe these two features with other theological terms, such as *the intrinsic* and *economic doctrines of God* or the distinction between *divine processions* and *missions*. The rule holds these two traits together.

28. Hägglund, "Die Bedeutung der 'regula fidei,'" 37.
29. Irenaeus, *On the Apostolic Preaching* 3.
30. Irenaeus, *On the Apostolic Preaching* 3.
31. Levering, *Participatory Biblical Exegesis*, 1.

The dogmatic and narratival features of the rule are, in Kelly's definition above, the "fixed" parts; like the framing of a building, they stabilize the rule. Through confession, Christians take up residence in this building and see the world from its perspective. Christians who confess this rule believe themselves to be living under the reign of the transcendent God, who is active in creation, leading his people toward an appointed telos.

Taking the two traits in turn, I begin with the basic dogmatic summary of God, including descriptions of the Father, Son, and Spirit. These titles derive from Matthew 28:19 and form three key subheadings that call for qualification. The rule is like a divine resume, describing the character and work of God. The early church filled in each heading with theological descriptors, drawn from the Bible, that resonated with its faith. In the words of R. R. Reno, "Premodern churchmen engaged in a vast, never-ending project of using doctrine to interpret Scripture and Scripture to illuminate doctrine."[32] Biblical descriptions of divine attributes fuse together in theological summaries of God's nature.

Second, the dogmatic statements are stitched together in a narrative of the history of salvation, which includes the economic activity of God, moving from creation to the future kingdom of God. The rule serves the "Christian hope of articulating and authenticating a world-encompassing story or metanarrative of creation, incarnation, redemption, and consummation."[33] The basic structure of the rule comprises a "framework or 'overarching story' by which the Scriptures [are] to be read and interpreted."[34] The rule always begins with a reference to creation; progresses to summarize the work of Christ, from incarnation to the ascension; and concludes with reference to the Spirit, the resurrection, and the future kingdom. I will spend more time explaining this narrative in another chapter, but the important point here is that narrative buttresses the dogmatic statements in the rule of faith.

Through both the dogmatic and the narratival features of the rule, the Scriptures provide the data—the words, concepts, and images—that compose the rule's wording. For the fathers, as I will argue below, the Scriptures are the perfect content of divine revelation. When the early church crafted the rule, it drew deeply from the well of Scripture, creating what I would call a symbiotic relationship between Scripture and the rule of faith. Cyril

---

32. Reno, *End of Interpretation*, 6.
33. Blowers, "Regula Fidei," 202.
34. Young, *Biblical Exegesis*, 18. For other examples of the rule of faith or truth, see Irenaeus, *Against Heresies* 1.10.1, 1.22.1, 3.4.2; Tertullian, *Against Praxeas* 2; Tertullian, *Prescription against Heretics* 13.1–6; Tertullian, *Concerning the Veiling of Virgins* 1.3; Origen, *On First Principles* 1.pf.4–10; Novatian, *On the Trinity* 9; Augustine, *On Christian Doctrine* 1.5.5–1.21.19.

of Jerusalem (ca. 313–86) compares the process of synthesizing Scripture to botany, arguing that the rule is like a mustard seed that is small but grows to contain many branches. Once fashioned, the rule "has embraced in few words all the knowledge of godliness in the Old and New Testaments."[35]

There are also several assumptions at play when ancient thinkers or communities articulate a rule of faith. Any theological controversies, or other desired points of emphasis, may color the descriptions of God. Irenaeus, for example, was engaged with Gnostics, who tended to devalue the body and the material world, so it is no surprise to find more emphasis on creation and resurrection in his rule. Terms and words are often interchangeable amid the stable subheadings of Father, Son, and Spirit. However, the fathers were always cognizant that the faith articulated in the rule, what terms were chosen, reflected a true comprehension of God.

Once the teaching of the church, with its dogmatic and narratival features, emerges out of Scripture and fashions a rule, the rule works deductively.[36] Certainly, the deductive process involves "attention to the meaning of words, their particular biblical sense, the syntax and the context of the text in question— the basic techniques of the *grammaticus* attending to the verbal configuration of a passage."[37] But the "deductive exegesis" of the early church worked from the theological assumptions of the rule of faith.[38] We can consider this by building on the marital image that I used earlier. Todd Billings compares the way the rule of faith shapes exegesis with marriage vows. When one declares their marriage vows, they enter into a relationship with another person and surrender a number of things.[39] They can no longer consider their lives and their actions apart from considering the needs of their spouse. This does not mean, as I described above, that their assumptions always remain static and unquestioned. Some features of the rule remained unchanged, such as the basic theological structure mentioned in Matthew 28:19 and the general dogmatic and narrative features. But within these fixed structures, Scripture functioned like a theological feedback loop that continually clarified and shaped the way the church articulated its faith in a broader culture.

Some might imagine that interpreting the Scriptures deductively is reading a particular metaphysic into them, but the fathers see it the other way around. God precedes revelation and the rule. God has always existed. Those who

---

35. Cyril of Jerusalem, *Catechetical Lectures* 5.12.

36. Athanasius's exegesis, for example, is not essentially literal, allegorical, or typological; "it is deductive." Young, *Biblical Exegesis*, 36.

37. Young, *Biblical Exegesis*, 40.

38. Young, *Biblical Exegesis*, 40.

39. Billings, *Word of God*, 27.

deny God are reading a newly invented, foreign metaphysic into Scripture. The fathers would never assume that an interpreter comes to a text as an objective observer. Their concern is to approach with assumptions that are consistent with the God revealed in the Scriptures (and that are expressed in the rule). Hilary (ca. 310–ca. 367) is a good example. The "best student," he writes, "does not read his thoughts into the book." But the student "lets it [i.e., Scripture] reveal its own"; he "draws from it its sense, and does not import his own into it, nor force upon its words a meaning which he had determined was the right one before he opened its pages."[40] So, any virtuous interpreter will approach the Word of God with the assumption that "God has full knowledge of Himself, and bow with humble reverence to His words. For He whom we can only know through His own utterances is the fitting witness concerning Himself."[41]

Other examples of this kind of logic appear in early Christian polemics against anyone who interprets Scripture, even as they deny the existence of God or confess a different god than the God *revealed in the text*. Their interpretations are foolish because they say in their heart, "There is no God" (Ps. 14:1), and then they try to read the very Scriptures that reveal the one true God. Take Athanasius's response to the Arian reading of Scripture. "It is plain from this," Athanasius writes, reflecting on Proverbs 8:22, "that the Arians are not fighting with us about their heresy; but while they pretend [to fight] us, their real fight is against the Godhead Itself."[42] While Athanasius certainly critiques the Arian reading of Scripture, he recognizes that their problem is not necessarily their method but rather their faulty conception of God. The Arians deny the deity of Christ and, consequently, fail to read Scripture rightly.

Early Christian biblical theology begins with the appeal to read the right metaphysic in Scripture, the metaphysic embedded *in Scripture*. The rule of faith articulates the metaphysic that emerges out of the scriptural revelation, so there is a cyclical relationship between the rule of faith and the Scriptures. The Scriptures epitomize the rule of faith and provide the data points with which the rule's contents are constructed. The rule, in turn, serves to guide the right reading of Scripture. The fathers assume that one could read any metaphysic into the Scriptures, but the rule summarizes the nature of God and calls the church to read Scripture in accordance with the God who has been revealed.

40. Hilary, *On the Trinity* 1.18.
41. Hilary, *On the Trinity* 1.18.
42. Athanasius, *Four Discourses against the Arians* 2.18.32.

Scripture and the Spiritual Life

Scripture and the rule of faith are seamed together in a cultural package with a third feature of an ecclesial biblical theology: liturgy. I define *liturgy* as broadly inclusive of both active participation in a worshiping community and the regular habits of a spiritual life. On the one hand, the spiritual exegete should be tethered to the institution of the church, the celebrations of the liturgical calendar, and the formal gatherings that lead stages of life (including baptism, marriage, training up children, and ultimately death). On the other hand, the spiritual life is not just lived in these moments but cultivates habits of prayer and fasting that will help them embody the teachings of the Scriptures. Many evangelicals have an uneasy relationship with liturgy that stems from their aversion to "cultural Christianity." But they do not normally notice the way their lives are already participating in cultural liturgies. Their lives have been formed through the cultural patterns and mores of the body politic. The term *cultural liturgies* was popularized by philosopher James K. A. Smith, and it explains how daily rituals slowly form our desires and loves. "Liturgies—whether 'sacred' or 'secular'—shape and constitute our identities by forming our most fundamental desires and our most basic attunement to the world," Smith writes.[43] He argues that we should question not *if* we are shaped by our cultural liturgies but rather *how* we are shaped by these liturgies. Smith uses the image of a local shopping mall to make this point. There is a profoundly "religious nature of cultural institutions," he writes.[44] The mall is not neutral; it is subtly and patiently acting as our pedagogue, leading us to inhabit and embrace a constellation of beliefs that inculcate us in the virtues of the consumer life. From this mundane example, we can see that liturgy—specifically, Christian liturgy—is "a pedagogy that teaches us, in all sorts of precognitive ways, to be a certain kind of person.[45] And the formation of liturgy offers a coordinated effort to embody the faith and to practice it in the world.

The early church understood the normative nature of liturgy. For instance, it used the rite of baptism to confirm that a person of faith retained "unchangeable in his heart the rule of truth."[46] Baptism was the ritual that demonstrated to the community that a convert assumed the essential contours of the church's faith and practice. Like Cortés burning his ships, one could not go back to the old world. Through the liturgy of baptism, converts found

43. J. Smith, *Desiring the Kingdom*, 25.
44. J. Smith, *Desiring the Kingdom*, 23 (italics omitted).
45. J. Smith, *Desiring the Kingdom*, 25.
46. Irenaeus, *Against Heresies* 1.9.4.

Ecclesial Biblical Theology

themselves part of the world defined by the rule of faith—a world where God reigns and the people live in union with him and communion with each other. As reflected in the New Testament, the early Christians baptized those who confessed the faith, and they gathered together for Eucharist meals (Acts 2:38–42; 8:36–39).

We can see an example of the rule of faith and liturgy forged together in many early Christian catechetical manuals, such as the work *On the Apostolic Tradition*, often attributed to the Roman bishop Hippolytus (ca. 170–ca. 235).[47] The text reports that most new converts work through a process of catechesis that lasts up to three years. When these neophytes are finally ready, the community chooses a place outdoors to baptize, preferring a place where the water is cool and flowing. Baptizands then remove their clothes (symbolizing the act of rebirth), and they are baptized individually, both men and women. During baptism, deacons go down with them into the water and ask them a series of questions:

> When the one being baptized goes down into the waters the one who baptizes, placing a hand on him, should say thus: "Do you believe in God the Father Almighty?" And he who is being baptized should reply, "I believe." Let him baptize him once immediately, having his hand placed upon his head. And after this he should say: "Do you believe in Christ Jesus, the son of God, who was born of the Holy Spirit and Mary the virgin and was crucified under Pontius Pilate and was dead [and buried] and rose on the third day alive from the dead and ascended in the heavens and sits at the right hand of the Father and will come to judge the living and the dead?" And when he has said, "I believe," he is baptized again. And again he should say: "Do you believe in the Holy Spirit and the holy church and the resurrection of the flesh?" And he who is being baptized should say: "I believe." And so he should be baptized a third time.[48]

Each one of these questions is a point in the rule of faith. In the act of baptism, baptizands confess each point of the rule. The rule is again confirmed when the deacon anoints each of their heads with oil and prays, "I anoint you with holy oil in God the Father Almighty, and Christ Jesus, and the Holy Spirit."[49]

Finally, after these things, the new members dry and dress themselves and join the community for the Eucharist. Once again, we see the doctrine of

---

47. This text is notoriously difficult to date, but the original portions of the text date to the mid-third century. Another relevant manual is the *Constitutions of the Holy Apostles* (often called *Apostolic Constitutions*). See *Constitutions of the Holy Apostles* 3.16–17.

48. Hippolytus, *On the Apostolic Tradition* 21.

49. Hippolytus, *On the Apostolic Tradition* 21.

God woven into the eucharistic rite. The deacon brings out milk and honey mixed together (symbolizing the promised land) and then water and wine. Three elders or deacons stand ready to receive them, and in each case, those who receive the elements take three sips each of the water, milk, and wine. As they sip, a trinitarian reflection is applied to the elements. As each person partakes, the elder says, "In God the Father Almighty," and the one who receives the food and drink responds, "Amen." Then they take a second sip and the leader adds, "And in the Lord Jesus Christ," and the one who receives responds again, "Amen." Finally, when they take a third sip, the elder responds a final time, "And in the Holy Spirit, and in the holy church," and the one who receives the elements responds, "Amen."[50]

This may sound odd to us today, but do not let that take away from the larger point; at every step, the liturgy reinforces the trinitarian metaphysic confessed in the community. Liturgy forms us. Liturgy reinforces the faith; new members are baptized, anointed, and eucharized in the trinitarian rule of faith. Following baptism, these new members are committed to a different conception of reality, a different vision of life with a whole new set of political and social entailments.

Many church fathers use the image of illumination to describe this event. In his account of baptism, the Cappadocian father Gregory of Nazianzus (329–90) describes this transition theologically as "illumination," and he defines it with a variety of poetic terms, including the "radiance of souls, transformation of life, engagement of the conscience toward God."[51] The experience of illumination, Gregory writes, is "a vehicle leading toward God," who is "unapproachable and ineffable, neither grasped by the mind nor expressed in language." God illuminates "every reason-endowed nature" and is "to intelligible realities what the sun is to sense-perceptible realities."[52] Just as the sun illuminates the world and shines on all things, dispensing light and life, so God illuminates the soul and shows forth the destiny of those who are seeking him. Irenaeus uses a similar image. "Just as those who see the light are illuminated by the light and share in its brilliance," Irenaeus writes, "so those who see God are in God and share his splendor."[53] With the soul illuminated, the baptized believer is ready to read and live the Scriptures.

---

50. Hippolytus, *On the Apostolic Tradition* 21.
51. Gregory of Nazianzus, *On Baptism* 4. In the same context, Gregory gives many other names to baptism, including gift, grace, anointing, robe of anointing, robe of incorruption, bath of rebirth, seal, everything honorable.
52. Gregory of Nazianzus, *On Baptism* 4.
53. Irenaeus, *Against Heresies* 4.20.5.

Not only does liturgy slowly form the believer, but the devotional life, a life of prayer, attunes the Christian to the right orientation of the heart. The recitation of basic Christian belief was a regular routine for the ancients. Augustine advises the catechumens, "Receive, my children, the Rule of Faith, which is called the Symbol (or Creed). And when ye have received it, write it in your heart, and be daily saying it to yourselves; before ye sleep, before ye go forth, arm ye with your Creed."[54] The rule guides catechumens' daily lives and their vision of the good life.[55] Once Christians are sealed in baptism, *On the Apostolic Tradition* assumes that "they shall be zealous to do good works, and to please God, living honorably, devoting themselves to the church, doing the things which they were taught, and advancing in piety."[56] The faithful are now living, serving, and advancing in piety in confession of this one true God. As early as the second century, Christians encouraged fasting and prayer as regular habits of the devotional life. The Didache, an early Christian handbook, advises its readers that their fasts and prayers should not be like the "hypocrites." They should fast on different days than the other religious groups around them and pray the Lord's Prayer three times throughout the day.[57] In his treatise on prayer, Origen (ca.185–253) reflects on Paul's injunction to "pray without ceasing" (1 Thess. 5:17). The apostle's command implies that "the whole life of a saint is one great continuous prayer."[58] The one who "prays without ceasing," Origen concludes, "combines prayer with right actions, and becoming actions with prayer." As the Didache does, Origen argues that prayer ought to happen three times a day, citing Daniel's example, "who, in spite of the grave danger that impended, prayed three times daily" (Dan. 6:10–12).[59] Alongside Origen, other patristic writings envision the Lord's Prayer as a key element in the life of prayer—indeed, the whole life of faith.[60] The ongoing performance of the spiritual life reinforces one's confession and leads the people of God toward virtue. In liturgy and a life of prayer, the rule is lived.

This extended discussion of the rule of faith and the spiritual life points to the incubator where Scripture and the rule coalesce in the lives of Christians. This triadic formula provides the church a context for nurturing good biblical

---

54. Augustine, *On the Creed* 1.1.
55. See Augustine, *Catholic and Manichaean Ways of Life*.
56. Hippolytus, *On the Apostolic Tradition* 21.
57. Didache 8.
58. Origen, *On Prayer* 7.
59. Origen, *On Prayer* 7.
60. Tertullian, Cyprian, and Origen, *On the Lord's Prayer*.

theology. This description and vision of God have serious implications for guiding the faithful toward a right reading of Scripture. Interpretation is not merely about applying the right method or doing the right exercises; these things have great value, but only within a proper orientation toward God. The mind, when left to its own rational ingenuity, fails to properly conceptualize God. The human mind "might be purged from falsities of this kind," but "Holy Scripture, which suits itself to babes has not avoided words drawn from any class of things really existing, through which, as by nourishment, our understanding might rise gradually to things divine and transcendent."[61] As Christians living in the world, we need to have our eyes daily trained in the right direction and our lives and affections oriented toward God.

Conclusion

This chapter shows us that we can learn much from the fathers. The early church understood the synergy between Scripture and the spiritual life in ways that we need to recover. Reading Scripture well was not just about learning methods but about viewing reality through the lens of Scripture. The fathers have shown us that the rule of faith provides the theological framing needed for an ecclesial biblical theology. The rule was the early church's social imaginary, the way it viewed all relations to God and world, and the same is true of us. The rule of faith emerges out of the Scriptures and, in turn, becomes the means by which we make sense of them. The Scriptures provide the church a metaphysic that describes reality and makes order out of complexity. Everything is downstream of the church's trinitarian confession. Like the fathers, we should begin to see Scripture and the world through the lens of the rule of faith, recognizing that we are already living the divine narrative revealed in Scripture.

Augustine realized this. I began this chapter discussing his conversion, a meandering path to the church that led him through the trifles of philosophy. Augustine broke himself against the Word of God, confessing the one true God and committing to live in continuity with that confession. Like Augustine, we are on a journey headed somewhere. We have been created for God, and our hearts are restless until they rest in him. Just as our Lord questions the apostles, "Who do you say that I am?" (Matt. 16:15), so he asks us the same question. We can teach our methods and apply our hermeneutics, but until we come to confess Christ, we will not have the right assumptions to

61. Augustine, *Trinity* 1.

guide us in the right direction. The fathers confessed and lived their biblical theology, and we should too.

Like the fathers, if we want to understand the Scriptures, we need to find ourselves in the church, where catechesis and liturgy help reinforce the rule of faith we confess. Scripture is often talked about outside the church, but the fathers show us that participation in the ecclesial life is essential to good interpretation. Reading Scripture well includes being catechized in the rule of faith and embracing the spiritual life, with all its liturgical and devotional entailments. Only within this ecclesial incubator can biblical theology mature, and this is where we need to find ourselves.

In the next chapter, I describe how Scripture communicates spiritual realities and the postures a spiritual interpreter must assume to comprehend the Scriptures.

SIGNS OF GOD

In 372, Gregory of Nyssa (ca. 330–94) reluctantly agreed to become a bishop. The previous year Emperor Valens (328–78), an Arian, created several new bishoprics by dividing the province of Cappadocia, and Nyssa, a small town in the region nestled between Caesarea and Ancyra, was home to one of the newly formed ecclesiastical offices. Gregory desired to live a quiet life teaching rhetoric, but his older sister, Macrina (ca. 327–79), and his older brother, Basil (ca. 330–79), encouraged him to accept the appointment.

While Gregory was not initially adept at ministerial work, things changed after 379, when the formidable Emperor Theodosius (347–95) assumed power. Though Gregory never studied in the great philosophical schools as Basil and his friend Gregory of Nazianzus (329–90) did, he was intellectually gifted and excelled in learning. He became a prominent religious figure in the late fourth century, assuming an important role in the Second Ecumenical Council of Constantinople, which formulated the final version of the Nicene Creed. While Gregory wrote many important theological works, in his later years amid the controversies just mentioned, he turned his attention to the spiritual life and the steady theme of seeking "perfection according to virtue."[1] In this season, it was only right that Gregory should write on Moses. The Jewish theologian Philo (ca. 20 BC–AD 50) had written on Moses's life, as had

---

1. Gregory of Nyssa, *Life of Moses* 2.

other Christians before Gregory. The story of Moses is iconic. He embodies the tensions of the spiritual life—a man chosen by God to lead his people, but who in weakness struggles to grow in godliness. In his book *The Life of Moses*, Gregory explores these tensions, using Moses's life as a paradigm for the Christian pursuit of virtue.

Gregory rehearses the basic storyline of Moses's life, drawing out the spiritual insights. Throughout his life, Moses experienced the joy of communion with God. One such episode is the famed account of the burning bush, where Moses first met God. The mysterious presence of God appeared in the fire. This tale, according to Gregory of Nyssa, is more than just a regular meeting between friends. Moses beheld God in the fire, a theophany of dazzling light. In that experience of revelation, Moses "came to know that none of those things which are apprehended by sense perception and contemplated by the understanding really subsists, but that the transcendent essence and cause of the universe, on which everything depends, alone subsists."[2] Through God and God alone, do all things exist and subsist.

What Moses beheld in the burning bush points to realities beyond the material world. He discovered a truth that oriented his life and the lives of all faithful believers in God. The glory of God would go before him, guiding his feet in the path toward the promised land. Moses understood in the burning bush, Gregory tells us, that there is no self-sufficiency of existence "without participating in true Being."[3] Only those in relationship with this God, who are walking the path toward him and his kingdom, will find the good life. This is not a life that takes pleasure in the things of this world, the things we see or touch; rather, it is a life that longs for the God revealed to Moses, the transcendent and lovely Creator of all things. Gregory argues that any notion that truth comes to us through mere observation of the material world or through the application of our rationality is consumed in the fire of the burning bush. Mere reason cannot direct a person toward the good life. Only those who confess the one true God have the spiritual perception to behold things as they really are.

In the burning bush, Moses meets God, discovering the nature of the divine being who will help him lead his people. Believing in God is one of the necessary first principles for the spiritual life. "The full knowledge of being comes about by purifying our opinion concerning nonbeing," Gregory writes.[4] For a true conception of things as they are, we should seek out not mere methods,

2. Gregory of Nyssa, *Life of Moses* 2.24.
3. Gregory of Nyssa, *Life of Moses* 2.25.
4. Gregory of Nyssa, *Life of Moses* 2.23.

Signs of God 37

strategies, principles, or applications, but God. Like Moses before the burning bush, we must take off our sandals and stand and behold God as he has been revealed through Moses and the prophets. Gregory writes, "In my view the definition of truth is this: not to have a mistaken apprehension of Being." Or to say it positively, "truth is the sure apprehension of real Being."[5]

Moses, for Gregory, becomes a paradigm of the true spiritual life—a life lived in communion and adoration of the one true God. Just as Moses at the burning bush "attained to this knowledge," Gregory writes, "so now does everyone who, like him, divests himself of the earthly covering and looks to the light shining from the bramble bush."[6] Those who behold God in the bush, sandals off and head humbly bowed in reverence, behold "the true light and the truth itself." Like Moses before the burning bush, interpreters must attune their heart to God at the beginning of their spiritual journey.

So far, I have argued that biblical theology, as the early church conceived it, involves the synergy of three things—Scripture, the rule of faith, and liturgy—and that these three things should also be ordered toward their proper end—beholding the glory of God. Biblical theology cannot exist apart from a trinitarian confession or from participation in the liturgical life of the community of faith. Now, in this chapter, I explain how the early Christians' vision of God, as articulated in the rule of faith, shaped their reading of Scripture.

I first discuss the crucial spiritual sense, the primary sense and purpose of reading Scripture. (I will return to the literal sense in the next chapter.) I explain how the early church discerned the spiritual sense by appealing to semiotic theory, which considers the relationship between the "signs" and the "things" of Scripture, or the ontological realities that it reflects. This discussion has the potential to get bogged down in the weeds, but it's essential to see how the fathers read Scripture as a prism revealing divine things. The rule of faith is essential here because it offers a description of God that converses with Scripture. Studying the spiritual association between text and referent demands careful evaluation of the words and terms in Scripture and how they communicate spiritual realities. The fathers show us that we should approach the text not lazily or arrogantly but with a humble, discerning posture.

Second, discerning the spiritual sense also entails several abiding postures that attune interpreters to a right reading of Scripture. These postures are derived from the church's doctrine of God expressed in the rule of faith, working in coordination with semiotics and creating an environment simmering with the collaboration between the rule of faith and Scripture. The signs of

5. Gregory of Nyssa, *Life of Moses* 2.23.
6. Gregory of Nyssa, *Life of Moses* 2.26.

Scripture point to the nature of God, and equally the nature of God frames our postures toward Scripture. A few basic attunements to the Scriptures found within the patristic writings include the assumptions that Scripture is God's self-revelation and that all interpretation must be worthy of God. The fathers also teach us that interpretation requires certain suppositions that flow from these two assumptions. They assume that Scripture is internally consistent—so Scripture ought to interpret Scripture—that we need divine assistance to comprehend Scripture, and that Scripture is our highest authority. Together, these postures create a culture for sound biblical theology.

With these items in place—a right view of God and a right orientation of the heart before the words of Scripture—the fathers show us our path forward and how we can make sense of God's revelation.

Scripture and the Spiritual Sense

The rule of faith discussed in the previous chapter is not some abstract concept or theory that stands aloof from interpretation; it actively participates in the granular details of exegesis. Once a Christian is baptized and catechized, they embrace a new identity and hold to a new vision of reality. When these catechized Christians open their Bibles, the faith expressed in the rule serves as a new pair of glasses through which they read everything in new color and texture. Reading by the burning light of revelation, they learn how Scripture's "various discourses both form and presuppose a larger theological vision."[7]

A perennial issue in interpretation, either in the ancient world or today, involves the question of referent. "Much of the history of biblical interpretation," William Yarchin argues, "concerns the question of referentiality in the Bible: to what extent are the texts of Scripture to be read for what they *plainly* state, and to what extent as figures of something other than their plain reference?"[8] Modern interpreters, by and large, hold a basic "referential theory of meaning, which assumes that our words and sentences are meaningful insofar as they successfully refer or point," and we must identify the *things* to which the *signs* in Scripture point.[9] In other words, as biblical scholar Kavin Rowe argues, in order to understand the Scriptures, we must explain the reality that stands behind and above the text.[10]

7. Jamieson and Wittman, *Biblical Reasoning*, 57.
8. Yarchin, *History of Biblical Interpretation*, xii.
9. O'Keefe and Reno, *Sanctified Vision*, 8.
10. Rowe, "Biblical Pressure and Trinitarian Hermeneutics," 311.

This is where the differences between ancient and modern interpretation become clear. Every interpretation of a sign, or a word in Scripture, requires a choice of referent, or a conscious decision to link that word with something else. Do the words of Scripture point to material things or spiritual things? Or both? How can one know the difference? More importantly, the assumptions that interpreters bring to the exegetical task shape these associations. Modern interpreters often assume what Charles Taylor describes as an "immanent frame," which considers only the immediate material world as the locus of truth. The immanent frame, Taylor writes, "constitutes a 'natural' order, to be contrasted to a 'supernatural' one, an 'immanent' world, over against a possible 'transcendent' one."[11] Interpreters with an immanent frame appeal to mere empirical observation and argue that "words and sentences should be best understood as referring to facts or states of affairs in the world."[12] Others, who appeal to phenomenology, draw "attention to how texts convey the consciousness or experiences of the author."[13] These assumptions inform postmodern hermenutics that privilege the author's tastes. Nestled between these choices, premodern interpretation assumes that the primary referents of Scripture, or the *things* to which Scripture points, are not merely material or phenomenological but spiritual.[14] God, and not merely some historical event outside of Scripture, is the starting point and the ultimate referent. In the ancient world, Christians argued that philosophers, other religious groups, and even (non-Christian) Jews could not truly comprehend the divine referent signified in Scripture, because they denied the fundamental conception of the divine. Only the truly "spiritual person," in Paul's words (1 Cor. 2:14–15), was able to do so, because the spiritual person came with the right faith expressed in the rule.

Once a Christian confesses the rule, this confession redirects the interpreter's perception of any given referent, like rewiring the connections in a circuit. The theological synthesis between text and referent is what the early church called the spiritual sense. It pointed to spiritual realities that were only spiritually discerned. "The natural person," Paul writes, "does not accept the things of the Spirit of God, for they are folly to him, and he is not able to understand them because they are spiritually discerned" (1 Cor. 2:14). Understanding the spiritual sense meant that Christian interpreters had "different assumptions about the meaningfulness of the scriptural text"—assumptions that informed their social

11. Taylor, *Secular Age*, 542.
12. O'Keefe and Reno, *Sanctified Vision*, 8.
13. O'Keefe and Reno, *Sanctified Vision*, 8.
14. I think this assumption is what frames the work of scholars such as David Yeago and Kavin Rowe, who further analytically describe the differences between judgments and concepts and the "biblical pressure" in Scripture toward a theological reading.

imaginary, or the way they perceived the theological realities, because Scripture had the power "to illuminate and disclose the order and pattern of all things."[15]

Basic biblical interpretation involves identifying the spiritual referent assumed in any word or passage. In other words, for the fathers, the literal sense is not opposed to the spiritual sense but closely tied to it. As theologian Henri de Lubac argues, "The Christian tradition understands that Scripture has two meanings," and the "most general name for these two meanings is the literal meaning and the spiritual ('pneumatic') meaning."[16] The only way to perceive the spiritual sense is through the literal, through the literal signs embedded in Scripture. The spiritual sense, de Lubac continues, is "contained and hidden in the letter," which means that the letter is good and necessary, "because it leads to the spirit."[17] The letter is the body of Scripture, and the literal sense is found in nothing other than the letter of Scripture. The words and terms, the signs, of Scripture are where the fathers find the literal sense. The church confesses that Scripture is not like any other book; its words are "words not taught by human wisdom but taught by the Spirit, interpreting spiritual truths to those who are spiritual" (1 Cor. 2:13).

Using Origen's analogy of the body, to understand the Scriptures, one must see them like a human person. Just as a person is composed of body, soul, and spirit, Scripture contains both literal and spiritual senses, according to the body and the soul, but also requires the Spirit to guide the interpreter in truth. The "principal object of the Holy Spirit," Origen tells us, "is to preserve the coherence of the spiritual sense, either in those things which ought to be done or in those things which have already been performed."[18] What this means, Origen continues, is that whenever the Spirit finds things "capable of being adapted to a spiritual meaning, he compose[s] a texture of both kinds in a single style of God."[19] The spiritual sense is essential for contemplating Christ and truly seeing him as the prophets reveal him. It is a key difference between Origen and his pagan interlocutors such as Celsus; the latter reads the Prophets and laughs at the silliness of the literal sense, while the former reads the literal sense and finds Christ. Origen argues that the literal sense covers the spiritual sense and clothes it like a veil, a garment, or a body.[20] An unending matrix of meanings is hidden in the words, meanings that are stitched together through the verbal connections in and among the scriptural

15. O'Keefe and Reno, *Sanctified Vision*, 7, 11.
16. De Lubac, *Medieval Exegesis*, 1:225.
17. De Lubac, *Medieval Exegesis*, 1:226.
18. Origen, *On First Principles* 4.2.9.
19. Origen, *On First Principles* 4.2.9.
20. Origen, *On First Principles* 4.2.7, 2.7.2.

witness. The literal sense is pregnant with the spiritual sense because it is bound with the latter, like a body to a soul (to use Origen's image). Drawing from Augustine and other early fathers of the church, Thomas Aquinas (ca. 1225–74) surmises that the literal sense is contained in the words of Scripture. Even if "commentators should adapt to the text of sacred Scripture some true things that the author does not intend," Aquinas writes, "there is no doubt that the Holy Spirit, who is the chief author of sacred Scripture, so understood." Meaning is not imposed upon the terms but found in them, as intended by the human and Divine Author. Every "truth," Aquinas continues, "that can be adapted to divine Scripture, without prejudice to the literal context, is the sense of Scripture."[21] So the literal sense is essentially the words in their arrangement within the fabric of revelation, framing truth that the divine Author intended.

I will spend more time explaining the association between the literal sense and the biblical narrative in the next chapter, but for my purposes here, it suffices to say that the focus of ancient exegetes was on the spiritual sense they could discern through the literal. The spiritual sense reveals God and God's work, thereby situating the reader within the theological-narrative substructure of Scripture.

In the early church, writers such as Origen and Augustine explained the spiritual sense with different terms and concepts that all bear a family resemblance. Take Augustine's description of the fourfold method of interpretation. In his work *On the Profit of Believing*, he writes, "All that Scripture therefore, which is called the Old Testament, is handed down fourfold to them who desire to know it, according to history, according to aetiology, according to analogy, according to allegory."[22] Augustine then walks through each of these points, observing that "history" is "when there is taught what has been written, or what has been done; what not done, but only written as though it had been done." History attends to the way the words appear on the page and how they present the narrative of events or actions. "Aetiology," Augustine continues, explains "for what cause anything has been done or said." This sense looks to the reason and purpose of the words, probing the spiritual intents in the text. The third feature is "analogy," which unites the two Testaments, showing that "the two Testaments, the Old and the New, are not contrary the one to the other." Finally, "allegory," or what Augustine also calls "figuration," is found when "certain things which have been written are not to be taken in

---

21. Aquinas, *Power of God* 4.a.1.
22. Augustine, *On the Profit of Believing* 5.

the letter, but are to be understood in a figure."[23] These are spiritual readings that are bound up in the letter, but they reflect realities and events that are only spiritually discerned.

Augustine makes similar observations in his unfinished literal commentary on Genesis.[24] While he uses different terms and often asks slightly different questions than other fathers do, a family resemblance exists in the ways that they all attempt to discern the spiritual sense. They all ask theological and moral questions of the text and try to grasp the theological unity of Scripture.

The spiritual sense, though, is complex, and throughout the early church, it was refracted into a kaleidoscope of terms that approach it from different vantage points. Part of the reason for this complexity is that the spiritual sense is not always easy to discern, and early Christian thinkers believed God wanted it that way. To them, the Holy Spirit intended the spiritual sense to be difficult to ascertain so that those who were unworthy of its truths would not have access to them and those who could access them would appreciate them more fully.[25]

But little consensus exists about the terms used to describe the object of the spiritual sense or how it is discerned. Terms such as *allegorical*, *typological*, *figurative*, *tropological*, and *prophetic* pervade early Christian writings. These terms coalesced in the medieval period with the development of what is called the quadriga, meaning the "fourfold sense" of Scripture. Like the four points on a cross, the quadriga comprised four perspectives on the text: the literal, the allegorical, the tropological, and the anagogical. These senses explain what the text says (the literal); what it calls us to believe (the allegorical); what it says about how we should live (the tropological); and what it says we should hope for (the anagogical). But by the time of Aquinas, the church found itself questioning the legitimacy of the quadriga to explain the totality of ancient exegesis. Still, these disparate points help capture the complexity of the spiritual sense. My point here is not to get lost in debates about the spiritual sense—I will discuss this in some detail in another chapter—but simply to recognize its complexity, while acknowledging that it is something the church must pursue.

Finding the Spiritual Sense: Text and Referent

In the early church, the spiritual sense involved the careful analysis between text and referent. We can already see the importance of discerning the right

23. Augustine, *On the Profit of Believing* 5.
24. Augustine, *Literal Meaning of Genesis* 2.5.
25. Origen, *On First Principles* 1.pf.8.

referent in the questions the Lord poses to the Pharisees in Matthew 22:41–45. He asks them, "What do you think about the Christ? Whose son is he?" They appear well informed and are quick to respond: "The son of David." But the Lord follows up with a second question. He quotes Psalm 110:1—"The Lord said to my Lord, 'Sit at my right hand, until I put your enemies under your feet'"—and queries them about the text's referent. "How is it then that David, in the Spirit, calls him Lord?" he asks. "If then David calls him Lord, how is he his son?" he continues. The Pharisees are speechless. Who is the true referent to the title "son," and why does David call him "Lord"? From our vantage point, the answers to these questions might seem obvious, but those who are not familiar with the incarnation might find this reading unpersuasive or naive.

The most developed and coherent explanation of text and referent—the signs of Scripture and the things to which they point, respectively—is found in Augustine's classic work *On Christian Doctrine*. Augustine offers a distinctively Christian understanding of semiotics, or the science of interpretation. He argues that reading Scripture requires that we observe the difference between "signs" (*signa*) and "things" (*res*). To name a *thing* is to describe reality, or what really exists; it is a metaphysical claim about God or creation.[26] *Signs*, on the other hand, are used to signify *things*, in the way we might use a flag to symbolize a nation or organization. All language, including scriptural language, functions this way, offering signs that signify reality. "Language, even the language of the scriptures," Frances Young explains, "belonged to a world of signs, a world of indirect knowledge occasioned by the Fall."[27] In the present age, the kingdom of God has not yet been realized among us, nor do we now behold the face of God as we will one day. Sin has separated us from God, and we need signs to help direct us back to communion with him.

Consider the way Scripture (e.g., John 10:11) uses the sign of a shepherd to signify something else—in this case, Christ. Of course, the sign of a shepherd is a concrete image that has a direct material referent: a person who cares for sheep. But in this case, the shepherd is an image that signifies a spiritual reality, which is Christ. We might be able to draw connections between a human shepherd, who cares for sheep in a field, and the person and work of Christ. A shepherd cares for sheep, protects them, leads them, feeds them, and so on. But this analogy can break down if pressed too far, for there are ways in which Christ is not like a shepherd. He can protect his sheep from much more than physical danger, and his food satisfies in ways that material food never will.

---

26. Augustine, *On Christian Doctrine* 1.6.
27. Young, *Biblical Exegesis*, 278.

Christ is the Great Shepherd (Heb. 13:20; 1 Pet. 5:4), who lays down his life for his sheep. Therefore, "a shepherd" is clearly a sign, but it also refers to a thing, and what that thing is makes all the difference in the world.

To make matters a bit more complicated, not all signs point to spiritual referents. Discerning the difference between spiritual and material referents is part of the challenging process of exegesis. The difficulty comes in the simple fact that all signs (e.g., "a shepherd") signify certain things (e.g., a flesh-and-blood shepherd), and they can signify other things as well (e.g., Christ). In other words, sometimes "a shepherd" refers to a simple flesh-and-blood shepherd and may not serve as a direct referent for Christ (Jer. 22:22; Zech. 11:17). Sometimes the signs signify just a material thing, not some other spiritual thing. The challenge of interpretation is understanding the things that "are spiritually discerned" (1 Cor. 2:14)—discerning the spiritual associations between text and referent, signs and things, and how the language of Scripture points to the ultimate Thing (that is, God).

This point gets to the basis of biblical theology described in the rest of this book. The sacred words of Scripture are the windows to know God. The fathers knew that "behind the signs of scripture was the reality of God, known in flashes of direct awareness"; the ancient theologians contemplated these signs, craving "more immediate access to the real world of 'things,' of God's very self."[28] When we open the pages of Scripture, we are reading no mere words; rather, we are reading revelation that gives us a glimpse of the divine through linguistic signs. For the early church, Scripture was "the orienting, luminous center of a highly varied and complex reality, shaped by divine providence."[29]

This discussion of signs and things, of text and referent, also raises a second question about the spiritual sense. The reason Augustine must explain this tension between text and referent is that the ultimate end of exegesis is love. A second rule, besides the rule of faith, is what he terms the rule of love. He understands that interpretation is not merely about the identity of signs and referents but also about our relations to these things. The rule of love is utilitarian in the best sense of the term, because not all things are the same— some things are to be "used" (*uti*) and some things are to be "enjoyed" (*frui*).[30] To enjoy a thing is "to cling to it with love for its own sake."[31] The things we

28. Young, *Biblical Exegesis*, 278–79.
29. O'Keefe and Reno, *Sanctified Vision*, 11.
30. Rowan Williams argues that Augustine's account of interpretation in *On Christian Doctrine* is "a set of variations on a single theme, the relation of *res* and *signum*, thing and sign, reality and representation." Williams, "Language, Reality, and Desire," 138.
31. Augustine, *On Christian Doctrine* 1.4.4.

enjoy make us happy and are loved as they are. Love is the theological virtue offering the perfect good, leading us to the object that makes us happy.

Using a thing, on the other hand, is "to employ it in obtaining that which you love, provided that it is worthy of love."[32] Love is the goal—or loving the right *thing* is the goal, I should say—because sometimes we can love things that ought not to be loved and love things that ought to be used. When we enjoy things that ought to be used, we divert our attention from things that are good, to lower things that hold us back from loving what is ultimately good. If we give too much attention to loving things that ought to be used, we can impede our growth and keep ourselves from loving the right thing. Nothing "better or more exalted" exists than God. To behold and contemplate the nature of God is to "place Him above all things mutable, either visible and corporal or intelligible and spiritual," says Augustine. Put simply, "All men struggle emulously for the excellence of God."[33] We have been created to enjoy God, to love God, and to behold the beauty of God. God is our homeland, our destination. But until we arrive at beholding God, at beatitude, we continue on our journey, a journey through a deeper love for God and neighbor.

Augustine establishes what he terms the rule of love that complements the rule of faith. The "two regulae"—the rule of faith and the rule of love—work together, "one with the focus on doctrine or belief (faith and hope), and the other on ethics (love)."[34] The rule of faith "lays out the 'things' to which Scripture points," which I discussed above; these are the things that are believed. The rule of love "teaches one how to relate to those 'things,'"[35] or how to walk in faith. To explain the essence of the rule of love, he turns to Matthew 22:37–40, "You shall love the Lord your God with all your heart and with all your soul and with all your mind. This is the great and first commandment. And a second is like it: You shall love your neighbor as yourself. On these two commandments depend all the Law and the Prophets."[36] This passage, Augustine tells us, "is the divinely instituted rule of love"; this rule ought to guide every interpretation of Scripture, every affection of our heart. The Lord's command in Matthew does not "leave any part of life which should be free and find itself room to desire the enjoyment of something else."[37] Tying these rules together means that all interpretation of Scripture should lead the

---

32. Augustine, *On Christian Doctrine* 1.4.4.

33. Augustine, *On Christian Doctrine* 1.7.7.

34. Andrews, *Hermeneutics and the Church*, 141. See Augustine, *First Catechetical Instruction* 4.8. For biblical passages that support this reading of the double love command, see Rom. 13:9–10 and 1 Tim. 1:5.

35. Andrews, *Hermeneutics and the Church*, 141.

36. Augustine, *On Christian Doctrine* 1.22.21, 1.26.27.

37. Augustine, *On Christian Doctrine* 1.22.21.

reader to greater knowledge and faith in God and God's relationship to the world, and a greater love for God and neighbor.

The purpose of reading Scripture is not just about gaining knowledge of God or the world but about love. Love is the aim of exegesis. The *Thing* we ought to love or enjoy is God, and we ought to use *things* here and now to lead us to our homeland, where we will see God and behold his beauty. When we sit down and open Scripture, we begin, in some small measure, to contemplate the things of God and to learn to enjoy God. In Augustine's words, "The things which are to be enjoyed are the Father, the Son, and the Holy Spirit, a single Trinity."[38] True happiness and satisfaction come only through enjoying God.[39] The desire to love God demands that, from the outset, Bible interpreters must confess that "God exists" and that "God speaks, communicates, and reveals himself to us in order that we might love him and, in turn, enjoy him."[40]

This discussion of text and referent, signs and things, and loving God is not unique to the bishop of Hippo. Many premodern interpreters are united with him in his spiritual discernment. Hilary makes the point that the problem with heresy is its failure to identify correct referents. "Heresy lies in the sense assigned, not in the word written," Hilary writes.[41] Many early Christian heresies stemmed from discerning an erroneous referent in the signs of Scripture. Origen, too, argues that the "unspeakable goodness of God" is "always read in the letter."[42] Gregory of Nyssa assumes that the linguistic expressions in Scripture describe the prior existence and activity of God. For Gregory, "religious language is grounded in what human beings perceive of God's operations: through contemplation of the works of God, certain particular and appropriate names are derived."[43] At every turn, the ancient church peered through the signs of Scripture to behold God.

An Example of the Spiritual Sense: Irenaeus and the Gnostics

While Augustine's description of signs and things is interesting, how does it actually work in practice? A good example is found in Irenaeus's debate with the Gnostics. The basic issue between Irenaeus and his interlocutors is a disagreement concerning the referents signified in the signs of Scripture.

38. Augustine, *On Christian Doctrine* 1.5.5.
39. Augustine, *On Christian Doctrine* 1.22.21, 1.26.27.
40. Holmes, *Theology of the Christian Life*, 3.
41. Hilary, *On the Trinity* 1.18.
42. Origen, *Homilies on Numbers* 9.7.5.
43. Young, *Biblical Exegesis*, 141–42.

They each encounter the same terms but perceive very different referents, differences that stem from contrasting assumptions about the nature of God. "These [Gnostics]," Irenaeus writes, "while seeking to explain the Scripture and parables, introduce another, greater God above the God who is the Creator of the world."[44] The Gnostics applied a foreign metaphysic to the Scriptures, which involved inventing a pantheon of gods and a myth that describes the creation and telos of the world. Then they forced the signs of Scripture to comport with that myth. Without the rule of faith and the rule of love, they have rejected the very God who created them, Irenaeus argues, and adapted the Scriptures (or the signs) "to the God whom they invented."[45] They read Scripture in correspondence with this god who does not exist, using those passages that are particularly difficult or ambiguous to support their factitious conceptions of their god.[46]

But Irenaeus is emphatic: any time an interpreter reads the Scripture, he or she must assume that when Scripture uses a term for God (*YHWH*, *Elohim*, *theos*, etc.), the one true God is the only referent in view. For "neither the Lord, nor the Holy Spirit, nor the apostles," Irenaeus writes, "would precisely and absolutely ever have named 'God' one who is not God, unless He truly was God." The only possible referent for any divine pronoun or title is "God the Father who has dominion over all things, and His Son who received from His Father power over creation."[47] Certainly there are places in Scripture that refer to "gods" and other such titles, designating some kind of other deity. In these cases, Irenaeus argues, the interpreter should read closely, noting the ways that Scripture does not "present them as gods absolutely, but with certain modifications and indication by which they are shown not to be gods."[48] These might be "gods" in some material sense, but they are not the one true, and absolute, God, Creator of all things.

This distinction between signs and referents is how we should understand Irenaeus's famous mosaic image. In *Against Heresies* 1.8.1, he compares the tesserae, or the tiles, of a mosaic to the signs of Scripture that portray the image of a king. Irenaeus argues that the Gnostics "endeavour to adapt with an air of probability to their own peculiar assertions the parables of the Lord, the sayings of the prophets, and the words of the apostles, in order that their scheme may not seem altogether without support."[49] In other words, they

---

44. Irenaeus, *Against Heresies* 2.10.2.
45. Irenaeus, *Against Heresies* 2.10.1.
46. Irenaeus, *Against Heresies* 2.10.1.
47. Irenaeus, *Against Heresies* 3.6.1.
48. Irenaeus, *Against Heresies* 3.6.3.
49. Irenaeus, *Against Heresies* 1.8.1.

assume that the signs of Scripture refer to a different god or gods embedded in their myth.

> By way of illustration, suppose someone would take the beautiful image of a king, carefully made out of precious stones by a skillful artist, and would destroy the features of the man on it and change around and rearrange the jewels, and make the form of a dog, or of a fox, out of them, and that a rather bad piece of work. Suppose he would then say with determination that this is the beautiful image of the king that the skillful artist had made, at the same time pointing to the jewels which had been beautifully fitted together by the first artist into the image of the king, but which had been badly changed by the second into the form of a dog. And suppose he would through this fanciful arrangement of the jewels deceive the inexperienced who had no idea of what the king's picture looked like, and would persuade them that this base picture of a fox is that beautiful image of the king.[50]

Both Irenaeus and the Gnostics are working with the same tiles, the same signs, but they assume that they correspond to different metaphysical referents. The Gnostics disassociate the natural referents to God, "violently drawing [them] away," in Irenaeus's words, "from their proper connection, words, expressions, and parables whenever found, to adapt the oracles of God to their baseless fictions." This kind of referential misapplication disregards "the order and the connection of the Scriptures, and so far as in them lies, dismember[s] and destroy[s] the truth." The Gnostics end up deceiving others by reappropriating the signs, or "transferring passages, and dressing them up anew, and making one thing out of another," fabricating interpretations that destroy the beautiful art of God as seen in the Scriptures.[51] The Gnostics begin with the wrong metaphysic and end up in the wrong place; they create meanings that do not reflect the God revealed in Scripture.

The fathers work in the other direction. In the pages of the New Testament and throughout the early church, there is an abiding concern to associate the words of Scripture with the nature and work of God. Exegesis is not an end in itself; to generate some isolated reading does not serve an inherent purpose. The end of exegesis is love, in the glory of God.

The Interpretive Postures of Biblical Theology

This whole discussion of the rule of faith and the spiritual sense points to the kind of culture in which biblical interpretation is nourished. Those who

50. Irenaeus, *Against Heresies* 1.8.1 (italics original).
51. Irenaeus, *Against Heresies* 1.8.1.

Signs of God

are baptized, anointed, and eucharized in the trinitarian God inhabit a culture defined by the Christian social imaginary. Christians perceive the world through that lens and contemplate the good work of God. Within this culture, there are several mores, or assumptions, that shape their approach to the text, logical entailments of their vision of God. These assumptions are involved in the application of method, but they are more important than method because they attune interpreters to the Scriptures. They create the kind of reading culture in which a reader can discern the spiritual sense. As Moses does before the burning bush, when we open the Scriptures, we must take off our sandals because we are standing on holy ground.

Given what they believed about God, early Christians approached the Scriptures with five assumptions that shaped the way they read the text. As I see them, these assumptions are closely aligned with Augustine's description of the purification of the mind, which should attend any interpretation. Since the interpreter's primary aim is to behold the glory of God, "the mind should be cleansed so that it is able to see that light and cling to it once it is seen."[52] The language of cleansing the mind might sound a bit odd to us at first, but what Augustine is getting at is how sinful humanity approaches God through the Scriptures. He turns to 1 Corinthians 1:21: "For since, in the wisdom of God, the world did not know God through wisdom, it pleased God through the folly of what we preach to save those who believe"—to explain how God saw fit to appear to those whose eyes are "weak" and "impure."[53]

This purification, "this process of cleansing," Augustine compares to a homeward journey. "Let us consider this process of cleansing as a trek, or a voyage, to our homeland," he writes.[54] For Augustine and the rest of the fathers, biblical interpretation is a journey toward beholding God within the cultural setting of a vibrant liturgical community. But we cannot journey to God without help. We need a docent who can direct us. We must contemplate material things, especially the Scriptures, and let that contemplation direct us toward the ultimate Thing—that is, God. "We have wandered far from God," Augustine continues; "if we wish to return to our native country where we can be blessed we should use this world and not enjoy it, so that the 'invisible things' of God 'being understood by the things that are made' [Rom. 1:20] may be seen, that is, so that by means of corporeal and temporal things we may comprehend the eternal and spiritual."[55] These assumptions that guide

52. Augustine, *On Christian Doctrine* 1.10.10.
53. Augustine, *On Christian Doctrine* 1.12.11.
54. Augustine, *On Christian Doctrine* 1.10.10.
55. Augustine, *On Christian Doctrine* 1.4.4.

interpretation are like the wisdom that guides a seasoned traveler on their journey. Only those who adopt these assumptions will be able to comprehend the things of God and journey to him through the Scriptures.

I imagine these five assumptions are like interlocking layers on a map that highlight the roads, contours, structures, and terrain and work together to lead the traveler home.[56] The first two portions include the assumptions that (1) Scripture is God's self-revelation and (2) all interpretation must be worthy of God. The colors of these two sections blend in harmony, conforming interpretive postures to the divine Word and shaping how interpreters read the signs of Scripture. Positioned around these two pieces are three more pieces that also flow together: (3) Scripture is internally consistent and harmonious, so Scripture ought to be used to interpret Scripture; (4) understanding divine revelation requires divine assistance; and (5) Scripture is the highest source of authority, such that no other source is more authoritative. Together, these five portions portray a beautiful vision of God.

Below, I discuss each of these assumptions, exploring how early Christian interpreters explain them.

Scripture Is God's Self-Revelation

The first layer of the map directing us to God is the assumption that Scripture is God's self-revelation. This conviction pervades the writings of the early church. Writing in the first century, Clement, bishop of Rome (died ca. 100), points out how the faithful have examined the Scriptures closely, seen that they are the "true utterances of the Holy Spirit," and known that "nothing of an unjust or counterfeit character is written in them."[57] The second-century theologian Clement of Alexandria (ca. 150–ca. 215) imagines Scripture as the voice of the divine Logos.[58] We read Scripture to hear God. Writing in the fourth century, John Chrysostom (ca. 347–407), the "golden-mouthed" preacher, refers to the Scriptures as a "door" to God. Those who want to seek and find God should enter the door of the Scriptures, for only the Scriptures "bring us to God, and open to us the knowledge of God."[59] The assumption

---

56. James Kugel argues that four assumptions about Scripture characterize all ancient interpretation: (1) the Bible is fundamentally a cryptic text; (2) Scripture is a relevant text; (3) Scripture is perfectly harmonious; and (4) all Scripture is divinely sanctioned. I agree with these assumptions generally, though I describe them more positively and identify *five* assumptions that flow from the ancients' vision of God. I also frame them logically, explaining how they are interrelated. See Kugel, *Traditions of the Bible*, 15–19. See also Behr, *Irenaeus of Lyons*, 129–30.

57. 1 Clement 45.2–3.

58. Clement of Alexandria, *Exhortation to the Heathen* 9.

59. Chrysostom, *Homilies on the Gospel according to St. John* 59.2.

that Scripture is the self-revelation of God is perhaps best expressed in Augustine's famous description of the Scriptures as the very "face of God." Citing Psalms 68:2 and 19:6 and Romans 12:11, Augustine argues that until we behold the beauty of God and see him face to face, we should "treat the Scripture of God as the face of God." When we consider Scripture, we should "melt in front of it," like wax on a candle.[60] These reflections are only a sampling of the constant refrain that the Scriptures offer the self-revelation of God.

Through the Scriptures, we encounter God and comprehend some small measure of his nature and mission. This means, contra Benjamin Jowett, that we cannot "interpret the Scriptures like any other book," because the Bible is not like any other book.[61] "Christians should reserve a special hermeneutic for the Bible that sees its diverse books and genres as one canon that functions in a particular way."[62] We find God in the Holy Writ. As John O'Keefe and R. R. Reno write, "To think in and through the scriptures is to have a sanctified vision," a vision of life from God's perspective.[63] The church's understanding of God and God's will is found in no other book than the Bible. The works of Homer and Plato, Walt Whitman or Jacques Derrida, may be interesting and even helpful in some regards, but they do not offer the self-revelation of God.

All Interpretation Must Be Worthy of God

If Scripture is the self-revelation of God, then it logically follows that all interpretation must be worthy of God. When they gaze on the words of God, ancient authors assume that the language of Scripture speaks truthfully of God. That biblical interpretation must be worthy of God is a common refrain among the writings of the church fathers.[64] In his catechetical work, Clement of Alexandria assumes that "truth is not found by changing the meanings (for so people subvert all true teaching), but in the consideration of what perfectly belongs to and becomes the Sovereign God." Such reading, befitting of God, is "demonstrated in the Scriptures again from similar Scriptures."[65] Conversely, those who misread Scripture are those "who do not quote or deliver the Scriptures in a manner worthy of God and of the Lord."[66] Origen makes a similar argument.

---

60. Augustine, *Sermon 22* 7.

61. Jowett, "On the Interpretation of Scripture," 458.

62. Billings, *Word of God*, 33.

63. O'Keefe and Reno, *Sanctified Vision*, 116.

64. This assertion is true despite Kugel's argument that the assumption is not well attested in the ancient world (Kugel, *Traditions of the Bible*, 18). The assumption might be less explicit before the apostolic writings, but early theologians often state that the Bible is divinely inspired.

65. Clement of Alexandria, *Stromata* 7.16.

66. Clement of Alexandria, *Stromata* 6.15.

In all places, Christian interpreters ought to aim for a meaning "worthy of God."[67] Both Basil and Gregory of Nyssa suggest that "God-fittingness" is a key feature of interpretation.[68] Reading divine revelation necessitates reading in ways that interpret God. It is not that Basil and Gregory always agree about Scripture's portrait of God's attributes, their qualities, or their potentialities, but they assume that Scripture speaks of God in a worthy manner.

Even when the words or narratives of Scripture appear to show God as capricious or violent, the fathers filter these passages through the classical attributes of God to demonstrate that each passage represents God accurately. Early-church scholar Brian Daley calls this style of reading "a hermeneutic of piety"; early Christians justify their exegesis with the claims that their reading is more "reverent" or more "appropriate to God" than other options.[69] Ancient Christians would never interpret Scripture in a way that denied or disparaged God as God has been revealed, which is why Augustine speaks of reading Scripture fearfully. We should "think and believe," he writes, that the Scriptures are "better and more true than anything which we could think of by ourselves, even when it is obscure."[70] If some of us were to interpret Scripture and deny that God is triune, or imagine that God is capricious or powerless, or believe that God is bound by time, our readings would be quite unworthy of God.

Even among potentially problematic texts, such as passages that present God with human or material attributes or passages that depict him judging with violence, an abiding principle that guides the fathers' interpretation is that "anything genuinely taught about God in Scripture must be worthy of God."[71] Origen applies this principle when he argues that not everything in Scripture—anthropomorphisms included—should be understood in the literal sense; instead, these images are given so that interpreters should diligently seek out the spiritual truth, eagerly searching for "a sense that is worthy of God."[72] God is spirit (John 4:24), so Christian interpreters should not think that God possesses anything material or bodily. With respect to passages that pose potential moral problems, such as Exodus 12:29, where God judges the Egyptian firstborn, writers such as Gregory assume that God's judgment is a just response to sin.[73] Such interpretations are just a few examples reflecting the general assumption that interpretation must be worthy of God.

67. Origen, *On First Principles* 4.2.8–9.
68. Basil, *Against Eunomius* 2.23–24; Gregory of Nyssa, *Catechetical Discourse* 24.5–7.
69. Daley, "Is Patristic Exegesis Still Usable?," 78.
70. Augustine, *On Christian Doctrine* 2.7.9.
71. Graves, *Inspiration and Interpretation of Scripture*, 124.
72. Origen, *On First Principles* 4.2.9.
73. Gregory of Nyssa, *Life of Moses* 2.91.

Scripture Interprets Scripture

The first two postures work together in a symbiotic way. Scripture is the revelation of God; thus, all interpretation ought to be worthy of God. The harmony between these assumptions points to a third: Scripture is self-referential and consistent. The fathers assume that we need revelation to interpret revelation, so Scripture ought to interpret Scripture. Early Christian biblical interpreters practiced the idea that "Scripture is such a timeless unity that passages from all over the biblical canon can be used to illuminate one another."[74] They argued that Scripture proclaimed one God, one economy, and one work of salvation, which were all detailed in the rule of faith, because Scripture was perfectly harmonious.[75] This did not mean that any revelation outside Scripture was viewed as unhelpful; rather, it meant that any good interpretation should result from biblical passages not being unequally yoked with extrabiblical passages.

This was such a common assumption that there is no shortage of exhortations among the fathers to read Scripture in continuity with Scripture. Irenaeus regularly uses the term "coherence" (*consonare*) to describe the assumption of the union of Scripture passages.[76] We find the same assumption in Clement of Alexandria, who argues that truth is found "in the consideration of what perfectly belongs to and becomes the Sovereign God" and that ascertaining this truth comes to us through "establishing each one of the points demonstrated in the Scriptures again from similar Scriptures."[77] Cyril of Jerusalem teaches this assumption to new believers in his *Catechetical Lectures*, saying, "Let no one therefore separate the Old from the New Testament." Anyone who denies that the Spirit of the Old Testament is not identical with the Spirit of the New Testament offends the Holy Spirit, "who with the Father and the Son together is honoured."[78] The union of the testaments creates a theological vision of life that will guide these catechumens. Tertullian (ca. 155–ca. 220) makes a similar argument, saying that the interpreter of Scripture should never assume any inconsistency, "for nothing is so much to be guarded as (the care) that no one [passage of Scripture] be found self-contradictory."[79] Finally, Augustine provides us with one of the most memorable summaries of this point: "the New Covenant veiled in the Old, and the Old Covenant revealed in the New."[80] This

---

74. Graves, *Inspiration and Interpretation of Scripture*, 72.

75. Kugel, *Traditions of the Bible*, 17.

76. Presley, *Intertextual Reception of Genesis 1–3*, 18–23.

77. Clement of Alexandria, *Stromata* 7.16.

78. Cyril of Jerusalem, *Catechetical Lectures* 16.4.

79. Tertullian, *On Monogamy* 11. In another place, Tertullian argues that the faithful ought to understand a few passages in light of the many. Tertullian, *Against Praxeas* 20.

80. Augustine, *Exposition of the Psalms* 105.36.

sampling shows the widely held assumption that the Scriptures are internally consistent and that, therefore, Scripture interprets Scripture.

The notion that Scripture interprets Scripture is related to what Rowe calls Scripture's "pressure." In brief, Scripture exerts pressure on its readers so that "there is (or can be) a profound continuity, grounded in the subject matter itself, between the biblical text and the traditional Christian exegesis and theological formation."[81] This concept assumes that the "two-testament canon read as one book pressures its interpreters to make ontological judgments about the trinitarian nature of the one God *ad intra* on the basis of its narration of the act and identity of the biblical God *ad extra*."[82]

The assumption that Scripture interprets Scripture does not mean that all Scripture is equally clear and understandable. On the contrary, given the divine origin of Scripture, patristic writers assume that portions of Scripture are difficult to understand. Many of them argue that unclear passages ought to be read with clear passages. Irenaeus explains this practice. On the one hand, he recognizes that "all Scripture, which has been given to us by God, shall be found by us perfectly consistent." But he also recognizes that not all Scripture is equally clear; some passages are more obscure than others. The unclear passages, or what he calls "parables," should be harmonized with those passages "which are perfectly plain," whereas the passages that have a clear meaning "shall serve to explain the parables." When Scripture is read with this kind of theological continuity, it proclaims, in Irenaeus's poetic imagery, "one harmonious melody in us, praising in hymns that God who created all things."[83] Irenaeus is not alone. Many others, such as Tertullian and Augustine, explain how interpreters ought to read unclear passages in continuity with clear ones.[84]

The fathers assume that the Bible is self-referential, and they have created a culture of interpretation that gathers around the Scriptures, meditates on them, and looks for the ways they collectively proclaim the truth of God; the

81. Rowe, "Biblical Pressure and Trinitarian Hermeneutics," 308. In a related way, de Lubac describes the "symbols of harmony" that unify the two testaments (*Medieval Exegesis*, 1:251). As he argues, "For the Christian there exist two successive 'Testaments,' which are not primarily or even essentially two books, but two 'Economies,' two 'Dispensations,' two 'Covenants,' which have given birth to two peoples, to two orders, established by God one after the other in order to regulate man's relationship with him." De Lubac, *Medieval Exegesis*, 1:227.

82. Rowe, "Biblical Pressure and Trinitarian Hermeneutics," 308.

83. Irenaeus, *Against Heresies* 2.28.3.

84. Tertullian, for example, argues "that uncertain statements should be determined by certain ones, and obscure ones by such as are clear and plain; else there is fear that, in the conflict of certainties and uncertainties, of explicitness and obscurity, faith may be shattered, truth endangered, and the Divine Being Himself be branded as inconstant" (*On the Resurrection of the Flesh* 21). See also Augustine, *On the Merits and Forgiveness of Sins* 3.7.

"compounding of texts with other texts" is characteristic of early Christian interpretation.[85] The fathers assume that Scripture provides an integrative framework for reality and the good life that is discerned through the fundamental unity of Scripture. Various interpretive schemas flow from these associations, such as typology, allegory, prophecy fulfillment, covenantal structures, and so on. All these strategies flow from basic assumptions concerning Scripture's self-referentiality.

Interpretation Requires Divine Assistance

The previous assumptions (Scripture is God's self-revelation, interpretation must be worthy of God, and Scripture interprets Scripture) suggest that biblical interpretation is not a mere human enterprise, devoid of spirituality. The convictions about the nature of Scripture, the contemplation of God, and associations among scriptural passages mean that interpreters depend on the Spirit to make sense of the biblical text. The fathers argue that understanding spiritual things necessitates the Spirit, so that only within the culture of the worshiping community can we make sense of divine revelation. The Spirit guides the faithful and illuminates their minds to understand ways of reading that are worthy of God and to discern his true nature.

That Scripture is truly understood only by those within the church and those indwelled by the Spirit of God is a constant refrain that can be found throughout the writings of the fathers. Only when the soul is purified is an interpreter able to see the "light and to cling to it once it is seen."[86] In his discussion of interpretation, Origen distinguishes between two types of *seeing God*: corporeal and spiritual. For the former, we need only physical eyes to see corporeal things, but for spiritual things, we need divine assistance. "It was by an act of grace that God appeared to Abraham and the other prophets," he writes. "The eye of Abraham's heart was not the only cause of his seeing God; it was God's grace freely offered to a just man that allowed him to see."[87] Cyril of Jerusalem captures this sentiment too. In an exhortation to catechumens, he reminds them that before they joined the church, they heard the Word but did not comprehend its meaning. While the Word echoed around them, they were "hearing of hope, and knowing it not; hearing mysteries, and not understanding them; hearing Scriptures, and not knowing their depth." But since these catechumens joined the church, the echo, Cyril writes, has been "no longer around thee, but within thee; for *the indwelling Spirit* henceforth

---

85. Young, *Biblical Exegesis*, 133.
86. Augustine, *On Christian Doctrine* 1.10.10.
87. Origen, *Homilies on Luke* 3.1.

makes thy mind a house of God."[88] Now these catechumens hear the Word proclaimed and understand through the Spirit.

Other fathers make a similar point. In one letter written to an anxious widow seeking advice, Basil of Caesarea reminds her that she has "the consolation of the Holy Spirit" and stands "in need neither of [his] assistance nor of that of anybody else to help [her] comprehend [her] duty." Instead, appealing to the Spirit's help in interpreting the Scriptures, Basil writes, "You have the all-sufficient counsel and guidance of the Holy Spirit to lead you to what is right."[89] Like Basil, Irenaeus reminds his faithful readers, "The Lord taught us that no one is able to know God unless taught by God. God cannot be known without the help of God."[90] In another place, Irenaeus is even more explicit: "Man cannot see God on his own. If God wills to be seen he will be seen by those to whom he wills to be seen, when he wills, and in what ways he wills."[91] Others, such as Ambrose, whose spiritual interpretation guided Augustine toward a clearer understanding of the Scriptures, acknowledge that many things are obscure in Scripture but that "God teaches and illuminates the minds of each, and pours into them the light of knowledge, if thou dost open the doors of thy heart, and dost give entertainment to the light of heavenly grace." "When thou art in doubt," Ambrose continues, "inquire diligently; for he that seeks finds, and to him that knocks it is opened."[92]

As I mentioned in the previous chapter, the fathers often use the language of "illumination" to describe this assumption concerning the Spirit's guidance. A good example of this language is found in the story of Justin Martyr's (ca. 100–ca. 165) conversion. Through a serendipitous meeting with an old Christian philosopher, Justin discusses the nature of philosophy, creation, the soul, and God. Finally, the old man implores Justin to seek the truth found in the Scriptures because, even before the times of the philosophers, the biblical writers "spoke through the inspiration of the Holy Spirit and predicted events that would take place in the future." He encourages Justin to pray that his mind be illuminated, saying, "Above all, beseech God to open to you the gates of light, for no one can perceive or understand these truths unless he has been enlightened by God and his Christ."[93] Justin reports that his mind is illuminated, and he does indeed convert to Christianity and commits himself

88. Cyril of Jerusalem, *Catechetical Lectures* pro.6.
89. Basil, *Letter 283*.
90. Irenaeus, *Against Heresies* 4.6.4. See also Origen, *Contra Celsum* 3.47, 7.42.
91. Irenaeus, *Against Heresies* 4.20.5.
92. Ambrose, *Exposition of Psalm 118 (119)* 8.59.
93. Justin, *Dialogue with Trypho* 7.

Signs of God 57

to teaching the Scriptures. Throughout his apologetic writings, Justin assumes that divine grace is necessary for understanding Scripture.

This emphasis on illumination does not mean that early Christian thinkers deny a place for rational faculties. While the Greek philosophers assume that all truth is achieved through reason, Christians "who believeth then the divine Scriptures with sure judgment," Clement of Alexandria writes, receive "in the voice of God, who bestowed the Scripture, a demonstration that cannot be impugned."[94] To receive Scripture is to receive the voice of God, which is beyond demonstration. "Faith, then, is not established by demonstration," he continues; "'Blessed therefore those who, not having seen, yet have believed.'"[95] Far from being rationally suspect, the Scriptures are mysterious, the fathers assume; they contain ever-increasing depth and profundity, beyond what mere human reason can attain. Even among texts that appear mundane, divine truths can be found. "The more simple and easy this Scripture appears in the way it is worded," de Lubac writes, "the more profound and majestic are its meanings."[96] Origen, for example, found the Scriptures to be an ever-increasing well of truth. "The further we progress in reading," he writes, "the greater grows the accumulation of mysteries for us." Origen compares studying Scripture to sailing on a vast ocean in a small boat. As the boat stays close to shore, one has little to fear, but as interpreters advance deeper into a "vast sea of mysteries," they encounter the swells and waves that toss about their little boat. Terrified with fear, the interpreter's only prayer is that "the Lord should see fit to give [them] a favorable breeze of his Holy Spirit," that they "shall enter the port of salvation with a favorable passage of the word."[97] The breeze of the Holy Spirit is the hope for divine illumination to comprehend the things of God.

Divine assistance also does not mean that a Christian interpreter ought to approach the Scriptures lazily or curtail the exegetical process, assuming that good interpretation comes easily. On the contrary, it is only through reading the Scriptures that they become clearer. Origen, for example, calls his readers to engage in daily study. "The more one reads the Scriptures daily," he writes, "the greater one's understanding is, the more renewed always and every day."[98] Similarly, Athanasius (ca. 296/298–373), the bishop of Alexandria, calls his readers to regular engagement with the Scriptures, saying, "The knowledge of our religion and of the truth of things is independently manifest rather than

94. Clement of Alexandria, *Stromata* 2.2.
95. Clement of Alexandria, *Stromata* 2.2 (quoting John 20:29).
96. De Lubac, *Medieval Exegesis*, 1:76.
97. Origen, *Homilies on Genesis* 9.1.
98. Origen, *Homilies on Genesis* 9.1.

in need of human teachers, for almost day by day it asserts itself by facts, and manifests itself brighter than the sun by the doctrine of Christ."[99] Cyril of Jerusalem uses the image of a bee to describe how the Christian ought to engage Scripture. *"Go to the bee, and learn how industrious she is,"* Cyril writes; "hovering round all kinds of flowers, she collects her honey for thy benefit: that thou also, by ranging over the Holy Scriptures, mayest lay hold of salvation for thyself."[100] Just as bees hover around flowers to gather honey, Christians ought to hover around the Scriptures and delight in the sweetness of salvation. Similarly, Jerome (ca. 342/347–ca. 420) writes to Paulinus (ca. 354–431), bishop of Nola, "I beg of you, my dear brother, to live among these books, to meditate upon them, to know nothing else, to seek nothing else." Is not this life of meditation on Scripture, Jerome asks, "a foretaste of heaven on earth?"[101]

Scripture Is the Highest Authority

All the assumptions discussed above—Scripture is God's self-revelation, biblical interpretation must be worthy of God, Scripture interprets Scripture, and interpretation requires divine assistance—created an interpretive culture in which Scripture was the primary curriculum. The goal of early Christian theologians was to contemplate the mind of Scripture and to perceive truth and reality through the text. This vision, cast through a matrix of Scriptures, helped fashion an ecclesial culture that was embedded within other ancient communities and that often competed for allegiance with their various authorities. Through all of this, the fathers held Scripture as the highest authority.

Many early Christian writers extolled the authority of the Scriptures. Gregory of Nyssa argues, citing the words of his older sister Macrina, "We always use the holy Scripture as the canon and rule of all our doctrine."[102] In another place, he argues, "Let the inspired Scripture, then, be our umpire, and the vote of truth will surely be given to those whose dogmas are found to agree with the Divine words."[103] Basil, addressing some doctrinal disputes, writes, "Let God-inspired Scripture decide between us."[104] Athanasius similarly argues, "But this all-inspired Scripture also teaches more plainly and with more authority, so that we in our turn write boldly to

---

99. Athanasius, *Against the Heathen* 1.1.
100. Cyril of Jerusalem, *Catechetical Lectures* 9.13.
101. Jerome, *Letter 53* 10.
102. Gregory of Nyssa, *On the Soul and the Resurrection* 3.
103. Gregory of Nyssa, *On the Holy Trinity*, 327.
104. Basil, *Letter 189* 3.

you as we do."[105] Athanasius argues that anyone who reads Scripture can confirm his arguments, because "an argument when confirmed by higher authority is irresistibly proved."[106] Clement of Alexandria uses the image of a craftsperson to argue that the Scriptures are superior to any other source of knowledge. Just as a craftsperson is skilled in a particular art, far superior to others who try the same art, so also are the Scriptures superior to anything else.[107] Augustine also argues that even ecclesiastical authorities are not more authoritative than Scripture: "For the reasonings of any men whatsoever, even though they be Catholics, and of high reputation, are not to be treated by us in the same way as the canonical Scriptures are treated. We are at liberty, without doing any violence to the respect which these men deserve, to condemn and reject anything in their writings, if perchance we shall find that they have entertained opinions differing from that which others or we ourselves have, by the divine help discovered to be the truth. I deal thus with the writings of others, and I wish my intelligent readers to deal thus with mine."[108]

The fathers trust the sacred Scriptures above all other things, not in the sense that they think the Scriptures answer every question, but in the sense that the Scriptures provide the theological vision needed to make sense of everything else. They would have agreed with C. S. Lewis's sentiments, "I believe in Christianity as I believe that the Sun has risen not only because I see it but because by it I see everything else."[109] Without this framework, Irenaeus writes, "man would always be in search without ever finding, because he had rejected the very method of investigation."[110] Appealing to the fathers' theological interpretation, Jens Zimmermann writes, "By grounding all human knowledge in the eternal Logos of Christ, early church theologians found a way to unify reason and faith, a way that duly considered both faith's dependence on reason and reason's inability to supersede faith."[111] Any interpreter needs a theological vision; otherwise they will bring whatever cultural or philosophical influences they inherit to the exegetical task. Without a rule of faith, there will be found as many interpretations as there are interpreters, or in Irenaeus's words, "as many interpreters of the parables as there would

105. Athanasius, *Against the Heathen* 3.45.
106. Athanasius, *Against the Heathen* 3.45.
107. Clement of Alexandria, *Stromata* 7.16.
108. Augustine, *Letter 148*.
109. Lewis, "They Asked for a Paper," 165.
110. Irenaeus, *Against Heresies* 2.27.2.
111. Zimmermann, *Incarnational Humanism*, 11. He goes on to add, "By abandoning this healthy correlation of reason and faith, modern Western conceptions of truth continue to suffer from rationalism, relativism and dualism" (11).

be, just so many truths would be seen at war with each other and setting up contradictory opinions."[112]

At the same time, most early Christian thinkers were well versed in the writings of the philosophers and rhetoricians. They even recognized that some philosophers, such as Plato, approached the truth of God more closely than others. But they approached the pagan writings in a few different ways.

First, they regularly defended the uniqueness and superiority of the Scriptures over pagan literature. Justin is a good example. In the story of his conversion, he debates an old Christian philosopher, who tells him that the authors of Scripture "did not use demonstration in their treatises, seeing that they were witnesses to the truth above all demonstration, and worthy of belief."[113] Cyril of Jerusalem makes a similar argument when he tells his catechumens that the mysteries of the faith require an exposition of the Scriptures. The salvation that the church offers "depends not on ingenious reasoning, but on demonstrations of the Holy Scriptures."[114] As Cyril does, Origen argues that the writings of the prophets and apostles do not need proof; rather, they are above all proof. The gospel "has a proof which is peculiar to itself, and which is more divine than a Greek proof based on dialectical argument." Unlike the philosophers, the Scriptures have "the proof of the Spirit and of power."[115] Chrysostom regularly contrasts the authority of the Scriptures with that of the pagan literature. In one homily, he exhorts his people to "disregard what this man and that man thinks about these things, and inquire from the Scriptures all these things; and having learnt what are the true riches, let us pursue after them that we may obtain also the eternal good things."[116] In another homily, Chrysostom states that we have put on "the mind of Christ" (1 Cor. 2:16; Phil. 2:5) so that our thinking is not derived from "Plato, nor of Pythagoras, but it is Christ Himself, putting His own things into our mind."[117] Finally, Gregory of Nyssa argues something similar, saying, "Thus does our reason, under the guidance of the Scripture, place not only the Only-begotten but the Holy Spirit as well above the creation, and prompt us in accordance with our Savior's command to contemplate Him by faith in the blessed world of life giving and uncreated existence."[118]

112. Irenaeus, *Against Heresies* 2.27.1.
113. Justin, *Dialogue with Trypho* 7.
114. Cyril of Jerusalem, *Catechetical Lectures* 4.17.
115. Origen, *Contra Celsum* 1.2.
116. Chrysostom, *Homilies on Second Corinthians* 13.
117. Chrysostom, *Homilies on First Corinthians* 7.12.
118. Gregory of Nyssa, *Against Eunomius* 1.23.

Augustine provides a reasoned defense of the authority of the Scriptures. His whole hermeneutical project "presupposes a community that centers around a single group of texts that have been recognized as authoritative, seen as the place to hear God's will."[119] In one insightful letter penned to Jerome, he writes:

> For I admit to Your Charity, I learned to show this reverence and respect only to those books of the scriptures that are now called canonical so that I most firmly believe that none of their authors erred in writing anything. And if I come upon something in those writings that seems contrary to the truth, I have no doubt that either the manuscript is defective or the translator did not follow what was said or that I did not understand it. I, however, read other authors in such a way that, no matter how much they excel in holiness and learning, I do not suppose that something is true by reason of the fact that they thought so, but because they were able to convince me either through those canonical authors or by plausible reason that it does not depart from the truth.[120]

One has no grounds for elevating any authority above the writings of the prophets and apostles. These writings are where we meet God. The prophetic and apostolic corpus "excels all the writings of all nations by its divine authority"; indeed, "Scripture has a sacredness peculiar to itself."[121]

Second, not only did the fathers defend the authority of the Scriptures against pagan literature; they also strove to converse with it and meet philosophy "argument for argument."[122] The fathers were invested in a cultural exegesis that aimed to engage the philosophical world. When Origen established his catechetical school in Alexandria in the third century, the Scriptures were at the center of the curriculum. But whenever he identified students who were intellectually gifted, he provided them with a detailed study of all philosophical streams and carefully worked through the insights and weaknesses of each.[123] This tactic is consonant with Basil's approach to ancient literature. Basil describes his own educational experience, saying, "Do not think it strange, then, if I say to you, who each day resort to teachers and hold converse with the famous men of the ancients through the words which they have left behind them, that I myself have discovered something of especial advantage to you." The Scriptures are more useful than studying the pagan writers. Using the image of a ship's rudder, which helps steady a sailing

---

119. Andrews, *Hermeneutics and the Church*, 134.
120. Augustine, *Letter 82* 3.
121. Augustine, *City of God* 11.1; Augustine, *Reply to Faustus the Manichaean* 11.5.
122. Wilken, *Spirit of Early Christian Thought*, 14.
123. Gregory Thaumaturgus, *Oration and Panegyric Addressed to Origen* 14.

vessel and keep it on course, Basil argues, "You should not surrender to these men [Greek authors] once for all the rudders of your mind, as if of a ship, and follow them whithersoever they lead." But gather from them "only that which is useful" and disregard that "which ought to be overlooked."[124] Like a skilled docent, the Christian is free to wander the trails of pagan literature and discern the more splendid parts but ignore that which is useless.

Third, far from ignoring general revelation, the fathers put the Scriptures in conversation with philosophy and aimed to maintain a healthy understanding of the relationship between faith and reason. As early as the second century, Irenaeus explains the classic formula of faith seeking understanding. "Action, then, comes by faith," Irenaeus writes, "as 'if you do not believe,' Isaias says, 'you will not understand.'" Irenaeus argues that the Scriptures demand of interpreters an epistemological humility. He assumes that human reason can comprehend a great deal, but some things must remain with God. "If, for example, anyone should ask us what God did before he created the world, we reply that the answer to this is in God's keeping." The Scriptures teach us that the world was formed by God, but "no Scripture reveals what God did before this." Irenaeus offers many other examples from creation, some concerning which modern science has managed to give plausible explanations, but certainly some metaphysical questions and questions of causation remain.[125] Irenaeus concludes that we are able to "explain some of the things [in Scripture], though we leave others in God's keeping," so that, both in this life and the next, "God may always teach and man may always learn from God."[126] God's revelation is the highest authority and always guides the faithful reader toward wisdom.

Conclusion

This chapter has continued to unveil the biblical theology of the early church, and there is much here that the contemporary church should recover. Like Moses before the burning bush, we need to learn to behold God in the Scriptures. For too long, modern reflection on the Bible has rejected the spiritual sense, preferring to focus on the mundane realities of this world alone. The fathers compel us to reconsider things. The signs of Scripture reveal to us the

124. Basil, *Address to Young Men* 1.
125. Irenaeus, *Against Heresies* 2.28.3. He appeals to the Pauline maxim "'Knowledge' puffs up, but love builds up" (1 Cor. 8:1) in his discussion of the philosophers who function without a basic existential framework. Irenaeus, *Against Heresies* 2.26.1, 2.27.2.
126. Irenaeus, *Against Heresies* 2.28.3.

spiritual sense latent in the literal. The sacred words of Scripture are like a prism that illuminates the things of God. The question of referent is as applicable today as it was in the ancient world; the same God who created all things still reigns and rules over creation, and we face the same fundamental questions about the nature and work of God as the ancients did. When we perceive God in Scripture, we should seek to understand him in ways that are becoming of his revealed self. The fathers show us how to read Scripture without suppressing the spiritual referent embedded in the literal sense. We will surely have reasonable disagreements about the nature of God and creation; the premodern tradition is filled with heated theological debates among those who share the same rule of faith. By and large, those theological differences were downstream of the common assumption that Scripture reveals spiritual things. This attention to assumptions is what makes premodern biblical theology so helpful. The fathers do not offer just a few interesting methods for reading Scripture; instead, they remind us to frame our basic postures toward the world and to celebrate the theological lens through which we see the world. God is the Creator and Sustainer of all things, and we have been created in the image of God, to love God.

The fathers remind us that we cannot treat the Bible like any other book. Once we confess Christ and join the community of faith, we embrace a culture that reads Scripture with unique attunements. These attunements are the basic assumptions about both the interpreter and the nature of the text itself, and they help frame the spiritual sense, including the convictions that Scripture is God's revelation, that all interpretation must be worthy of God, that Scripture should interpret Scripture, that interpretation requires divine assistance, and that Scripture is the highest authority. These assumptions are involved in the application of method, but they transcend method, because they set interpreters on the right path. And they can guide us too. God is the God of Scripture. When we read the Bible, we must learn to read in ways that are worthy of God, always respecting him, his revelation, and the very words of Scripture. These assumptions form an ecclesial culture in which exegesis takes place, guiding readers of Scripture in the right direction, toward God. We need to live amid this community, guided by the assistance of the Spirit and always respecting Scripture as our final authority in all matters of faith and practice.

In the next chapter, I explain the literal sense in more detail by examining the narrative that unfolds in Scripture.

NARRATIVES OF SCRIPTURE

Irenaeus, bishop of Lyons in the second century, encountered various Gnostic sects courting members of his congregation. In his day, the term *Gnostics* became a catchall for different groups that shared some basic assumptions about the spiritual and material worlds. These groups tended to imagine the existence of a good, spiritual world above, which stood in stark contrast to an evil, material world below. The Gnostics created various myths or stories about these spiritual realities above and the creation of the world at the hands of rebellious, wicked gods. Irenaeus worked to catalog and refute these different streams of Gnosticism. Eventually, his project ballooned into a five-volume work commonly known as *Against Heresies*, which begins with a detailed account of the theological system of a Gnostic sect called the Valentinians.

Describing the Valentinian system can feel a bit like entering the strange world of a science fiction novel. All things, they assume, begin with "the perfect Aeon that was before all." This perfect Aeon dwells in a heavenly realm called the Pleroma and goes by many different names, which they interchange regularly: First Being, First Beginning, First Father, and Profundity.[1] Each of these names sheds light on different attributes of this original perfect being. Surrounding this Aeon is a host of other aeons with all kinds of names, such as Silence, Mind, Word, Life, and Church. There are thirty in all, a pantheon

---

1. Irenaeus, *Against Heresies* 1.1.1.

of spiritual beings, which exist in a hierarchy descending to the last one, named Sophia (or Wisdom). In a moment of weakness, Sophia committed a grievous act; she embraced passion and devised to comprehend the greatness of First Father. Through this incomprehensible act, Sophia became isolated from the others and brought forth a degenerate offspring called the Demiurge.

Born of vanity and other vices, the Demiurge embodied depravity and ignorance, being unaware of the true spiritual realities above him. The Demiurge, in turn, fashioned the material world, the creation partaking in the nature of its wicked creator. The result was that creation was infused with all the depraved passions of "fear, grief, and perplexity."[2] The crowning achievement of the Demiurge's creative program was creating the "earthly element of man," which he thought he would rule. But he did not know that behind him, his mother, Sophia, was working too. She deposited the seed of a divine spark in the earthly covering of humankind—the perfect element of human beings that longs to ascend to the heavenly realm.[3] In time, a spiritual savior appeared from the heavens to initiate some into the mysteries of the unseen realm and the knowledge of the divine spark.[4] Truly spiritual ones "are spiritual, not by conduct, but by nature and so will be saved entirely and in every case."[5] The truly spiritual are released from any concern for the sins of the body, and the body will pass away, so they are free to enjoy all the passing pleasures of this life.[6]

These Gnostics, Irenaeus reports, not only create this myth, but they then turn to the Scriptures and conform certain passages to defend this account of reality. One of their favorites is Isaiah 45:5, "I am the LORD, and there is no other," which they interpret to mean that the Demiurge is ignorant and prideful, unaware of the superior aeons above him.[7] They interpret all the other passages in the Old Testament like this, so the story of salvation, from the Gnostic point of view, is the story of freedom from the Demiurge and the material world he created. The Gnostics also use many passages in the New Testament to describe the work of the savior, who is often called Jesus Christ—though "Jesus" and "Christ" represent two different elements of the savior. The spiritual element is the living Jesus who freely abandons his mortal body, whereas the fleshly part is Christ that is crucified. They also sift

2. Irenaeus, *Against Heresies* 1.5.4.
3. Irenaeus, *Against Heresies* 1.5.6.
4. Irenaeus, *Against Heresies* 1.6.1.
5. Irenaeus, *Against Heresies* 1.6.2.
6. This is just one of the many Gnostic myths Irenaeus encountered in the early church. Throughout *Against Heresies* 1, he details various Gnostic groups that have their own versions of this myth. The names, characters, and events differ, but the same basic storyline remains.
7. Irenaeus, *Against Heresies* 1.5.4.

through the words and actions of the savior to discover knowledge of the spiritual realm above.

Irenaeus responds to this myth by offering an entirely different conception of God, creation, humanity, and salvation history. The trouble with the Gnostics is not that they cite the Bible; the trouble is that they come to it with a fabricated myth, not the truth found in its pages. "It is necessary," Irenaeus writes, "that we begin with the first and greatest principle, with the Creator God who made heaven and earth and all things in them, whom these individuals blasphemously call the fruit of degeneracy."[8] The Gnostic reading of the Bible begins with different first principles, and everything flows from there. For Irenaeus, the one true God created all things through his Word, bestowing on all things, both spiritual and material, "form and order and the principle of their creation."[9] From this premise, the Scriptures resound together like a harp; they harmonize into a unified "system of truth" that sings "one harmonious melody" about God and God's work of salvation.[10] This melody of salvation declares a different story, the true narrative, or "tradition," that "proclaims one God almighty, the Creator of heaven and earth, the Fashioner of man, who brought on the flood, and called Abraham, who led the people out of the land of Egypt, who conversed with Moses, who gave the law and sent the prophets, and who has prepared fire for the devil and his angels."[11] Irenaeus knows the Gnostic myths, but he chooses a different story—the story of the one true God who is at work in creation and is ushering humanity to their appointed end.

In chapter 1, I described the synergy between Scripture, the rule of faith, and liturgy in the fathers' approach to Scripture. These things exist in a hermeneutical dance, mutually informing and guiding the people of God. Then, in the previous chapter, I examined these points in more detail, exploring the ways in which the rule has shaped the fathers' reading of the signs of Scripture, as well as the assumptions that have influenced their general exegetical posture.

In this chapter, I explain another piece of the puzzle of early Christian biblical theology: the narrative of salvation history. I first consider the literal sense that the fathers find in the letter, the very words of Scripture and explain how the literal sense is understood as a narrative that coordinated Scriptures in a history of salvation. Early Christian theologians pay close attention to "the way the words go," but they are concerned with not merely isolated

8. Irenaeus, *Against Heresies* 1.2.1.
9. Irenaeus, *Against Heresies* 1.2.4.
10. Irenaeus, *Against Heresies* 2.25.1–2.
11. Irenaeus, *Against Heresies* 3.3.3.

terms or phrases but also the relations of words, stories, and books that unite Scripture's revelation. The literal sense forms a narrative of Scripture, a complex and beautiful tapestry of redemption traced out along the storyline of Scripture. The world depicted in Scripture is the "real" world—that is, the proper intellectual perception of reality. It's a spiritual perception that helps make sense of this world. It does not simply offer some nice anecdotes or postulates; it gives a sweeping vision of the whole. When the fathers read the biblical text, every passage is mapped onto a larger web of linkages and interconnections to portray a single, beautiful, and complex story of God's salvation history.

The story of Scripture is the substructure supporting the work of God in the world. It offers a decorated arena that stages the events of human history. For the early church, only "one public history" contains the real and honest acts of God and humanity.[12] Tracing out the narrative of Scripture is where the modern discipline of biblical theology has shined. Many works chart the storyline of the Bible, such as Vaughan Roberts's book *God's Big Picture: Tracing the Storyline of the Bible*, or Craig G. Bartholomew and Michael W. Goheen's popular treatment *The Drama of Scripture: Finding Our Place in the Biblical Story*. These books originate from the same impetus as that of the early church; they seek to find the unity of the Scriptures.

Second, for the early church, the "narrative" vision of Scripture is a complex unity, because it contains the spiritual sense. It is simultaneously a single narrative that moves from creation to new creation and many episodes congealing together under the providential working of God in creation—like a single tree, with many branches twisting and interlacing. The single ideal narrative legitimizes the meshwork of intertextual connections between points running along the storyline. The narratives bind together through various theological and covenantal themes, and I provide several examples. The unity of the narrative helps situate the particular stories so that interpreters can make sense of their inner connectivity and fashion their own retellings of the stories.

Third, I discuss the assumptions that are associated with the literal sense, including the notion that interpreters find their identity in the biblical narrative, which is always christologically conceived. In other words, the person and work of Christ is like the mortar binding together the bricks of the biblical narrative; everything is built in and through Christ. The fathers assume that strategies of intertextuality can more intimately bind the narrative together.

12. O'Donovan, *Desire of the Nations*, 2.

Narratives of Scripture

The narrative structure allows for dynamic cross-referencing, with various intertextual bindings reinforcing the narrative.

The Death of Narrative

Many years ago, the biblical narrative was, to use Hans Frei's famous expression, "eclipsed." But things did not start out that way. For centuries before the rise of historical criticism in the eighteenth century, the reading of the Bible was, as Frei writes, "usually strongly realistic, i.e. at once literal and historical, and not only doctrinal or edifying." Premodern Christians who contemplated the events of Scripture "envisioned the real world as formed by the sequence told by the biblical stories." The narrative was totalizing. It was a sequence that "covered the span of ages from creation to the final consummation to come." This sequence of events served a purpose. It framed the beginning and end of things and the human approach to the social and political worlds, providing "the governance both of man's natural environment and of that secondary environment which we often think of as provided for man by himself and call 'history' or 'culture.'"[13] The people saw themselves as participants in a larger narrative and conducted their lives, creating a culture, in response to this narrative.

Then came the philosophers. As the eighteenth century developed, Enlightenment thinkers broke up the narrative and disconnected the individual stories from real events. They turned to natural revelation, which they privileged over special revelation, and began speaking about the world in ways that untied the theological threads of Scripture. Scholars slowly dissected the individual portions and appended them to various human authors, genres, and other literary features, thus reversing the direction of interpretation. Life was perceived no longer through the lens of Scripture but through the rational or emotional ingenuity of the human mind. Without spiritual coherence, the narrative unity of Scripture died. Frei comments on this fatality: "As the realistic narrative reading of the biblical stories broke down, literal or verbal and historical meaning were severed and literal and figural interpretation, hitherto naturally affiliated procedures, also came apart."[14] Once the literal and historical meanings were ripped apart, and the spiritual sense excised, essentially, the whole tapestry of precritical readings lay dead on the floor. Even today, many of us have been taught to read the Bible in atomized ways "as if it were merely a mosaic of little bits—theological bits, moral bits,

13. Frei, *Eclipse of Biblical Narrative*, 1.
14. Frei, *Eclipse of Biblical Narrative*, 6–7.

historical-critical bits, sermon bits, devotional bits."[15] When we read the Bible this way, we lose the narrative anchoring that stabilizes these moral, cultural, and devotional bits.

Not everyone has followed the philosophers down their rabbit hole. Biblical theologians have worked against the tide, trying to bring order out of disorder. Scholars from Geerhardus Vos to Brevard Childs, along with movements such as the biblical theology movement of the mid-twentieth century, have tried to reconnect the biblical narrative in different ways. They agree that Scripture has a narrative, though they disagree about the details. The number, order, and arrangement of the covenants, for example, remain hotly contested to this day. While we have yet to put all the pieces back together, the contributions of these biblical theologians and movements demonstrate that when the narrative of Scripture evaporated, the Christian community lost something sacred.

From my vantage point, we can also see that ever since the destruction of the biblical narrative, intellectuals have been busy constructing other narratives with authoritarian power. Jean-François Lyotard's famous definition of postmodernism—"incredulity toward metanarratives"—testifies to the modern fear of totalizing narrative, a way to unite all narratives under the political and social order of a single narrative.[16] Lyotard is principally speaking about modern, oppressive metanarratives, such as those that led to the destructive wars of the twentieth century, but even still, narratives continue to orient our lives.

All human communities function on the basis of a story, because stories unavoidably shape our values and purposes. Philosopher Alasdair MacIntyre argues that "man is in his actions and practice, as well as in his fictions, essentially a story-telling animal." Without stories, we tend toward nihilism and despair. "I can only answer the question 'What am I to do?'" MacIntyre continues, "if I can answer the prior question 'Of what story or stories do I find myself a part?'"[17] We shouldn't question whether we find ourselves in a story; rather, we should question what story we are already a part of. MacIntyre shows, contra the Enlightenment philosophers, that we are not principally individual actors constructing reality, but we are already participating in some story. We enter human history as performers on a stage, not at the beginning, *ab initio*, of a drama, but *in medias res*, in the middle of a story already unfolding.[18]

15. Bartholomew and Goheen, *Drama of Scripture*, 12.
16. Lyotard, *Postmodern Condition*, xxiv.
17. MacIntyre, *After Virtue*, 217.
18. MacIntyre, *After Virtue*, 215.

Christians in the ancient world knew this implicitly. They were born into a world that contradicted the narrative of Scripture. In a way eerily similar to our postmodern situation, the early church was engulfed in a world that did not sympathize with the biblical narrative. The Roman view of history, a view the Christians rejected, was largely cyclical.[19] History was conceived as "a revolving wheel," constantly repeating the same reality.[20] While some historians of the Greco-Roman world describe events in linear terms, they still assume that history is part of the cycles of nature, which move from birth to death and back again. Such historians assume an immanentizing of history that envisions history in natural terms, with no telos and few notions of transcendence. "The pagan and Christian inhabitants of the Roman Empire lived in two radically different mental worlds," writes Ernst Breisach. The Romans identified "the world of the past, present, and future with the Roman state; their historians spoke of the glory of the Roman Republic, great battles, and heroic deeds."[21] The web of these competing narratives amounted to conflicting discourses about reality.

To illustrate the differences between the Roman and Christian views of reality, I turn to the German literary critic Erich Auerbach, who, in his work on realism, famously contrasts the different approaches to narrative of Homer and Moses. He compares Homer's *Odyssey* with Moses's stories in Genesis. Homer creates a separate world, an alternative reality—a world where gods and humans are intertangled in an epic of cataclysmic proportions. But whereas Homer tries to make us forget our world for a while by creating a separate reality, Moses "seeks to overcome our reality: we are to fit our own life into [his] world, feel ourselves to be elements in its structure of universal history."[22] Moses's narrative envelops the world in which we live. The God who created the world, the God introduced in the opening lines of Genesis, is the one true God who rules and reigns over all creation and is, through his providential care, leading creation toward an appointed end. Hans Boersma captures this difference, saying, "In contrast to Hellenistic interpreters of Homer, the church fathers treated salvation history as indispensable."[23] The biblical narrative seeks to pervade our world, our reality. Either we conceive of Scripture as a story, or the story of Scripture is absorbed into some other story.

Ancient Christians, armed with the Scriptures, envisioned history differently through Scripture. They found themselves in the scriptural world—a

---

19. Bebbington, *Patterns in History*, 31–33.
20. Bebbington, *Patterns in History*, 21.
21. Breisach, *Historiography*, 77.
22. Auerbach, *Mimesis*, 15.
23. Boersma, *Scripture as Real Presence*, 23.

world reminding them that God is transcendent and providential, working out a plan of redemption within the fabric of creation. Working against the grain of Roman culture, "a distinctly Christian view of history evolved in the discussions among the church fathers, through interpretations of the Christian texts and under the impact of events."[24] Frances Young describes how "Christianity is particularly 'word-oriented' and text-based" and how "this enabled the formation of a powerful 'totalizing discourse' enshrining an encompassing world-view or ideology."[25] The "totalizing discourse" of the Scriptures offers a narrative that redescribes reality, recasting the events of "history" in light of Scripture. Early Christian writers assume a conceptualized vision of the whole of the Bible, from beginning to end. Time and time again, they tell the biblical story as if it were the one true story, emphasizing that it tells the story of our world, culminating in the final and future kingdom of God.

Many scholars recognize that the fathers assume a coherent metanarrative in Scripture. "The church's reading of Scripture has usually presupposed its narrative unity," writes Richard Bauckham—"that is, that the whole of the Bible—or the Bible read as a whole—tells a coherent story."[26] Brian Daley makes a similar argument. "From the first stages of Christian biblical interpretation, evident in the New Testament writings themselves," he writes, "early Christian exegesis approached individual passages against the assumed background of a single story of God's work in the world to give and to restore life."[27] Daley traces a summary of the narrative and moves from creation to the Christ event. Both Bauckham and Daley argue that the narrative arrangement of Scripture is not alien to Scripture itself, since several parts contain summaries of its own narrative (e.g., Ps. 106:6–46; Acts 7:2–53).[28] The fathers understand that not all of Scripture may be classified as narrative, but an ideal narrative remains, conceptualized as the totality of the events that move progressively from creation to new creation. This narrative is not unified in the same way that a narrative written today is unified. But it is recasting time and history through the key turning points of the biblical narrative.

The recovery of the biblical narrative takes us back to the early church—to a world where the narrative of Scripture was the assumed basis for biblical interpretation. The ancients understood that the world, the divine economy,

24. Breisach, *Historiography*, 77.
25. Young, *Biblical Exegesis*, 257.
26. Bauckham, "Reading Scripture as a Coherent Story," 38.
27. Daley, "Is Patristic Exegesis Still Usable?," 74.
28. Bauckham, "Reading Scripture as a Coherent Story," 41–42. For a discussion of the history of summarizing Israel's story and a list of summaries of that story, see Hood and Emerson, "Summaries of Israel's Story." These authors show the narrating impulse within the Old Testament itself.

was the stage on which the biblical narrative was unfolding. When we begin reading Scripture, we are not transported into another world, nor do we read the narrative of some far-off, distant land. We are reading the story of this world, the narrative of this creation. We find our place in the story of God and let that story shape us.

Narrative and the Literal Sense

For the fathers, the literal sense is closely tied to a larger narrative of Scripture, formed through the work of the Creator. Like a stained-glass window that is intricately arranged, the narrative of Scripture unites all the disparate portions of Scripture in a beautiful tapestry that is embedded with a spiritual sense. The interpreter looks through this window to the world outside to perceive the world through this theological lens, reading it within the context of the unfolding narrative of God's providential work.

Frei describes the precritical approach to the scriptural narrative by underscoring three key elements: history, sequence, and unity. First, "if it seemed clear that a biblical story was to be read literally, it followed automatically that it referred to and described actual historical occurrences."[29] Premodern readers understood that competing interpretations of reality existed, different stories that tried to make sense of the world. But only the Bible, because it was given by God, provided an authoritative description of history. The literal reading of Scripture in the premodern period was a reading that was "strongly realistic" and assumed that the stories of Scripture "together went into the making of a single storied or historical sequence."[30] With Frei, Lindbeck argues that the amalgam of Scripture connections forges a reality that redescribes our world—or "redescribes reality." In other words, it is "the text, so to speak, which absorbs the world, rather than the world the text."[31]

The fathers are not all that concerned with "what actually happened"; they are more concerned with the right way to conceive of what happened and to see how their participation in past events guides them toward a future telos. They trust that the Scriptures report to us, through the prophets and the apostles, a right understanding of what happened. Using Gregory of Nyssa's *Life of Moses* as an example, John O'Keefe and R. R. Reno write that, for modern scholars, "history is the sequence that the narrative refers to, and we query the accuracy." But, they continue, "Gregory never meant a

29. Frei, *Eclipse of Biblical Narrative*, 2.
30. Frei, *Eclipse of Biblical Narrative*, 1.
31. Lindbeck, *Nature of Doctrine*, 118.

reconstructed life of Moses conceived as a truth alongside and in competition with the text. His *historia* is a rhetorically motivated reconstruction of the scriptural narrative, designed to make the episodes depicted in scripture more accessible to the reader. It is, we might say, a Cliff Notes version." Gregory simply did not care to ask "what Moses' life was *really* like."[32]

Second, Frei adds that, for premoderns, "narrating sequential segments in time must fit together into one narrative."[33] Only one story, one narrative, exists for premoderns. This means that the Bible, despite its literary diversity, tells a coherent, sequential narrative that expresses the literal sense in concrete terms. The fathers manage to hold in tension an ideal narrative presented in the text and summary narratives that tell the story of salvation in abbreviated form.

Such management is similar to the way that French literary theorist Gérard Genette distinguishes between *narrative*, *story*, and *narration*. He suggests that *narrative* refers to "the signifier, statement, discourse or narrative text itself," which is simply the words on the page that relate the events in their order and arrangement. The *story*, on the other hand, refers to the "the signified or narrative content," or the history of the events in which they actually occurred. Finally, the act of narrating involves "the producing narrative action and, by extension, the whole of the real or fictional situation in which that action takes place."[34] Genette argues that these three exist in mutual relations: "As narrative, it lives by its relationship to the story that it recounts; as discourse, it lives by its relationship to the narrating that utters it."[35]

Genette's classifications help envision how the fathers conceive of the narrative in different senses—though they do not share Genette's metaphysics. For the fathers, there is a "story," a metanarrative of salvation history that is conceived in the mind of God and unfolding in creation, or what I call the "ideal story." The Holy Spirit, through the prophets and apostles, narrates this story in various written forms, producing inspired narratives, the written Scriptures themselves, that depict the work of God in Christ. The people of God—even those in the present day—receive these narratives and the larger story, or metanarrative, of which they are part and then narrate this story in their lives. In the act of narrating the story, they acknowledge their participation in it. In other words, the narratives they read in Scripture assume a larger story, and they find themselves living in this story.

32. O'Keefe and Reno, *Sanctified Vision*, 15 (italics original).
33. Frei, *Eclipse of Biblical Narrative*, 2.
34. Genette, *Narrative Discourse*, 27.
35. Genette, *Narrative Discourse*, 29.

Finally, Frei's work further illustrates the notion of participation in the previous point. Premodern interpreters envisioned the unity of Scripture as a single narrative, continuous with the real world and embracing "the experience of any present age and reader."[36] Readers of Scripture found their place within the story of Scripture, not the other way around. The literal sense, then, is the story we are part of, the sequence of events that situates the reader in a drama of salvation. In the early church, "biblical interpretation became an imperative need," Frei continues, "but its direction was that of incorporating extra-biblical thought, experience, and reality into the one real world detailed and made accessible by the biblical story—not the reverse."[37] Certainly, theological discourse has developed throughout the church's history, and with it, conceptions of the biblical narrative have changed, but the fundamental substructure of the narrative moves from creation, through the Old Testament, to Christ and the church. This narrative structure, the literal sense, was the essential framework for the spiritual sense that influenced the construction of Christian doctrine. As Frei argues, "a realistic or history-like (though not necessarily historical) element is a feature, as obvious as it is important, of many of the biblical narratives that went into the making of Christian belief."[38] But this element is more than just a factor in making Christian belief; it is the logical entailment of conceiving the nature of God.

For the fathers, the biblical narrative, or the literal sense, is downstream of the Creator. The Scriptures record the work of God, who formed the narrative. The narrative, in turn, forms the essential literal sense as the interpreter follows the way the words go along the path of the narrative. The narrative, or literal, sense contains the figural, which is embedded within the narrative substructure.

A Story of Narratives

As ancient Christians approached the text, they came with a narratival framework that regularly cast Scripture in various chronological relationships. Below, I show how the fathers assume a narrative that moves from Genesis to Revelation and captures the whole work of God in the world. Patristic interpreters interpret stories in their immediate literary context, tracing the literal sense as the events unfold. But any interpretation of individual stories in Scripture is organically part of this narrative and interconnected with

36. Frei, *Eclipse of Biblical Narrative*, 3.
37. Frei, *Eclipse of Biblical Narrative*, 3.
38. Frei, *Eclipse of Biblical Narrative*, 10.

other scriptural accounts in various ways. Second, the fathers are able to present the narrative of Scripture in different levels of detail, like blueprints that give a detailed plan of a building but do not describe all the intricacies of the structure. These two features help explain how the fathers approach the Scripture and find coherence and unity.

First, patristic writers conceive of the narrative unity of Scripture by narrating the events of history in an ordered account of salvation history, but all of these narrative summaries *assume* a larger comprehensive story. Early Christians understood themselves as living within a "world-encompassing story or metanarrative of creation, incarnation, redemption, and consummation."[39] When Christians in the patristic period read Scripture, they felt convicted that its stories were not dissociated or cobbled together by haphazard editors but rather were historically and theologically united, telling a single narrative. Christians themselves were participating in this narrative. The "body" of Scripture, according to Origen, is "the common and narratival sense" or "the sequence of the narratival meaning."[40] The narrative sense is useful, because it "is witnessed by the entire multitude of believers, who believe quite faithfully and simply; nor does it need much argument, because it is openly manifest to all."[41] Describing the complexity of the narrative sense, Origen writes, "The principle of the Holy Spirit is to preserve the coherence of the spiritual sense, either in those things which ought to be done or in those things which have already been performed." In other words, the narrative is found among the deeds performed in creation. The narrative is the "narrative of the visible creation," which he summarizes as "the creation and formation of the first human being, and then the offspring which followed from him in succession; some of the actions done by the righteous amongst them are recounted, and occasionally also certain of their transgressions are mentioned, inasmuch as they were human; and then also a number of things done shamelessly and wickedly by the impious are described." "In a wonderful manner," Origen continues, "the account of battles is presented, and the alternation, now of the conquerors, now of the conquered." This quick summary of the narrative captures the literal reading that provides a "covering and veil of the spiritual meaning."[42] So when the Spirit found things performed in history "capable of being adapted to a spiritual meaning, he composed texture of both kinds in a single style of narrative, always concealing the secret sense more deeply."[43] The

39. Blowers, "Regula Fidei," 202.
40. Origen, *On First Principles* 4.2.4; 4.2.5.
41. Origen, *On First Principles* 4.2.6.
42. Origen, *On First Principles* 4.2.8.
43. Origen, *On First Principles* 4.2.9.

Spirit frames the narrative in a variety of ways, including length, style, or the presence of the miraculous, which may or may not seem useful on the surface.

The narrative of Scripture moves from creation to the kingdom of God. The fathers assume this is a general story that progresses in a unity of time, binding together events in creation. We can see this underlying assumption in the way Augustine "envisioned the real world as formed by the sequence told by the biblical stories."[44] No other source provides a coherent understanding of reality outside Scripture—not Platonists, Stoics, Epicureans, Pythagoreans, or Aristotelians; nor empiricists, Romantics, Hegelians, or postmodernists; nor anyone else. No other rationally derived system of coherence provides an authoritative divine window into perceiving reality.

Second, situated within the narrative—or, as MacIntyre argues, *in medias res*—the fathers recognize that biblical interpreters are already participating in the narrative. Augustine is interested in giving young catechumens a scriptural framework so that they are not overwhelmed with the details of Scripture. The literal or narrative sense is the elementary sense that the catechumens must grasp. The unified narrative brings together Old and New Testaments, Jew and gentile, Israel and all nations. The narrative of the Scriptures is "written for our sakes unto whom the consummation of the ages has reached" (Rom. 15:4).[45] For Augustine, the Scriptures form an all-encompassing worldview that moves from creation to consummation, the church being absorbed into that story. This is why he argues that this narrative is the basis for catechesis. When his friend Deogratius writes to him and asks him how to catechize new converts, Augustine tells him to begin with a narrative, a basic literal interpretation of the Scriptures. Any new catechumen needs to have a grasp of the whole story of Scripture. The catechist must narrate the whole, from Genesis to Revelation, including the story of the church. "The narration [of Scripture] is complete," Augustine writes, "when the beginner is first instructed from the text: 'In the beginning God created heaven and earth,' down to the present period of Church history."[46] Otherwise, catechumens will not be able to comprehend the individual parts of Scripture. Without the basic narrative of salvation history, the individual stories are individual actors, like a set of short stories without any larger plot binding them together. Augustine also knows that when he preaches, his congregation needs to be living the same story. They need to have in their mind's eye the story of Scripture. Time doesn't permit the rehearsal of the basic narrative every Sunday. The spiritual sense (which is

44. Frei, *Eclipse of Biblical Narrative*, 1.
45. Augustine, *First Catechetical Instruction* 3.6.
46. Augustine, *First Catechetical Instruction* 3.5.

assumed in the literal sense) is what guides the faithful in their conformation to the likeness of Christ.

The teacher does not need to recite all the Scriptures from memory. Augustine has the good sense to recognize that this would be time consuming. But the instructor "ought to present all the matter [the summary of Scripture] in a general and comprehensive summary, choosing certain of the more remarkable facts that are heard with greater pleasure and constitute the cardinal points in history." This narrative retelling focuses on Scripture's turning points, the events that compel the story in various directions. The teacher should "relate in our own words all that is contained in these books [of Scripture]"—in other words, present the Scriptures in summary form.[47] Reporting a game of baseball or softball is a helpful analogy: one has no need to recount every out or every pitch; it suffices to recount some of the key turning points as the game progresses through successive innings, culminating in the final score. Not all points of the narrative are rehearsed all the time; this means that an ideal narrative exists, a narrative that is assumed but can be described in a variety of ways. In the same context, Augustine uses the image of a parchment that is rolled up and tied. The teacher, as it were, metaphorically unties the parchment and unrolls the contents into view, so that the hearer can admire the whole text. When early Christian writers recount the narrative, they do not always rehearse all of its points. Instead, they provide different versions of the story that draw on different events.

Finally, love is the purpose of the story. Love summarizes the story, providing a window into its conceptual unity. As Augustine writes, "With this love, then, set before you as an end to which you may refer all that you say, so give all your instructions that he to whom you speak by hearing may believe, and by believing may hope, and by hoping may love."[48] The aim of relating the biblical narrative is the love of God and neighbor; the narration of Scripture should lead us not to pride or envy but to love. So for Augustine, at the end of the narrative, teachers should set forth before catechumens the hope of the resurrection, the future judgment that awaits, "the kingdom of the good and faithful, and that city in heaven and its joys."[49] Augustine compares the summary of the narrative to the gold that binds together a set of gems. The catechists ought not to let their hearts and tongues "stray into the more tangled mazes of controversy," but instead, Augustine writes, "the simple truth of the narration that we employ be like the gold which holds together in

47. Augustine, *First Catechetical Instruction* 3.5.
48. Augustine, *First Catechetical Instruction* 4.8.
49. Augustine, *First Catechetical Instruction* 7.11.

Narratives of Scripture

harmonious arrangement the jewels of an ornament without becoming itself unduly conspicuous."[50] In other words, the catechists should not get bogged down in the weeds but instead should focus on the whole narrative, framing the story of Scripture in one consecutive sequence of events.

Assuming a Larger Narrative

When the fathers write, preach, or teach, they *assume* a larger narrative, even if they summarize that narrative in different ways. They do not constantly rehearse the biblical narrative, nor do they pause or explain it often; instead, they assume that those who have been catechized understand it. By way of analogy, let's say that two people have read the same novel and begin to discuss it. They immediately theorize about the characters or the events and begin to draw logical connections between them. They do not reread the novel; they assume that each has read the novel and discuss its connections and implications.

Below, I provide three examples of the scriptural narrative that illustrate Augustine's narrative strategy mentioned above. These examples, taken from Origen, Eusebius (ca. 260/265–339), and Irenaeus, are different in length and detail, building in progression from the shortest to the longest narrative. The first example is a summary of the biblical narrative found in Origen's account of the rule of faith. He moves from creation to the calling of the gentiles in quick fashion, touching on the more memorable figures of both testaments.

> The particular points, which are clearly handed down by the preaching of the apostles are as follows: First, that "there is one God, who created and arranged all things," and who, when nothing existed, made all things; he is God from the first creation and foundation of the world, the God of all the just, of Adam, Abel, Seth, Enosh, Enoch, Noah, Shem, Abraham, Isaac, Jacob, the twelve patriarchs, Moses, and the prophets; and that this God in the last days, as he had announced beforehand by his prophets, sent our Lord Jesus Christ to call first Israel to himself and second the Gentiles, after the unfaithfulness of the people of Israel. This just and good God, the Father of our Lord Jesus Christ, himself gave the law and the prophets and the Gospels, who is also the God of the apostles and of the Old and New Testaments.[51]

In this example, Origen simply recounts the narrative of Scripture as part of the fabric of Christian belief. He assumes that his narrative summary presents

50. Augustine, *First Catechetical Instruction* 6.10.
51. Origen, *On First Principles* 1.pf.4.

a genuine account of the sequence of events in salvation history. The miraculous work of God has been woven into these events, and they are simply viewed as part of the chronological narrative flow.[52] God has created the world as well as a line of followers that moves from Adam to Christ. Christ, in turn, calls the apostles, who form the church and minister to God's people. In chapter 1, I described Paul Blowers's argument that explains the narrative character of the rule of faith. The rule of faith was essential during the "root struggle for 'Christian' identity—understood precisely as identification with and 'in' a narrative—in the early Christian communities."[53] The rule gave early believers a theological framework that situated them *within* the drama of salvation.

Eusebius gives us a second example that is a bit longer and more detailed. The opening of his ecclesiastical history records a summary of salvation history. This summary provides a framework for making sense of the rest of his account, conceiving all things through the lens of the biblical narrative. He argues that the teaching of Christ was not proclaimed in the past because humanity was not capable of grasping the teaching of Christ in all its wisdom and virtue at that time.[54] He summarizes the course of history, from creation to the incarnation, in the following way:

> The life of men in ancient times was not in a situation to receive the doctrine of Christ in the comprehensive fullness of its wisdom and its virtue. Immediately in the beginning after that happy state, the first man, neglecting the divine commands, fell into the present mortal and afflicted condition and exchanged his former divine enjoyment for the present earth, subject to the curse. The descendants of this one, having filled our earth and proved themselves much worse, excepting one here and another there, commenced a brutal and disorderly mode of life. . . .
>
> Upon these men, leading lives of such wickedness, the omniscient God sent inundations and conflagrations as upon a forest scattered over the earth. He cut them down with successive famines and pestilence, with constant wars and thunderbolts as if to suppress the dreadful and obdurate disease of the soul with his more severe punishments.
>
> Then it was when the excess of malignity had nearly overwhelmed all the world like a deep fit of drunkenness overshadowing and beclouding the minds of men, that the first begotten wisdom of God, existing before all creatures, and the selfsame preexisting Word, induced by his exceeding love of man, appeared at times to his servants in visions of angels, at others, in his own person. As the salutary power of God, he was seen by one and the other of the pious in

52. See Graves, *Inspiration and Interpretation of Scripture*, 82–83.
53. Blowers, "Regula Fidei," 202.
54. Eusebius, *Ecclesiastical History* 1.2.

Narratives of Scripture

ancient times in the shape of man because it was impossible to appear in any other way. And as by these pious men, the seeds of godliness had been already scattered among the mass of mankind, and the whole nation that claimed its origin from these ancient Hebrews, continued devoted to the worship of God—to these, therefore, as to a multitude still affected by former corrupt practices, he imparted through Moses, images and signs of a certain mystical Sabbath and circumcision and instructions in other spiritual principles but did not yet grant the privilege of an immediate initiation.

Their law obtained celebrity and like a fragrant odor was spread abroad among all men. By means of this law, the dispositions of men, even among most of the Gentiles, were improved by legislators and philosophers everywhere, who softened their wild and savage ferocity so as to enjoy settled peace, friendship, and mutual intercourse. Then it was when men at length throughout the whole world and in all nations had been previously prepared and fitted for the reception of the knowledge of the Father, that he himself again appeared, the master of virtue, the minister of the Father in all goodness, the divine and celestial Word of God. He appeared in a human body, in substance not differing from our own nature, at the commencement of the Roman empire. He performed and suffered such things as were to follow according to prophecy, namely, that man and God, the author of miraculous works would dwell in the world, and would be exhibited to all the nations as the teacher of that piety which the Father would approve.

In these prophecies, also, were foretold the extraordinary facts of his birth, his new doctrine, and his wonderful works, as well as the manner of his death, his resurrection from the dead, and finally his divine return to the heavens. The prophet Daniel, under the influence of the divine Spirit, foreseeing his kingdom in the end, was inspired thus to write and describe his vision, in adaptation to human capacity.[55]

Eusebius's account is detailed and developed. I am sure certain parts of his narrative retelling are disquieting for some, but we have no need at this point to get lost in the details. Also, I could explain his brief interpretation of key events, but that would take away from the larger point. Simply put, this example demonstrates the coherence of the literal sense in Eusebius's thought. His account gives a theological framework that helps make sense of the rest of the biblical witness.

A third and final example of the narrative of Scripture comes from Irenaeus's *On the Apostolic Preaching*. There, he offers a narrative that spans several chapters, beginning with creation and progressing, with varying levels of detail,

---

55. Eusebius, *Ecclesiastical History* 1.2. Immediately following this quote, Eusebius cites Dan. 7:9–10 and 13–14 to illustrate the nature of the future kingdom.

to the coming of Christ.[56] Page after page contains one scriptural reference after another. Many paragraphs are simply long quotations of Scripture. Irenaeus wants to immerse new believers in the narrative that they are already participating in. Like Origen's, Irenaeus's account of salvation history is linked with his rule of faith and other summaries of salvation history that are found in various forms throughout his work.[57] He begins his story with creation: "This One [God], by the Word, established the whole world; and in this world are also the angels; and for this whole world He legislated that each should keep to their own place and not overstep the boundary determined by God, each one accomplishing their appointed work."[58] The next few paragraphs discuss the creation of Adam and Eve, then the fall, followed by Cain and Abel, and so on. Noah receives several chapters, along with Abraham and Moses. Irenaeus rushes through a summary of the united kingdom under David and Solomon and the work of the prophets during the divided kingdom. "Hither the prophets were sent from God," he writes; "by the Holy Spirit they admonished the people and returned them to the God of the patriarchs, the Almighty, and were made heralds of the revelation of our Lord Jesus Christ, the Son of God, announcing that his flesh would blossom from the seed of David."[59]

All these summary narratives presume a general story that comprises the whole of Scripture. Their authors assume that the narrative depicted in Scripture is historical and reflects events that have transpired in creation. The narrative impulse of the fathers situates them within this drama of salvation, which unfolds before them. They can recount this story in different ways at various lengths, while reflecting the work of God in creation.

Types of Narratives

Second, the early church understood the narrative of Scripture to be multilayered, with many narratives intertangled. As in an epic novel, such as *Brothers Karamazov*, many subplots weave together into a single story. Several different figures enter and exit the stage as the narrative progresses, congealing under the providential working of God. The fathers map every passage onto a larger web of linkages with Christ at the center. These various kinds of intertextual connections portray a beautifully complex story of God's salvation history that is unending in its depth and profundity.

56. Irenaeus, *On the Apostolic Preaching* 9–32.
57. Including *Against Heresies* 3.3.3, 3.4.2, 3.15.3, and 3.16.6.
58. Irenaeus, *On the Apostolic Preaching* 10 (slightly modified).
59. Irenaeus, *On the Apostolic Preaching* 30 (slightly modified).

Narratives of Scripture

In the next chapter, I will explain some of these intertextual connections with more specificity as they relate to the person and work of Christ. Here, however, I want to focus on the way that the narrative (or literal) sense helps us perceive the unity of Scripture. The biblical narrative lays the groundwork for various chronological arrangements, forming intertextual bindings, which create smaller narratives that reinforce the story.

I argue for two types of "narratives," which I call "thematic" and "covenantal." Other kinds of narrative binding might exist, but these two types show the elasticity of narrative structure within patristic interpretation. The first type is thematic narrative. This kind of narrative tells the story of Scripture or a portion of Scripture with a focus on a specific theme. It shows how Scripture consistently portrays a specific idea, how that theme develops throughout the biblical narrative, or both. This is not altogether different from the ways in which modern biblical theologians trace doctrines or topics throughout the Scriptures, though I wonder if the fathers have a clearer understanding of the metanarrative that undergirds these accounts. Themes are often virtues or vices or other types of images or symbols that are interpreted in a progressive fashion.

We already see this practice in the New Testament. The genealogies of Jesus in Matthew 1 and Luke 3 are good examples. The authors structure the accounts with persons who unite the people of God in the line of Christ. Another example is Hebrews 11–12, which offers an organized narrative centered on the theme of faith. The narrative moves from creation to Christ and the church to the final revealing of the kingdom of God. What is important here is not simply that people have had faith but that people from creation to Christ have *continuously* had faith. These people are thematically connected; they are unified in their belief in God and God's work of salvation. In Hebrews 11:39–40, the author explains that "all these, though commended through their faith, did not receive what was promised, since God had provided something better for us, that apart from us they should not be made perfect." The New Testament community is drawn into the story. The author assumes a narrative continuity that binds his account together. In other words, since Scripture tells a unified narrative, he can isolate specific episodes within the narrative to create a narrative focused on the theme of faith.

Something similar is going on in the opening chapters of 1 Clement. The letter is written to the church of Corinth, which has experienced division. Some younger members of the congregation have rebelled against the elders of their community and expelled them. The letter aims to heal the divide and uses images from Scripture to demonstrate their sin. The first eighteen chapters bind together a narrative of salvation history tailored to several themes.[60] In 1 Clement 3, the author, Clement of Rome, chastises the community for refusing to walk in accordance with the divine commands, because some in the church have followed their own desires and "assumed that attitude of unrighteousness and ungodly jealousy." In 1 Clement 4–7, Clement unites together several figures and events around the topic of jealousy.

Catchwords are the glue that binds the narratives together. The fathers focus on the words and images, both explicit and implicit, in the stories. In the case of 1 Clement, Clement uses the catchwords "jealousy" (*zēlos*) and "envy" (*phthonos*) and explains how figures in the Old Testament express jealousy and envy or are affected by someone else who is jealous or envious.[61] He discusses Cain's actions that culminate in Abel's murder, observing, "You see, brothers, jealousy and envy brought about a brother's murder." Then he laces a series of figures, including Joseph's brothers, Moses and the Hebrews, Aaron and Miriam, Dathan and Abiram, the Philistines, Saul and David, and Peter and Paul.

> Because of jealousy our father Jacob ran away from the presence of Esau his brother. Jealousy caused Joseph to be persecuted nearly to death, and to be sold into slavery. Jealousy compelled Moses to flee from the presence of Pharaoh, king of Egypt, when he was asked by his own countryman, "Who made you a judge or a ruler over us? Do you want to kill me just as you killed the Egyptian yesterday?" Because of jealousy Aaron and Miriam were excluded from the camp. Jealousy brought Dathan and Abiram down alive into Hades, because they revolted against Moses, the servant of God. Because of jealousy David not only was envied by the Philistines but also was persecuted by Saul, king of Israel.[62]

The only reason why Clement can compose this thematic narrative is because a larger ideal story unites these accounts. He connects Peter and Paul with Old Testament figures. Like those in the Old Testament, they, too, are examples of "patient endurance" in the face of persecution.[63] Alongside Peter and Paul, there is added "a vast multitude of the elect who, having suffered many torments and tortures because of jealousy, set an illustrious example among us."[64]

---

60. For a more detailed discussion of this, see Presley, "Reading Community." Also, see the structured chart of these narratives in Clayton Jefford's introduction to the Apostolic Fathers (Jefford, *Reading the Apostolic Fathers*, 116–17).

61. Ambrose has a similar collection of Old Testament figures that embody virtue. See Ambrose, *On the Duties of the Clergy* 24.105–15.

62. 1 Clement 4.

63. 1 Clement 5.

64. 1 Clement 6.

The "elect" are those of the Corinthian and Roman communities who have suffered with the apostles.[65]

Another example of a thematic narrative is Origen's study of prayer. Here, the focus is not a virtue or vice per se but an act of devotion. In a brief survey, Origen catalogs examples of prayer in the Old Testament. "As far as I can discover, I find that the first time the term 'prayer' is used is when Jacob, fleeing from the wrath of his brother Esau, went to Mesopotamia, in compliance with the instructions of Isaac and Rebecca," Origen writes.[66] He works his way through Scripture, evaluating different senses of prayer. The term "prayer," he continues, "which often differs in meaning from 'invocation,' is here employed in the case of one who promises in a vow to do certain things if God grants him certain other things."[67]

A good example of prayer "used in the ordinary way" is when Moses prays to end the plagues at Pharaoh's behest. Another example is Numbers 30:2, where Moses says to the people, "When a man makes a vow to the LORD or takes an oath to obligate himself by a pledge, he must not break his word but must do everything he said" (NIV). Origen cites other examples, showing the tensions between these senses of prayer. His whole analysis demonstrates the kind of thematic-narrative construct that illuminates the theological coherence of Scripture.

Second, another specific type of narrative is an arrangement of God's covenants and promises with his people. Covenantal coherence is a subset of narrative coherence and arranges events according to the covenants or "epochs" of scriptural history.[68] These are like signposts or landmarks, staged periodically throughout the biblical narrative, signifying the turning points of salvation history.

Throughout the early Christian tradition, theologians arranged the covenants in various ways. A good example of a covenantal narrative is found in Irenaeus's writings. Irenaeus uses the term *testamentum* "to refer to a specific period or administration in God's economy," speaking of the Old and New Testaments.[69] Then, he draws on imagery of Scripture, such as the treasure of

---

65. Clement also has a few other thematic-narrative constructions. Then, in 1 Clement 7, he uses a few short images for repentance. Finally, in 1 Clement 9–12 and 17–18, he discusses the theme of salvation. Donald Hagner argues that Clement uses the example of Hebrews to model his narrative structures. See Hagner, *Use of the Old and New Testaments*, 184.

66. Origen, *On Prayer* 3.1.

67. Origen, *On Prayer* 3.2.

68. Ferguson, "Covenant Idea in the Second Century."

69. Duncan, "Covenant Idea in Irenaeus of Lyons," 48. For other discussions of Irenaeus's interpretation of the covenants, see Presley, "Biblical Theology," 25–48, and Graham, "Irenaeus and the Covenants," 393–98.

things "new and old" and the reference to the fact that "one sows and another reaps," to explain the general unity of the testaments.[70] He uses the specific covenants to explain God's narrative of redemption. In several key places, he mentions covenants with Adam, Noah, Abraham, Moses, and David, as well as the new covenant.[71] For example, couched within his discussion of the fourfold Gospel canon, he argues that "four principal covenants were given to the human race: the first, of Adam before the deluge; the second, of Noe after the deluge; the third, the law under Moses; and the fourth, which renews man and recapitulates in itself all things, that is, which through the Gospel raises up and bears men on its wings to the heavenly kingdom."[72] The covenantal arrangement moves progressively through the Old Testament, leading up to the Christ event.

While Irenaeus discusses the covenants in many different places, *On the Apostolic Preaching* 31–42 provides a general commentary on the covenantal arrangement of the specific promises to Adam, Abraham, and David.[73] Irenaeus previews this discussion with an allusion to the prophets, who "were made heralds of the revelation of our Lord Jesus Christ, the Son of God, announcing that his flesh would blossom from the seed of David, that He would be, according to the flesh, son of David, who was the son of Abraham, through a long succession."[74] While Irenaeus sees Christ as fulfilling the covenants, he also imagines the covenants in a narrative relationship. As Susan Graham concludes, "Irenaeus builds his history between creation and incarnation around the covenant narratives concerning Noah, Abraham, and Moses."[75] She argues that these covenants form "real relations between God and humanity," which occur within "real events in human history." The reality of these events stresses the historicity of these relationships. These narratives are unified in a progressive fashion and directed toward "the growth and progress of humanity toward God."[76]

70. Irenaeus, *Against Heresies* 4.9.1. The outline of *Against Heresies* 4 focuses on the unity of the two testaments. *Against Heresies* 4.1–19 uses dominical sayings in the Gospels, 4.20–35 looks at prophecies, and 4.36–41 examines some parables.

71. Irenaeus, *Against Heresies* 3.11.8; Irenaeus, *On the Apostolic Preaching* 22–24, 90. Irenaeus discusses the covenants in many places; see *Against Heresies* 3.10.3–5, 3.12.3–15, 3.17.2, 4.4.2, 4.9.1–3, 4.11.3, 4.12.3, 4.15.2, 4.16.1–5, 4.17.1–5, 4.24.1–3, 4.28.2, 4.32.1–2, 4.33.14, 4.34.2–4, 4.36.6, 5.9.4, 5.33.1, and 5.34.1.

72. Irenaeus, *Against Heresies* 3.11.8. Some scholars question the covenant with Adam, because later Greek texts differ and identify the Noahic, Abrahamic, Mosaic, and new covenants as the four covenants, instead of the Adamic, Noahic, Mosaic, and new covenants.

73. Irenaeus discusses the covenant with Noah and the new covenant as well.

74. Irenaeus, *On the Apostolic Preaching* 30.

75. Graham, "Irenaeus and the Covenants," 393.

76. Graham, "Irenaeus and the Covenants," 394.

The Adam-Abraham-David linkage binds together the Old Testament in a literal sense, but it does so in a way that assumes an underlying narrative. Referring to the Abrahamic covenant, Irenaeus writes that Christ has "fulfilled the promise to Abraham, by which God promised him to make his seed as the stars of heaven."[77] In Genesis 12:1–3, the Lord promises Abraham that his descendants will be as numerous as the stars in the heavens and as the sand on the shore. He promises him that they will receive land and blessing. "Christ accomplished this," Irenaeus says, "being born of the virgin, who was of the seed of Abraham [Gen. 15:5] and establishing believers in Him 'as lights in the world' [Phil. 2:15], making the Gentiles righteous by means of the same faith as Abraham."[78] Christ was born among the descendants of Abraham and accomplished salvation for the people of God, so that they can shine like stars in the world.

Irenaeus also discusses the covenant with David and the new covenant. As he puts it, Christ has also fulfilled God's promise to David "to raise up, from the fruit of his 'womb,' an Eternal King, whose reign would have no end." Christ is the true Davidic King that the people of God have been waiting for. In continuity with the Abrahamic promise, Irenaeus envisions the Davidic promise as fulfilled in the birth of a messianic king who is "of the seed of David" and who reigns eternally.[79] He links both the promise of a descendent in 2 Samuel 7:12 and the reference to "the fruit of the womb" in Psalm 131:11 LXX to the birth of Christ. Christ, the Son of God, has become has the fruit of the virgin, descended from David. Bringing these elements together, Irenaeus refers to Christ as "the Son of God become the Son of David and the Son of Abraham: for, in accomplishing and recapitulating these things in Himself, in order to obtain life for us, 'the Word of God became flesh' by the economy of the Virgin, in order to undo death and vivify man."[80] Then, in *On the Apostolic Preaching* 89–90, he argues that the law has been fulfilled in Christ and that now, as Jeremiah 31 proclaims, "our calling is 'in the newness of the Spirit and not in the oldness of the letter.'"[81] "These promises," he writes, have been "inherited by the calling of the Gentiles, in whom also the New Covenant was opened."[82]

Alongside Irenaeus, Augustine provides another good example of a covenantal narrative. He treats the covenants in several places, particularly as part

---

77. Irenaeus, *On the Apostolic Preaching* 35 (slightly modified).
78. Irenaeus, *On the Apostolic Preaching* 35.
79. Irenaeus, *On the Apostolic Preaching* 36.
80. Irenaeus, *On the Apostolic Preaching* 37.
81. Irenaeus, *On the Apostolic Preaching* 90 (slightly modified).
82. Irenaeus, *On the Apostolic Preaching* 91.

of his larger treatment of salvation history that spans the second half of his *City of God*. Augustine frames his portrait of the covenants with Paul's words in Galatians 4:22: "Abraham had two sons, one by a slave woman and one by a free woman." These sons, Paul argues, are to be understood allegorically for the two covenants. Augustine applies the image of a city to this allegory, a city that symbolizes both covenants: one given on Mount Sinai and leading to bondage, the other given through grace and pointing toward the heavenly Jerusalem. "We find, therefore, that the earthly city has two aspects," he writes. "Under the one, it displays its own presence; under the other, it serves by its presence to point towards the Heavenly City."[83] The "citizens of the earthly city are produced by a nature vitiated by sin," he continues, "while the citizens of the Heavenly City are produced by grace, which redeems nature from sin."[84]

In *City of God* 16.16, Augustine is even more specific. Referring to the promises to Abraham in Genesis 12:1–2, he writes, "Two things are here promised to Abraham. . . . The first is that his seed should possess the land of Canaan," and "the second, and far greater, promise, concerns not his bodily seed, but his spiritual, whereby he is not only the father of the nation of Israel, but of all the nations that follow in the footsteps of his faith."[85] In the next few paragraphs, Augustine weaves together a running commentary on Genesis's account of Abraham, combined with discussions of the fulfillment of the Abrahamic promises. The sign of circumcision, central to the Abrahamic covenant, signifies "the renewal of nature by the sloughing off of old age," whereas the eighth day symbolizes "Christ, who rose again after the completion of seven days, that is after the Sabbath." The name changes (Abram to Abraham and Sarai to Sarah) also signify the new covenant presented in a veiled manner, in the old. "For what is that which we call the Old Testament but a hidden form of the New? And what is that which we call the New Testament but the revelation of the Old?"[86] The relationship between the new and old covenants is found elsewhere, in his work *A Treatise on the Spirit and the Letter*. "The law of works, which was written on the tables of stone, and its reward, the land of promise, which the house of the carnal Israel after their liberation from Egypt received, belonged to the old testament," he writes. On the other hand, "the law of faith, written on the heart, and its

83. Augustine, *City of God* 15.2. For further discussion of the covenants, see Augustine, *On the Proceedings of Pelagius* 13–15; Augustine, *Against Two Letters* 3.6–13; and Augustine, *Treatise on the Spirit* 34–42.
84. Augustine, *City of God* 15.2.
85. Augustine, *City of God* 16.16.
86. Augustine, *City of God* 16.26.

Narratives of Scripture

reward, the beatific vision which the house of the spiritual Israel, when delivered from the present world, shall perceive, belong to the new testament."[87]

In *City of God*, Augustine shows that his view of the covenants is more complex, referring to the covenant that God makes with Adam. "Many covenants, indeed, are called God's covenants, apart from the two chief ones, the old and the new, which all may learn by reading them," he writes. "And the first covenant, made with the first man, is undoubtedly this: 'In the day that thou eatest thereof, thou shalt die the death.'" In addition to the Adamic covenant is the Mosaic covenant; "a more explicit Law was given later, and the apostle says, 'Where no law is, there is no transgression.'"[88] Between these two covenants, Augustine comments on the sign of circumcision, saying, "Circumcision was instituted as a sign of rebirth because, thanks to the original sin by which God's covenant was first broken, birth itself brings a not-undeserved ruin upon the infant, unless rebirth redeems him."[89]

Augustine turns to the Davidic covenant in *City of God*, book 17. "When many things had gone prosperously with King David, he thought to make a house for God: namely, that temple of most excellent fame which was afterwards built by his son King Solomon." Augustine discusses what God promises to David and his successors, arguing that anyone who thinks that "this grand promise [is] fulfilled in Solomon greatly errs." Solomon certainly builds a temple of splendor, but the promise also says, "His house shall be faithful, and his kingdom forevermore before me." Solomon's house does not last forever, and it is filled with immorality and idolatry. "We must not doubt here, or see the fulfillment of these things other than in Christ our Lord, Who was made the seed of David according to the flesh."[90] Augustine observes the way Psalm 89 reiterates several points expressed in the Davidic covenant and the differences between the earthly and heavenly kingdoms promised.[91]

Irenaeus and Augustine do not interpret the covenants in the same way, but such dissimilarity is tangential to the larger point that they both assume that the covenants form a connected network of texts within the storyline of Scripture. The point is not to get lost in the nuances of either interpretation of the covenants. Rather, the point is that thematic and covenantal narratives are subsets of a larger narrative of salvation history. The only reason the fathers can trace themes or covenants throughout Scripture is because the story of God is bound together. The subgenres of thematic and covenantal narratives

87. Augustine, *Treatise on the Spirit* 41.
88. Augustine, *City of God* 16.27.
89. Augustine, *City of God* 16.27.
90. Augustine, *City of God* 17.8.
91. Augustine, *City of God* 17.9–10.

also reinforce the larger narrative by revealing the theological network that organizes and laces the narrative together.

The Implications of a Narrative Reading

What are the implications of a unified narrative (or the literal sense of Scripture) for biblical theology? I see at least three key implications. First, the narrative of Scripture situates the reader within the unfolding drama of salvation. When interpreters open Scripture, they step into the true world, the world of the text. This world, as I have argued, is linked to the real world but also transcends it. Origen, for example, "contextualized the interpreter of Scripture—scholarly commitments included—within the Christian drama of salvation. By examining this drama as it was inscribed on Scripture's pages, ideal interpreters also participated in it."[92] Any interpreter must ask concerning each passage they study, Where is this passage in the narrative of salvation history? Narratives, Todd Billings argues, "present an imaginative world to inhabit, often with a shock value that calls the reader's world into question." With narrative, the "reader can imaginatively enter into the world revealed by the text."[93] Bartholomew and Goheen write, "In order to understand our world, to make sense of our lives, and to make our most important decisions about how we ought to be living, we depend upon some story. . . . We need a large background story if we are to understand ourselves and the world in which we find ourselves. Individual experiences make sense and acquire meaning only when seen within the context or frame of some story we believe to be the true story of the world: each episode of our life stories finds its place there."[94] God holds together the beginnings and the ends. A new sense of rootedness and identity emerges from the concept of narrative. I will argue that we simply cannot conceive of biblical interpretation—or anything else, for that matter—without conceiving of ourselves as situated within this divine economy.

Second, this narrative is christologically conceived. I will discuss christological interpretations in more detail in the next chapter, but I only want to point out that salvation history is contingent upon the Christ event. That event is the locus of human history and the turning point of salvation. The fathers believe that all Scripture is historical, in the sense that the events it reports occurred in the time and manner reported. But historicity "does not

92. Martens, *Origen and Scripture*, 6.
93. Billings, *Word of God*, 44.
94. Bartholomew and Goheen, *Drama of Scripture*, 18.

contain the whole purpose of Scripture in itself."[95] More is going on than meets the eye. Prior to the first advent of Christ, everything points toward that advent. Afterward, everything points back to it, as the second advent of Christ is anticipated. We live in the in-between times, and our situatedness is always christologically conceived.

The christological narrative is often summarized in the general creation, fall, and re-creation narrative that unfolds. Christ is the source and the object of all revelation; no part of Scripture does not in some way ultimately reveal him. "This thoroughgoing christocentricity and the different understanding of historical reality," John McGuckin continues, "marks off [the patristic writers'] exegesis from contemporary interpreters."[96] The fathers cannot neglect to perceive Christ in Scripture.

Third, the story of Scripture lays the intellectual and theological groundwork for specific intertextual connections such as typology, prophecy and fulfillment, or figural readings. Any interpretation that draws connections between texts in the story of Scripture assumes a larger story of Scripture. Like a physician who focuses on the symptoms rather than the underlying causes, some interpreters can make intertextual connections without addressing the underlying narrative that undergirds those connections. The stories of the Old Testament scattered throughout the Law and Historical Books tell one story with an infinite number of textual arrangements.

Conclusion

When Irenaeus begins his critique of the Gnostics, he understands that the main issue at hand is not their method but the theological assumptions they bring to the hermeneutical task. Irenaeus sees the story of Scripture as the field on which the work of God is performed. It lays out a substructure supporting the work of God in the world, forming the arena where the people of God navigate the journey of salvation history. But the story of Scripture is a complex unity, simultaneously a single narrative and many narratives congealing together. Thematic and covenantal narratives are special cases that bind the narrative together; their reading strategies guide their intertextual postures.

The fathers' perception of the scriptural narrative raises important questions for us and our conceptions of Scripture. The Christian life is a matter not just of confessing God but also of conceiving the work of God in Scripture in a unified way and perceiving ourselves as part of its narrative. The modern

95. De Lubac, *Medieval Exegesis*, 1:227.
96. McGuckin, *St. Cyril of Alexandria*, 190.

discipline of biblical studies tends to atomize Scripture, dissecting it into pericopes, genres, and other literary units—conceptual unities that sever any assumed unity of Scripture at large. Critical biblical scholars and postmodern theorists alike rarely approach Scripture with an assumed narrative of salvation history; rather, they choose to come with other assumptions that break up or divide the unified work of Christ. Biblical theologians, on the other hand, have always been interested in the narrative of Scripture; but as I have already mentioned, they tend to construct narrative accounts unconnected to the theological assumptions discussed in the previous chapters, and they fail to explain the tension between the ideal story and the narratives that support it. The fathers take the claims of Scripture seriously; perceive a seamless unity between Scripture and the world, which involves a single, beautiful, and complex story of God's salvation history; and map every passage onto this story through a web of linkages and interconnections.

In the next chapter, I discuss these interconnections in more detail, showing that the biblical narrative is the field on which they work their christological connections, and that should be the case for us too.

CHRIST IN ALL THINGS

The second-century philosopher Celsus clearly made an impression with his popular critique of Christianity, titled *On True Doctrine*. This erudite pagan philosopher harbored serious concerns about Christianity's growing impact on Roman culture. While his original text is lost to history, his criticisms were so influential that more than half a century after his death, the church father Origen crafted a careful response to them. Origen methodically walked through each of Celsus's arguments, providing large quotes of the philosopher's work, coupled with his own rejoinders. When he was done, Origen's response swelled into an eight-volume text titled *Contra Celsum*.

Celsus's criticisms of Christianity are unrelenting, especially his disparagements of the Scriptures. The only true source of wisdom comes through the Greek mind, Celsus concludes. If anyone wants to find truth, they will sit at the feet of the great philosophers, not the Scriptures. In one instance, Celsus contrasts quotes from Plato and from the Scriptures to show the intelligence of the former and the foolishness of the latter. Unlike the Scriptures, the truth is "better expressed among the Greeks, who refrained from making exalted claims and from asserting that they had been announced by a god or the son of a god."[1] If anything is true in the Scriptures, it is only because the biblical writers have borrowed their ideas from Plato.

---

1. Origen, *Contra Celsum* 6.1.

Among his criticisms of Scripture, Celsus finds Old Testament prophecies regarding Christ to be comical. The writings of the prophets are "incoherent and utterly obscure utterances," he writes. Most of them do not make sense.[2] On occasion, he admits that the prophecies make some interesting claims, even if they are completely unbelievable. Besides, he suspects that some Christians have manipulated the words of Scripture to cohere with the life of Christ, thereby doping simple people into believing that Christ has fulfilled the writings of the prophets.[3] But even when Celsus admits that Scripture persuasively predicts the work of Christ, he states that the relevant "prophecies could be applied to thousands of others far more plausibly than to Jesus."[4] Many other figures have accomplished things similar to what Christ has accomplished.

In the face of all these criticisms, Origen implores his readers to consider the prophets again. "The life of each prophet is to be found in the Bible," he writes. Origen catalogs a brief summary of prophets, including Moses, Jeremiah, Isaiah, and Daniel and his companions. In each case he notes the unity of their life and prophecies. Isaiah, for example, "surpassed every ascetic practice when he went naked and barefoot for three years." Daniel and his companions abstained from meat and chose water and vegetables instead. Before these prophets, there were others that lived and proclaimed the word of God. Noah, Isaac, Jacob, and "countless others prophesied unto God and foretold the story of Jesus Christ." Each one was chosen, not due to their sophistication or intellectual acumen, but "by providence to be entrusted with the divine Spirit and with the utterances that He inspired on account of the quality of their lives."[5] Their lives are walking illustrations of virtue, in word and deed. God has used the prophets to proclaim his message through them, leading his people down the righteous path.

The notion of spiritual perception is the key difference between Origen and Celsus. Origen knows this. Where Celsus sees foolishness, Origen sees prophets who "looked upon God and the invisible things which are not seen with the eyes of the senses, and on that account are eternal." All their messages converge on the person and work of Christ. Christ is the key that unlocks the prophets' mysteries. While the prophets' messages are varied and disparate, they were all looking forward to the coming of one person. The only way to make heads or tails of the prophets is by comparing them to the life of Christ. "It is only a person who is wise and truly in Christ who could give as

2. Origen, *Contra Celsum* 7.11.
3. Origen, *Contra Celsum* 2.27.
4. Origen, *Contra Celsum* 2.28.
5. Origen, *Contra Celsum* 7.7.

Christ in All Things

a connected whole the interpretation of the obscure passages in the prophets by 'comparing spiritual things with spiritual' and by explaining each phrase he found in the text from the common usage of that phrase elsewhere in scripture."[6] Celsus does not enjoy the gift of the Spirit and lacks the spiritual perception essential to the true interpretation of Christ. But Origen, connecting the spiritual with the spiritual, recognizes that the spiritual exegete can discern Christ in the Prophets.

In previous chapters, I built the framework of an early Christian vision of biblical theology. I argued that good theology flourishes in the coordination between Scripture, the rule of faith, and liturgy. I also argued that interpretation demands a proper view of God and a vision of God as the telos of interpretation. Then, in the previous chapter, I discussed the narrative of Scripture, to which I tied the literal sense. Interpreters must have a coherent narrative vision of the Scriptures to comprehend the spiritual sense.

In this chapter, I first describe the nature of the spiritual sense, woven into the literal, with particular attention to the person and work of Christ. Earlier, I discussed the spiritual sense as it relates to the doctrine of God, including the nature and work of God. Here, I give that sense a more particular flavor, directed to the Son of God—which is not unconnected with the former discussion. The doctrine of God provided a theological boundary to interpretation; in this chapter the person and work of Christ does the same. Second, I argue that a unified reading of the spiritual sense is also multilayered, progressing through the economic activities of the Son of God. Like a coin with two sides, the spiritual sense considers both Christ's person (ontological) and Christ's work (economic). Both senses must be held together. At times, these kinds of readings may be defined as typological or allegorical, but terms such as *typology* or *allegory*—or other related terms—simply do not capture all the nuances of christological readings. Instead, I argue that the interpreter should attend to the different kinds of christological orientations—what I call the personal, prophetic, and partitive perspectives. These are my own general classifications that describe the strategies I find in early Christian interpretation. Third, I argue that the spiritual sense requires a diversity of intertextual connections and linkages. The person and work of Christ is the glue that binds the spiritual sense together, but passages can be connected through various textual relationships. Such intertextual work requires linguistic, or philological, skills that take time to hone. Ancient students of Scripture committed the text to memory, attended closely to linguistic patterns, and studied the meaning of individual terms. Together, these features depict the vision of the

---

6. Origen, *Contra Celsum* 7.11.

spiritual sense, illuminating the ways that the early church fathers interpreted the spiritual things with the spiritual things.

Christ and the Spiritual Sense

The literal sense, discussed in the previous chapter, pays close attention to the letter and the literary unity of terms and accounts, assuming a unified narrative moving from creation to new creation. Within the fabric of the literal sense, the fathers also assume a secondary sense, a spiritual sense that transcends the literal. The spiritual sense comprehends, in a variety of ways, the work of God in Christ. I take it that this is what Paul is getting at when he contrasts the spiritual reader with the "natural person" who cannot accept the things of the Spirit, which are only spiritually discerned. Those who are indwelled by the Spirit of God, who have confessed the one true God in baptism and become partakers of the Spirit, are able to discern this spiritual sense. They have what Paul calls "the mind of Christ" (1 Cor. 2:16) that discerns spiritual insights, perceiving the beauty of Christ's work in Scripture.

When Paul proclaimed Christ to the ancient world, he did not reason as one of the philosophers; rather, he spoke only of Christ. Faith does not rest on reason-fashioned wisdom or sensory experience observing the works of creation. "For I decided to know nothing among you except Jesus Christ and him crucified," Paul writes (1 Cor. 2:2). Christ reveals "a secret and hidden wisdom of God, which God decreed before the ages for our glory" (v. 7). This secret and hidden wisdom, or the spiritual sense, is comprehended only through the Spirit. "Now we have received not the spirit of the world," Paul writes, "but the Spirit who is from God, that we might understand the things freely given us by God. And we impart this in words not taught by human wisdom but taught by the Spirit, interpreting spiritual truths to those who are spiritual" (vv. 12–13).

Paul shows us that the spiritual sense is discerned only by a Christian, a spiritual believer. Those outside the faith can rationally comprehend all kinds of interpretations, employing their God-given reason to interpret according to any scheme they desire. But they lack faith in God, and their lack of faith is a barrier to a true understanding of the Scriptures. Only after the spiritual meaning is discerned will the reader "have the 'truth' of it."[7] The spiritual exegete is able to see that "Jesus Christ brings about the unity of Scripture, because he is the endpoint and fullness of Scripture. Everything in it is related

7. De Lubac, *Medieval Exegesis*, 1:227.

to him. In the end he is its sole object."[8] Many roads, many of Scripture's intertextual connections, lead to Christ. The intricate associations between the narrative and spiritual senses imply that the Spirit of God has worked to enlighten "holy souls" through the Scriptures by concealing "in ordinary language, under the cover of some history and narrative of visible things, hidden mysteries."[9] These mysteries act as "stumbling blocks or interruptions of the narratival sense" for those without the Spirit.[10]

Many interpreters have tried, with varying degrees of success, to classify these spiritual readings under the headings of *typology*, *allegory*, or something else. John O'Keefe and R. R. Reno, for example, argue that typology moves "beyond analysis of particular words and images toward the larger, unifying patterns of the Bible." They stress the structural sense of typology, which builds unifying schemes through textual integrations across the Scriptures. The fathers use typological exegesis "to explore this larger coherence and describe the architecture of the text."[11] The range of meaning perceived in scriptural terms serves as the anchor that links texts to Christ. Contrasting typology with allegory, O'Keefe and Reno argue that allegories are "interpretations that claim that the plain or obvious sense of a given text is not the true meaning, or at least not the full meaning." In the hands of the allegorist, the words of Scripture "stand for something else; they speak for another reality, another realm of meaning."[12] Allegory is less concerned with the unifying structures of Scripture and more concerned with discerning the spiritual realities behind the text. Distinguishing allegory and typology is common among works on patristic exegesis. Typology looks for the connections between persons, places, and institutions across Scripture, whereas allegory perceives the spiritual realities behind Scripture. Further, this distinction is often put forward to sift out the wheat of good interpretation from the tares of bad interpretation in patristic exegesis. When the fathers use typology, their interpretations are tolerable, or even laudable, but their allegories are bad because they supposedly read their own spiritual realities into the text.

While it is possible to classify some readings in these ways, the sharp distinctions between these categories do not hold. This is why more and more scholars today see very little difference between typology and allegory. Even O'Keefe and Reno recognize that typology and allegory are "part of the same family of reading strategies, often referred to by the fathers as 'spiritual,'

8. De Lubac, *Medieval Exegesis*, 1:237.
9. Origen, *On First Principles* 4.2.8.
10. Origen, *On First Principles* 4.2.9.
11. O'Keefe and Reno, *Sanctified Vision*, 69.
12. O'Keefe and Reno, *Sanctified Vision*, 89.

that seek to interpret the scriptures in terms of the divine economy."[13] Given our discussion of metaphysics in the previous chapters, we can note that the fathers perceive a close connection between the ontology of God and God's work within the divine economy, making it difficult to distinguish these types of interpretation. The literal gives way to the spiritual; both senses hold together in the very wording of the text.

Alongside others, I argue that the intertextual connections throughout Scripture are more diverse and complex than these categories permit. Descriptors such as *allegorical, typological, figural, tropological,* and *teleological* are all subsumed under the spiritual sense, giving a variety of ways of conceiving of the spiritual sense. These are all forms of nonliteral exegesis that are connected with but transcend the literal sense. Patristics scholar Peter Martens's recent work on this topic drives the point home. Martens shows that the categories of literal and allegorical interpretation, imposed on Origen, have misconstrued his exegesis, but not in ways that disassociate the literal and the spiritual senses.[14] Martens's article summarizes a century of Origenian studies that assume that typology is good and allegory is bad and that impose their own methodological standards on the Alexandrian exegete: "Typology and allegory are *competing* forms of nonliteral exegesis, the former the successful variety, the latter its unsuccessful, nonliteral twin," Martens writes. "To the extent that Origen is an allegorist, he troubles; to the extent that he is a typologist, he is tolerable and perhaps even laudable."[15] In other words, many contemporary Christian scholars apply labels to Origen's exegesis that comport with modern sensibilities of what constitutes good or poor exegesis. Whatever spiritual renderings the modern exegete likes they label *typology,* and whatever they do not like they label *allegory.* Imposing this kind of inconsistent allegory-typology distinction on Origen is "decidedly less helpful," "even misleading," and more in line with popular versions of typology and allegory that circulate in contemporary works in biblical and theological studies.[16] Origen does indeed distinguish between "proper" and "improper" interpretation; he has some sense of good and bad nonliteral interpretation. But he does not draw these distinctions along the allegory-typology lines that have captivated so much of modern scholarship.

Others have noted that we need to move beyond the failed categories of typology and allegory. Elizabeth Clark, in *Reading Renunciation,* describes how these categories are no longer helpful for discussing interpretation in

---

13. O'Keefe and Reno, *Sanctified Vision,* 90.
14. Martens, "Revisiting the Allegory/Typology Distinction."
15. Martens, "Revisiting the Allegory/Typology Distinction," 295.
16. Martens, "Revisiting the Allegory/Typology Distinction," 315.

the fathers. They simply do not do justice to the complexity of the work of Christ.[17] Commenting on Origen, Denis Farkasfalvy also describes how in the Origenian tradition, the three senses beyond the literal sense (i.e., the allegorical, tropological, and eschatological) have all been "called comprehensively 'the spiritual meaning' of the Scriptural text."[18] These scholars, along with many others, recognize that we need better ways to contemplate the premodern tradition's spiritual interpretation of Scripture, ways that conceive of the unity of Scripture in the one person of Christ, who comes to us in two natures and performs the work of salvation on our behalf.

With these other voices, I think we need to move beyond pitting allegory and typology against each other and redirect our energies toward evaluating what constitutes good christological interpretation. Toward this end, I work from some general christological categories, using the nature of the person and work of Christ to explain the spiritual sense. The fathers come to Scripture confessing the one true Christ, complete in his deity and humanity, and respecting the salvific events accomplished in him. They see the unique ways that Scripture reveals the specific movements of Christ's work but also the ways in which all things are summed up in him.

The Spiritual Sense: Personal, Prophetic, and Partitive

The fathers adopt a spiritual way of reading tailored to the person and work of Christ, which I subsume under the headings *personal*, *prophetic*, and *partitive*. These three kinds of readings are ways that the spiritual exegete can perceive both, simultaneously and in varying degrees, the ontological referents linked with the signs of Scripture and the economic tapestries of the salvific events recorded throughout Scripture. We need to see these ways of reading as interconnected, like the different skills used to craft a beautiful mosaic with different colors and arrangements. The ontological and the economic senses dance together; they should not be pitted against each other with categories such as typology and allegory.

When the fathers employ a *personal* reading, they are always trying to discern the theological antecedents to specific signs in Scripture. Often they are attempting to discern how specific scriptural language and images point to the Son, the Second Person of the Trinity. While I will focus on Christ, at times, the Scriptures signify the Father or the Spirit, the people of God, or others. Second, the *prophetic* sense considers the coherence between prophecies

17. Clark, *Reading Renunciation*, 73–74.
18. Farkasfalvy, *Inspiration and Interpretation*, 127.

of the Old Testament and the coming of the Son. This kind of reading is not antithetical to the personal sense but coordinated seamlessly with it. The same one who has worked throughout the history of salvation has become incarnate and performed the work of salvation. The fathers apply what I call a "two-advent" hermeneutic, meaning that they read Scripture with the totality of Christ's two comings in view. Third, *partitive* exegesis explains how we read Scripture with attention to the two natures of Christ concurring in one person. Such exegesis requires a discussion of what is known as the hypostatic union and the *communicatio idiomatum*, or the communication of divine and human attributes in the one person of Christ. In all these ways, we can see the elasticity of the spiritual sense and the complex ways in which Scripture speaks of Christ.

Before I explain these ways of reading, I want to show that all three (the personal, the prophetic, and the partitive) are represented in the church's rule of faith. These categories reflect the way the church has been trying to make sense of the ontological and economic unity of Christ. As mentioned in an earlier chapter, the rule of faith typically follows a triadic formula with specific attributes assigned to the Father, Son, and Spirit. If we look to the "second point" of the rule of faith—the description of the Son—each of these ways of reading is represented. Consider the second article in Irenaeus's rule of faith: "the Word of God, the Son of God, Christ Jesus our Lord, who was revealed by the prophets according to the character of their prophecy and according to the nature of the economies of the Father, by whom all things were made, and who, in the last times, to recapitulate all things, became a man amongst men, visible and palpable, in order to abolish death, to demonstrate life, and to effect communion between God and man."[19] The titles "Word of God," "Son of God," and "Christ Jesus our Lord" all point to the importance of *personal* interpretation; they are titles that identify and characterize the Second Person of the Trinity. Each of them is derived from different Scripture passages— for example, "Word of God" is from John 1:1–2, 14; "Son of God" is from Psalm 2:7, Matthew 3:17, 17:5, John 5:26, and Hebrews 1:1–5; "Christ Jesus" is from Matthew 1:21, 16:16, and Mark 1:1; and "our Lord" is from John 13:13 and Acts 2:36. It is not enough to contemplate these individual titles; the point is that they all refer to the *same* person. True, different titles capture distinctive attributes, but they are, to use an Irenaean analogy, like the tiles of a mosaic revealing different attributes of the same person.[20] The references to "prophets" and "prophecy" in Irenaeus's second article are something

19. Irenaeus, *On the Apostolic Preaching* 6.
20. Irenaeus, *Against Heresies* 1.8.1.

different. They explain how a *prophetic* reading of Scripture anticipates the key moments in Christ's life, including his birth, life, death, resurrection, and second coming. All these moments are summarized in Irenaeus's reference to the recapitulating work of Christ that accomplishes salvation for his people. Finally, the *partitive* reading is expressed in the importance of Christ, the Son of God, becoming "a man amongst men, visible and palpable," both natures concurring in one person.

I could apply the same analysis to any summary of the rule of faith in the early church, including those in Tertullian's, Origen's, and Augustine's writings, discussed earlier. While the labels *personal*, *prophetic*, and *partitive* are my own, I think they capture the fathers' spiritual attunements to Scripture. These three senses are embedded in the rule of faith, representing the different ways the fathers harmonize Scripture with the melody of Christ.

Below, I look at each of these senses in more detail and provide examples of how they can be used to read Scripture.

Personal: Making Sense of the Presence of Christ

Early Christian interpreters were attentive to the identity and activity of the Son in the Scriptures, especially in the Old Testament. Any persons presented with divine attributes were subjected to close theological scrutiny. Such interpreters were always attentive to the ways in which texts could help illuminate the nature of God and the relation of persons within the Trinity. They did not always agree, but they always strove to read in ways that were worthy of God or reflected a true understanding of the relationship of the Father and the Son. They were always watchful for the antecedents of pronouns, titles, and figures in the Scriptures. The identification of these antecedents is not always straightforward and is often influenced by the immediate literary context, in conversation with any actions associated with these pronouns, titles, and figures.

The word *person* (Greek *prosōpon*) was one of the earliest terms used to describe the nature of the person and work of God.[21] The key is that the fathers assume a trinitarian doctrine of God, and based on this assumption, they try to make sense of the divine titles and activities within Scripture. "The patristic writers," John McGuckin writes, "regard the text as a continuous narrative of the Logos himself." Each moment of the Scriptures involves the activity of the Word. "It was the Word who spoke through all the prophets, the Word who inspired the psalms, the Word who appeared to Abraham, Moses,

---

21. Slusser, "Exegetical Roots of Trinitarian Theology," 463.

and Jacob, and so on."[22] Finding the person of the Son in the Old Testament demands that the interpreter believe in Christ and seek wisdom from God. These are the things that illuminate the Scriptures and help biblical theologians see the person of the Son in the Word of God.

The fathers assume that the Son of God is the antecedent to many divine titles, and they often group these titles together to show the unity of the prophetic testimony. A good example of this is found in the second-century apologist Justin Martyr. Responding to his Jewish interlocutor, Trypho, Justin writes that the Second Person of the Trinity "is called at one time the *angel of great counsel*, and a *Man* by Ezekiel, and the *Son of Man* by Daniel, and a *child* by Isaiah, and *Christ* and *God* [and] *who is adored* by David, and *Christ* and *Stone* by many prophets, and *Wisdom* by Solomon and Joseph and Judah, and a *Star* by Moses, and *Dawn* by Zechariah, and the *Suffering One* and *Jacob* and *Israel* by Isaiah, and a *Rod*, and *Flower*, and *Cornerstone*, and *Son of God*." This person is the same one, Justin continues, "who has now come, and been born, and suffered, and ascended to heaven; who shall also come again."[23] For Justin, the Son of God is identified in many different places in the Old Testament and given many different titles—titles that signify the unity of the Word of God within the fabric of the Old Testament.

Others, such as Origen and Tertullian, have similar collections. In his rule of faith, Origen offers a mingled series of divine titles drawn from Scripture. He writes, "Jesus Christ himself, who came, was born of the Father before all creatures. After ministering to the Father in the foundation of all things, *for by him were all things made*, in the last times, emptying himself, he became human and was incarnate; being God, when made human he remained what he was, God."[24] The same phenomenon appears in Tertullian's summary of his rule of faith: "Him we believe to have been sent by the Father into the Virgin, and to have been born of her—being both Man and God, the Son of Man and the Son of God, and to have been called by the name of Jesus Christ."[25]

In addition to the basic identification of titles and names, the fathers also consider the identity of persons speaking in the text. The term *prosopological exegesis* is rather new, but the concept is as old as Christian exegesis.[26] It is an

22. McGuckin, *St. Cyril of Alexandria*, 190.
23. Justin, *Dialogue with Trypho* 126.
24. Origen, *On First Principles* 1.pf.4 (italics original).
25. Tertullian, *Against Praxeas* 2.
26. The original term, coined by Carl Andresen, is *prosopographic*, which is a more general description focusing on the identity of the person (*prosōpon*), who is either speaking or acting in a text (*graphē*). Andresen's term may be better because it moves beyond mere "speakers" to include a discussion of actors who perform actions in a narrative, not just spoken terms. Andresen, "Zur Entstehung und Geschichte des trinitarischen Personbegriffes."

attempt to explain how Christian exegetes have interpreted the relationship between the person of the Son and the various speakers and actors woven into Old Testament narratives. The language of *prosopological* signifies the reading of Scripture in a way that perceives the antecedent identity of the person speaking in a text. There is an assumed human author who, through the Spirit, drafts Scripture with an embedded spiritual sense tailored to the divine subject. The identity of the person speaking in any given text may not be the human author, as in many of the examples mentioned above. Interpreters cannot merely assume human antecedents.

Justin Martyr tutors his readers in this pattern of prosopological exegesis. Writing to a Roman audience, he remarks that "when you hear the sayings of the prophets spoken as in the person of someone, you must not suppose that they are spoken by the inspired persons themselves, but by the divine Word who moves them."[27] The human author composes Scripture, but only at the inspiration of the Word of God. The Word at times is the principal actor in the dialogue. "For sometimes," Justin continues, "He speaks things that are to happen, in a manner of one who foretells the future; sometimes He speaks as in the person of God the Master and Father of all; sometimes as in the person of Christ; sometimes as in the person of the people answering the Lord or His Father." The performance of the Son in the Scriptures is comparable to a drama drafted by a Greco-Roman playwright; one person composes the whole drama but introduces several other "persons who converse," Justin writes.[28] Similarly, the Scriptures have a human author who, through the divine Spirit, introduces a divine Actor. The Christian cannot assume that the antecedent to every title, pronoun, or other form of personal identification is just the human author. Bible readers must attune themselves to the ways they perceive the divine nature through the words of Scripture.

Other patristic writers, such as Irenaeus and Tertullian, give us definitions of prosopological exegesis. Irenaeus describes a series of prophetic texts fulfilled in Christ (*On the Apostolic Preaching* 42–86), and he explains that the interpreter cannot assume the human prophet is the only person involved in proclaiming the divine word. Commenting on Psalm 110, Irenaeus writes, "It is necessary to affirm that it is not David nor any other one of the prophets, who speaks from himself—for it is not man who utters prophecies—but [that] the Spirit of God, conforming Himself to the person concerned, spoke in the prophets, producing words sometimes from Christ and at other times from

---

27. Justin, *First Apology* 36.
28. Justin, *First Apology* 36.

the Father."[29] Tertullian does something similar in his work *Against Praxeas*. He draws on several scriptural proofs that use dialogical interchanges between the Father and the Son, such as Psalm 2:7: "You are my Son; today I have begotten you." From this passage and others (e.g., Ps. 110:1; Isa. 45:1; 53:1–2), Tertullian argues that a "distinction in the Persons of the Trinity" is furnished in the rule of faith, so that "He who speaks, and He of whom He speaks, and to whom He speaks, cannot possibly seem to be One and the Same."[30] It is possible to distinguish the identity of the divine persons expressed in the language of Scripture, especially the person of the Son—who is always one with the Father and the Spirit.

As discussed previously, Irenaeus recognizes that one can read the Old Testament with a different metaphysic and that reading with a Christian metaphysic requires Scripture to interpret Scripture. He knows that the word *God* can be applied to any god the reader chooses. He critiques the Gnostics for just this sort of thing. But in this case, he assumes that the interpreter is "believing Christ and seeking wisdom and understanding from God, in order to understand what was said by the prophets."[31] On the one hand, Irenaeus assumes John 1:1 plainly teaches that "there is a Son to God, and He is, not only before His appearance in the world, but also before the world came to be."[32] Thus, Irenaeus cannot set aside this truth when he interprets Genesis 1:1. The texts are bound by their singular witness to the one true God revealed as Father, Son, and Spirit. The one revealed in the pages of the New Testament is the same with the Father in Genesis. "If anyone, therefore, reads the Scripture attentively, he will find in them a discourse about Christ," Irenaeus writes, for "he is the treasure hidden in the field."[33] All Christian readings of the Old Testament should assume the existence of the one true God and the revelation of the Son of God.

From the very opening pages of Scripture, Christian exegetes assume the presence of the Son of God in various theophanic accounts or dialogical portions.

Prophetic: Making Sense of Christological Prophecy and Fulfillment

Alongside the personal sense, there is a prophetic sense that is tied to the economic unfolding of the history of salvation. While the personal sense is

29. Irenaeus, *On the Apostolic Preaching* 49.
30. Tertullian, *Against Praxeas* 11.
31. Irenaeus, *On the Apostolic Preaching* 52.
32. Irenaeus, *On the Apostolic Preaching* 43 (slightly modified).
33. Irenaeus, *Against Heresies* 4.26.1.

focused on the *ontological* antecedents assumed in the text, the prophetic looks to the *economic* links between passages, though these two senses are not entirely distinct. The intertextual connections between specific passages transcend the mere notion of prophetic prediction. This kind of reading I call a two-advent hermeneutic, which provides a theological vision that captures the unitive work of Christ. It carefully reads the individual passages to understand how they envision both Christ's first and second advents, including reflection on his incarnation, resurrection, ascension, and second coming. The one Son of God, appearing and working in the Old Testament, is, through the Spirit and from the perspective of the Old Testament period, also anticipating future work in his incarnation. Reading the Old Testament is always an anticipatory reading—a reading that longs for the coming of Christ in two movements.

The Muratorian Fragment, one of the earliest scriptural canon lists, dating to the second century, gives insight into this two-advent hermeneutic. The text lists the canonical Gospels and then mentions that Christ's "twofold coming" frames their content. The first advent was "in lowliness when he was despised, which has taken place," the text reads, but the second advent will be different. The second will be "glorious in royal power, which is still in the future."[34] Like two acts of a drama, the Gospels, each in their own way, tell the story of Christ's advents, framing every miracle, every sermon, every act with this two-advent hermeneutic in mind. The Gospels all demonstrate that one sovereign Spirit has declared in the Gospels the same events "concerning the nativity, concerning the passion, concerning the resurrection, concerning life with his disciples."[35] Like a short biography, the Gospels trace the highlights of Christ's life, touching on the decisive moments of his first advent. On the other hand, they also all anticipate his second coming in glory and power. The Bible reader should always be vigilant to observe how Scripture speaks of Christ's two comings in unified ways, able to move seamlessly between them as they compose the unified work of Christ.

This kind of reading necessitates that the fathers defend the prophets and the nature of prophecy. "There were certain persons among the Jews, who were prophets of God," Justin writes, "through whom the prophetic Spirit announced beforehand things that were to come to pass before they happened." These prophets, Justin continues, "predicted that Jesus our Christ would come born of a virgin, growing up to manhood, and healing every disease and every sickness and raising the dead, and hated and unrecognized and crucified, and dying and rising again and ascending into heaven, and both being

34. Muratorian Fragment 23–26.
35. Muratorian Fragment 20–22.

and being called Son of God."[36] Origen defends a two-advent hermeneutic against Celsus. "Now it escaped the notice of Celsus," Origen writes, "that the prophecies speak of two advents of Christ: the former characterized by human suffering and humility, in order that Christ, being with men, might make known the way that leads to God, and might leave no man in this life a ground of excuse, in saying that he knew not of the judgment to come; and the latter, distinguished only by glory and divinity, having no element of human infirmity intermingled with its divine greatness."[37] A pagan like Celsus will always search and never come to a true knowledge of the Scriptures, unless he confesses these two advents.

Defending the prophets is just preparatory work for identifying the connections between prophecies and their fulfillment in Christ. Reading the Old Testament requires both attention to the presence of the Son and the Spirit's anticipation of the future work of the Son. This pattern of interpretation entails attending to Scripture's links to Christ's birth, life, death, resurrection, ascension, present session, and second coming. A prophetic sense of reading unites these specific moments and passages that relate to the work of Christ during his first and second advents. "Jesus is thus a scriptural exegete by virtue of himself, by virtue of all his being, and by virtue of all his mystery. He is an exegete, in principle, from the moment of his Incarnation."[38]

As mentioned above, we can see the same kind of two-advent hermeneutic in various presentations of the rule of faith. Tertullian writes, "We believe Him to have suffered, died, and been buried, according to the Scriptures, and, after He had been raised again by the Father and taken back to heaven, to be sitting at the right hand of the Father, and that He will come to judge the quick and the dead."[39] Origen, too, writes, "He assumed a body like to our own, differing in this respect only, that it was born of a virgin and of the Holy Spirit. And that this Jesus Christ was born and did suffer in truth, and not in appearance, and truly died our common death, and did truly rise from the dead, and after the resurrection, having sojourned a while with his disciples, was taken up."[40] Even Augustine weaves a commentary like this together in *On Christian Doctrine*.[41]

Below, I discuss the fathers' two-advent approach to Scripture, beginning with the first advent, tailored to the birth, life, death, resurrection, and

36. Justin, *First Apology* 31.
37. Origen, *Contra Celsum* 1.56.
38. De Lubac, *Medieval Exegesis*, 1:239.
39. Tertullian, *Against Praxeas* 2.
40. Origen, *On First Principles* 1.pf.4.
41. Augustine, *On Christian Doctrine* 1.11.11–1.15.14.

Christ in All Things

ascension of Christ. Then I discuss the second advent, anticipating Christ's return.

FIRST ADVENT

The fathers speak of prophecy and fulfillment in many places—too many places to count, in fact. Patristic writers often group prophetic passages together and offer an associated commentary on the person and work of Christ. So here, I just focus on passages in which the fathers gather prophecies and arrange them according to the life of Christ.

Irenaeus is a good example. In one long section of his work *On the Apostolic Preaching*, he shows how every moment of Christ's life has fulfilled prophecy.[42] He discusses Christ's birth, life and miracles, suffering, death, and resurrection, in each case explaining how Christ has fulfilled prophecy. "For with God," Irenaeus tells us, "there is nothing without purpose or due signification." Through the patriarchs and the prophets, the Son of God "was prefiguring and declaring beforehand future things."[43] In Irenaeus's work, Isaiah is often the organizing prophet; Irenaeus begins nearly every section with a reference to a specific moment of Christ's life fulfilling Isaiah, and then he links Isaiah with other prophets.

Turning to Christ's incarnation as an example, Irenaeus provides a collection of Scripture references that anticipate the birth of Christ, beginning with Isaiah 7:14.

> And that this Christ, who was with the Father, being the Word of the Father, was going to be incarnate and be a man and undergo birth, and be born of a Virgin and walk with men, the Father of all effecting His Incarnation, Isaias says in this way: "Therefore the Lord Himself will give you a sign: Behold, the Virgin shall conceive and bear a Son, and you shall call Him Emmanuel. He shall eat butter and honey. Before He knows or chooses evil, He will select the good, for before the child knows good from evil, He shall reject the evil, to choose good"—he made known that He was going to be born of a virgin, and that He would be truly a man he announced by His eating and by calling Him a child and also by giving Him a name, for this is the custom for infants.[44]

Irenaeus often introduces a prophecy, cites an associated passage, and then explains briefly how that prophecy has been fulfilled in Christ. The person of the Son, who was with the Father, would become incarnate, Irenaeus tells

42. Irenaeus, *On the Apostolic Preaching* 52–86.
43. Irenaeus, *Against Heresies* 4.21.3.
44. Irenaeus, *On the Apostolic Preaching* 53 (slightly modified).

us. The divine plan precedes the prophecy, and texts recording the prophecy prove that God has planned to fulfill it all along. Isaiah 7:14 is fulfilled in the simple facts that Christ has been born of a virgin and is truly human, eating and drinking and possessing a name. These things signify that the Word of God has become human and dwelled among God's creatures.

Similar to the way the incarnation shapes his reading of Isaiah 7:14, Irenaeus argues that every moment of Christ's life fulfills prophecy. Scripture proclaims that Christ "would heal those whom He healed and raise the dead whom He raised, and be hated and despised and flogged and put to death and crucified, as He was hated and despised and put to death."[45] Each of his healings and miracles, his sufferings, and especially his death and resurrection from the grave all reveal the truth of the prophets. Irenaeus analyzes these movements of prophecy and fulfillment and concludes, "If, then, the prophets have prophesied that the Son of God was going to appear on earth, and have prophesied also where on earth, and how, and what manner He was going to appear, and the Lord took upon Himself all these prophecies, firm is our faith in Him and true is the tradition of preaching."[46]

After several paragraphs including collections of prophetic sayings, Irenaeus writes, "So, that He is begotten, and in what manner He is begotten, and where the Son of God was going to be born, and that He is the Christ, the one eternal King—the prophets made known in this way."[47] Each of these specific references provides a prophetic kaleidoscope of the incarnation. The incarnation is the ordering image, and the prophets reference the specific features of the incarnation that fill out the picture. Such features include the notions that the Son of God will be born, the manner in which he will be born, the location of his birth, and his messianic identity. All of these features fill out the conditions and the nature of the incarnation.

Other fathers provide further examples of these kinds of collections. Take the opening chapters of Eusebius's *Ecclesiastical History*. There, Eusebius begins his narrative detailing "the principal and more important points" of Christ's narrative.[48] Then he walks through some key events of the Son's preexistence, incarnation, and life. Origen also treats many of these events in *On First Principles*, arguing that the Gospels frequently append a prophetic fulfillment to every act of Christ, "that it might be fulfilled what was spoken by this or that prophet."[49] These kinds of prophetic arrangements reveal how

45. Irenaeus, *On the Apostolic Preaching* 66.
46. Irenaeus, *On the Apostolic Preaching* 86 (slightly modified).
47. Irenaeus, *On the Apostolic Preaching* 66 (slightly modified).
48. Eusebius, *Ecclesiastical History* 2.1.
49. Origen, *On First Principles* 91.

the fathers apply a two-advent hermeneutic. They approach Scripture looking for the ways in which the writings of the prophets and the apostles cohere in Christ. Repeatedly, the fathers read Scripture with an eye toward the prophecies that correspond to the key moments of Christ's work.

SECOND ADVENT

Not only is the first advent anticipated in the Old Testament; the second advent is as well. The fathers simultaneously look backward to see how Christ has fulfilled the Old Testament in his first coming and then read in hope of his second coming. Returning to Irenaeus, we can see that he defines *prophecy* as "a prediction of things future, that is, a setting forth beforehand of those things which shall be afterwards."[50] He acknowledges that prophecies may seem unusual before they are fulfilled. "For every prophecy, before it is fulfilled," Irenaeus writes, "is an enigma and contradiction for men. But when the time has come and what was prophesied has taken place, then the prophecy can be given a clear explanation."[51] More is to be revealed in the second coming; Irenaeus is certain of that. This vision of God and the blessed life is a theme I will discuss in more detail in another chapter. But it shows that Irenaeus expects a future fulfillment; more will be revealed.

Much of the final book in his five-part refutation of Gnosticism covers key prophecies related to the Lord's second coming. To provide a brief example, Irenaeus argues that the righteous will be joyful at the resurrection. Again, Isaiah is the leading voice: "That he who created man in the beginning promised man a regeneration after he has been decomposed in the earth, Isaiah tells us as follows: The dead shall rise again, and those who are in the tombs shall rise, and those who are on the earth shall rejoice. For thy dew is health for them" (Isa. 26:19). Irenaeus then adds other passages in a supporting role, such as Ezekiel 37:12–14, "Behold, I will open your graves, and raise you from your graves. And I will bring you home into the land of Israel. And you shall know that I am the Lord, when I open your graves, to bring my people back from the graves, and I will put my Spirit with you, and you shall know that I, the Lord, have spoken and I will do it, says the Lord."[52]

In rapid succession, Irenaeus marshals the prophets to proclaim the resurrection at the second coming. Irenaeus's interlocutors, the Gnostics,

---

50. Irenaeus, *Against Heresies* 4.20.5.
51. Irenaeus, *Against Heresies* 4.26.1.
52. Irenaeus, *Against Heresies* 5.15.1 (italics omitted).

believe that only the soul is saved, and they undermine the hope of the Lord's return, denying a future resurrection. The prophets tell a different story. The Lord has promised, Irenaeus writes later, "that He would drink a new mixture of the cup in the kingdom with his disciples" (Matt. 26:29). The apostles confirm this promise too.[53] Together with the proclamation of the prophets, all Scripture testifies to the coming of the Son, when God's creatures will be brought to perfection and behold his glory.[54] Those who love God will, through Christ, "see God and hear his voice and be glorified by hearing his voice, to the extent that the rest cannot look upon his glorious face."[55]

Justin Martyr provides another example. In conversation with his Jewish interlocutor, he defends the two advents of Christ. The prophets compel us, Justin writes, "to admit that two advents of Christ were predicted to take place—one in which He would appear suffering, and dishonored, and without comeliness; but the other in which He would come glorious and Judge of all."[56] The first advent has shown power and glory through suffering. But the second will be an even greater, more "glorious advent," when Christ "shall come on the clouds as the Son of man, so Daniel foretold, and His angels shall come with Him."[57] Justin speaks of the kingdom of God that will be established in other passages as well. Writing to the emperor Antoninus Pius, he writes, "When you hear that we look for a kingdom, you uncritically suppose that we speak of a human one; whereas we speak of that with God."[58] The anticipation of a coming kingdom, with Christ returning in glory, has percolated down into the populace. The Romans are jittery about any foreign invader, but as Justin writes, Christians are awaiting not a foreign earthly power but rather a divine ruler to come again, just as the prophets have predicted.

Many other patristic writers illustrate these points, applying a two-advent hermeneutical framework in conversation with the prophets.[59] Anyone who reads the Old Testament and does not see Christ's two advents like a hidden treasure remains captivated in the narrative of Scripture. The spiritual sense, refracted through Christ, anticipates the coming of the Lord in suffering and glory, and the exegete who reads in faith will see it.

---

53. Irenaeus, *Against Heresies* 5.36.3.
54. Irenaeus, *Against Heresies* 5.2.3.
55. Irenaeus, *Against Heresies* 4.26.1.
56. Justin, *Dialogue with Trypho* 49.
57. Justin, *Dialogue with Trypho* 31.
58. Justin, *First Apology* 11.
59. See, e.g., Tertullian, *Apology* 21; Tertullian, *Against Marcion* 3.7; and Hippolytus, *Treatise on Christ and the Antichrist* 44.

Partitive: Making Sense of the Two Natures of Christ

Finally, with the personal and prophetic senses, we must also consider the partitive. Partitive exegesis attends to the unity of the divine person, assuming that any interpretation of the person and work of Christ must presume that both natures are always present. The Gospels are a primary focal point for this sense, though other books contribute to the conversation. The fathers have learned to read Scripture in ways that honor each nature concurring in his person. Christ is one subject with two predicates, one Christ who is both divine and human. In recent years, scholars have increasingly begun using the term *partitive exegesis* to stress the importance of interpreting "twofold" language about Christ, especially in the Gospels. "For the Nicenes," John Behr writes, "Scripture speaks throughout of Christ, but the Christ of the kerygma, the crucified and exalted Lord, and speaks of him in a twofold fashion." "This kind of 'twofold' speech about Christ," Behr continues, "demands a turn to 'partitive exegesis,'" which means that "some things are said of him as divine and other things are said of him as human—yet referring to the same Christ throughout."[60] These natures should not be confused, conflated, or separated. But we must learn the art of interpreting Christ in these "two registers in order to contemplate the whole Christ."[61]

Identifying the unity of Christ requires that interpreters take two theological points seriously: the hypostatic union and the communication of idioms (or the *communicatio idiomatum*). The hypostatic union is expressed in the Definition of Chalcedon, which speaks of "this one and only Christ—Son, Lord only-begotten—in two natures," and it does so "without confusing the two natures, without transmuting one nature into the other, without dividing them into two separate categories, without contrasting them according to area or function." When we read the Gospels, we should not confuse, change, divide, or separate the natures. We should not speak about Christ as if he is divine in one moment (say, when he heals) and human in another moment (say, when he eats). When we speak of the Son, we proclaim that "the distinction between the natures was never abolished by their union, but rather the character proper to each of the two natures was preserved as they came together in one person and one hypostasis." This summary of the doctrine of Christ implies that all discussions of Christ in the Scriptures have this confession as their framework. We should not speak of Christ in ways that deny or diminish one of his two natures.

Turning to the communication of idioms, the notion of an *idiom* refers to simply attributes or aspects used to describe the person of Christ, as in

60. Behr, *Nicene Faith*, 14.
61. Jamieson and Wittman, *Biblical Reasoning*, 153.

the many examples listed above. R. B. Jamieson and Tyler Wittman give us a helpful framework here: "Since Christ is a single divine person who subsists in both a divine nature and a human nature, Scripture sometimes names him according to one nature and predicates of him what belongs to the other nature."[62] In other words, Scripture assigns properties of one nature to the other nature (and vice versa). Close readers of Scripture might scratch their head at this kind of apparent confusion, applying divine attributes to a human person and human attributes to a divine person. How can the Son of God suffer and the man Jesus raise the dead? The only way the church has made sense of these realities is to affirm that Jesus Christ is both divine and human, without confusing or separating these natures.

Cyril of Alexandria (ca. 376–444) is a good example of this kind of partitive exegesis. "Confessing that the Word was united to flesh substantially, we adore the one Son and Lord Jesus Christ. We do not set up a division and distinguish the man and God," Cyril writes. "Nor do we speak of the Word of God separately as Christ and, likewise, the one born of woman separate as another Christ."[63] When Cyril turns to the Gospels, he reminds Nestorius (ca. 386–ca. 451) that these theological claims have exegetical import: "We do not allocate the statements of our Savior in the Gospels either to two hypostases or indeed to two persons, for the one and only Christ is not twofold, even if he be considered as from two entities and they [be] different." He compares the unity of Christ to the human person, who is composed of body and soul, "one from both." Christ is also an "inseparable unity," one person in two natures.[64] This means that interpreters must also assume that Christ is one subject and one actor, even if the text seems to stress one nature or the other.

Partitive exegesis means learning to interpret Scripture in a twofold way, always assuming that both natures concur in the same person; when the obvious and literal sense stresses one nature, the other must be assumed as well. The reality of the incarnation demands that the Christian exegete assume that both natures concur at all times and places. Certain passages may accentuate Christ's human nature, while others may put his divine nature on display. After the incarnation, every interpretation of the Son of God in Scripture must assume the unity of both natures concurring in one person. Every meal, every miracle, every message all exhibit both natures in unity. Cyril argues that Christians confess the Lord Jesus Christ exists "in one person [*prosōpon*]. As the Word he is born divinely before all ages and times, but in these last times

---

62. Jamieson and Wittman, *Biblical Reasoning*, 142.
63. Cyril of Alexandria, *Letter 17* 9.
64. Cyril of Alexandria, *Letter 17* 13.

of this age the same one was born of a woman according to the flesh." When we seek to understand the person of Christ, "we attribute both the divine and human characteristics, and we also say that to the same one belongs the birth and the suffering on the cross since he appropriated everything that belonged to his own flesh, while ever remaining impassible in the nature of the Godhead."[65] We cannot partition out the divine and the human natures; they compose one indivisible subject and agent. Only one incarnate Word exists, and of him we may simultaneously predicate divine and human properties and actions. The Christian interpreter must not divide these natures or conceive of Christ as one or the other. Instead, the marriage between these natures demands that interpreters understand that "all the sayings in the Gospels are to be attributed to one *prosōpon*, and to the one enfleshed hypostasis of the Word, just as according to the Scriptures there is One Lord Jesus Christ (1 Cor. 8.6)."[66] In the same letter, Cyril puts this rule succinctly: "If anyone interprets the sayings in the Gospels and the apostolic writings, or the things said about Christ by the saints, or the things he says about himself, as referring to two prosopa or hypostases, attributing some of them to a man conceived of as separate from the Word of God, and attributing others (as divine) exclusively to the Word of God the Father, let him be anathema."[67]

Gregory of Nazianzus describes the union of the two natures in the one person in a similar way, with the same implications. "He remained what he was; what he was not, he assumed. No 'because' is required for his existence in the beginning, for what could account for the existence of God? But later he came into being because of something, namely your salvation, yours, who insult him and despise his Godhead." Speaking about the incarnation, he continues, "He was begotten—yet he was already begotten—of a woman. And yet she was a virgin. That it was from a woman makes it human, that she was a virgin makes it divine. On earth he has no father, but in heaven no mother. All this is part of his Godhead."[68]

Gregory's rhetorical skill is on display when he describes—using a collection of passages from the Gospels—the unity of both natures existing and acting in unity. What I mean by christological twofold interpretation involves the two-natures reflection Gregory displays in this passage:

> As man he was put to the test, but as God he came through victorious—yes, bids us be of good cheer, because he has conquered the world. He hungered—yet

65. Cyril of Alexandria, *On the Unity of Christ* 133.
66. Cyril of Alexandria, *Letter 17* 8.
67. Cyril of Alexandria, *Letter 17*, anathema 4.
68. Gregory of Nazianzus, *Theological Orations* 29.19.

he fed thousands. He is indeed "living, heavenly bread." He thirsted—yet he exclaimed: "Whosoever thirsts, let him come to me and drink." Indeed he promised that believers would become fountains. He was tired—yet he is the "rest" of the weary and the burdened. He was overcome by heavy sleep—yet he goes lightly over the sea, rebukes winds, and relieves the drowning Peter. He pays tax—yet he uses a fish to do it; indeed he is emperor over those who demand the tax. He is called a "Samaritan, demonically possessed"—but he rescues the man who came down from Jerusalem and fell among thieves. Yes, he is recognized by demons, drives out demons, drowns deep a legion of spirits, and sees the prince of demons falling like lightning. He is stoned, yet not hit; he prays, yet he hears prayers. He weeps, yet he puts an end to weeping. He asks where Lazarus is laid—he was man; yet he raises Lazarus—he was God.[69]

Gregory's discourse continues with many other parallels between Christ's divine and human natures, and he concludes all of these christological readings, saying, "If the first set of expressions starts you going astray, the second set takes your error away."[70] Every interpretation must assume both natures, and what God has brought together, let no interpreter put asunder.

Given these theological assumptions about Christ, partitive exegesis, alongside the personal and prophetic senses, is essential to good interpretation. The Son of God is active in the narrative of the Old Testament, anticipating his incarnation through prophetic utterances. This selfsame one becomes incarnate and takes on human nature—the assumption that shapes the way we understand the two natures of Christ concurring in one person. Just as all roads lead to Rome, so all exegesis leads to Christ.

Some Implications for Christological Interpretation

Finally, given the theological assumptions discussed above, the Scriptures cohere around these points in a number of different ways. Alongside the hermeneutical assumptions mentioned earlier, I argue that three general practices guide christological readings: reading texts closely, observing catchwords, and noting different kinds of intertextual relationships.

First, the fathers apply close readings of texts, which involves intensive meditation and memorization. This style of reading "focuses on precise detail, on the 'how' of the text's construction."[71] This close reading attends to the various literary contours of individual passages, including chronology

69. Gregory of Nazianzus, *Theological Orations* 29.20.
70. Gregory of Nazianzus, *Theological Orations* 29.20.
71. Clark, *Reading Renunciation*, 119.

and the separation of features of a text.[72] The assumption that Scripture interprets Scripture itself assumes that interpreters know the sacred Word. Good interpreters inhabit the Scriptures; they take up residence within them. This reality is what O'Keefe and Reno call "intensive reading"; the fathers are always examining the details of their texts.[73] Interpreters need to have a sense of the words and sentences and an ability to navigate various associative strategies discussed in this chapter.

In essence, in order to understand the Scriptures, interpreters need to know them and understand reality through them, always attentive to the personal, prophetic, and partitive features of their texts. Irenaeus argues that an interpreter with a "sound mind" will "eagerly meditate upon those things which God has placed within the power of mankind, and has subjected to our knowledge, and will make advancement in [acquaintance with] them, rendering the knowledge of them easy to him by means of daily study."[74] The slow, steady internalizing of Scripture provides the data that allows one to recognize Scripture's unity in a vision of wisdom.

Other fathers follow Irenaeus's line of reasoning and assume that biblical exegetes eventually develop a greater knowledge of Scripture. In one homily on Genesis, the renowned orator John Chrysostom compares the reading of Scripture to a treasure. The reader who finds even a "tiny nugget gains great wealth," he writes. He also compares reading Scripture to "a spring gushing with everflowing waters in a mighty flood." Many have and will be swept away by the rushing water of the Scriptures. "Our forebears drank from these waters to the limit of their capacity," Chrysostom writes, "and those who come after us will try to do likewise, without risk of exhausting them."[75] The flood of Scripture is ever and ever increasing. Augustine also encourages intense familiarity with the Scriptures. In his work on hermeneutics, he encourages readers to get to know the writings of the Old and New Testaments, to memorize their words, to study their language, and to analyze their terms. He assumes that after one does this, the obvious parts of Scripture, especially the parts that describe the church's faith and practice (or what he calls "commands for living or rules for believing"), will be obvious and plain to the reader. From these clear passages, the interpreter can make sense of the obscure passages.[76]

Second, catchwords are the basis for linking texts, though the exactness of correspondence is not always the basis for intertextual links. Any given

---

72. Clark, *Reading Renunciation*, 119–22.
73. O'Keefe and Reno, *Sanctified Vision*, 46.
74. Irenaeus, *Against Heresies* 2.27.1.
75. Chrysostom, *Homilies on Genesis 1–17* 3.1.
76. Augustine, *On Christian Doctrine* 2.9.14.

catchword may convey a range of meaning or senses that can be conceptually united with a host of other terms in Scripture. This point takes us back to Augustine's semiotics. The identity of a sign in Scripture requires careful consideration of that sign and the links between it and the thing to which it points. The unity of things hinges on catchwords. Interpreters are free to move about the canon and look for intertextual connections that clarify the theological truths communicated in Scripture's signs. Several fathers speak of the "exactness" of Scripture to "underscore divine teaching's intentionality, reliability, and attention to detail."[77] The exactness of Scripture focuses on the precision of the words chosen by the divine Author.[78] The specific titles and activities mentioned above are all united in the one person of the Son. As discussed in a previous chapter (concerning Augustine's signs and things) and in this chapter (concerning Christ), God's ontology and the natures of Christ and creation are limiting factors for the range of possible linkages among biblical texts.

Third, a close reading of texts and a linking of catchwords lead to all kinds of intertextual interpretation. The term *intertextuality* is the product of twentieth-century literary criticism and has been used to describe the production of texts. Elizabeth Clark points to poststructuralist Julia Kristeva's famous definition of intertextuality: "Every text builds itself as a mosaic of quotations; every text is absorption and transformation."[79] She has been influenced by other literary critics, such as Mikhail Bakhtin, who links postmodern intertextuality with Hellenistic modes of reading. These postmodern authors reject the stability that the theological metaphysics brings to the interpretive task. They focus on what they can do with texts—a text's productivity.

The premodern interpreters are linking texts, but doing so with very different assumptions. They assume that the divine Author enables the biblical exegete to link passages under the direction of the Spirit. So given the assumptions about the person and work of Christ mentioned above, the Scriptures naturally theologically cohere because they are given through the inspiration of the Spirit. One can associate Scripture passages and connect them to Christ in a wide variety of ways. Frances Young, for example, uses the imagery of music—a symphony of notes playing in harmony with each other—to describe the father's intertextuality of the early church, with Origen as her immediate example.[80]

77. Jamieson and Wittman, *Biblical Reasoning*, 50.
78. See Martens, *Origen and Scripture*, 168–81.
79. Clark, *Reading Renunciation*, 122.
80. Young, *Art of Performance*, 2–3; Young, *Biblical Exegesis*, 133.

Thus, according to Clark, in a general sense, intertextuality simply entails that "texts are placed next to each other to reinforce a point." Such placement certainly occurs throughout the fathers' writings. They draw texts together in a variety of relations. But Clark takes the point further. She argues that in the fathers, "intertexts, whether overt or hidden, have the ability to reinforce or to constrain the text in ways that produce new textual meaning."[81] Her assertion is partially true, but it is not quite how the fathers would see it. They would surely affirm the ways in which intertextual relationships "reinforce" or "constrain" the interpretation of other texts, as well as the many other ways textual correspondence can be described. But for them, that reinforcement and constraint are directly related to the nature of God and the human person mentioned in the previous chapters. The purpose is not to create "new" meaning, because God has always existed; the purpose is to seek out what God has communicated to all people through the prophets and apostles. Intertextuality does not create *ex nihilo*; instead, intertextual relationships reveal what has existed all along. Texts can combine to clarify partially revealed doctrines.

It may be helpful to consider David Yeago's distinction between judgments and concepts: "Judgement-making," Yeago writes, "is an operation performed with words and concepts."[82] Unity in theological discourse is sought at the level of judgments, not concepts, because the same judgment can be rendered in different terms, which give insight into a judgment's force and implications. Many valid verbal and conceptual renderings can be made of the same judgment. Those who are part of the church and partake of the same Spirit often make similar theological judgments while using different concepts. The fathers make theological moves that they believe particularize and clarify the theological judgments that they affirm.

The fathers themselves point to this kind of intertextuality that flows from the assumption that Scripture interprets Scripture, discussed earlier. For example, Clement of Alexandria argues, "In order to interpret all of Scripture, you cannot 'lump everything together,' to use a proverbial expression. Rather, Scripture should be broached in the most dialectical ways possible, if one wants to find the coherent result of divine teaching in it."[83] Origen describes the same method of intertextuality, saying, "The Hebrew [Origen's unnamed Jewish teacher in Alexandria] said that the whole divinely inspired Scripture may be likened, because of its obscurity, to many locked rooms in one house. By each room is placed a key, but not the one that corresponds to it, so that

81. Clark, *Reading Renunciation*, 125.
82. Yeago, "New Testament and the Nicene Dogma," 159.
83. Clement of Alexandria, *Stromata* 1.

the keys are scattered about beside the rooms, none of them matching the room by which it is placed." The struggle of scriptural interpretation, Origen continues, is finding "the keys and match[ing] them to the rooms that they can open." Exegetes can understand even obscure passages when they take "the points of departure for understanding them from another place because they have their interpretive principle scattered among them."[84] This does not mean that the tradition always agrees on the proper way to integrate texts. Besides appealing to typological, allegorical, and figural readings, scholars have different ways of classifying the fathers' methods of interpretation. As Farkasfalvy writes, "The exegete aims at discovering in a diversity of ways: by verbal similarities, by thematic analogies or symbolism, by historical or geographic connections, and so on."[85]

Scripture's interpretation of Scripture is the basis for christological interpretation. The fathers show us how to think through and with the Scriptures, linking them in an unending display of textual unity that proclaims Christ.

Conclusion

This chapter has taken us deeper into the spiritual sense, framing a christological reading that should guide the way we think about Scripture. Origen does not let Celsus's rejection of the prophetic writings go unanswered. He knows that Christ is found in the Prophets. The testimonies of the Old Testament are melodies that sing about Christ, and only the person who confesses Christ can hear the music. I hope that we can learn to hear the music too. I think we need to reconsider our conversations about typology and allegory and move on to think about the relationship between Scripture and Christ with different categories. Such a reconsideration, I think, entails adopting a posture that reads the Prophets closely, paying attention to the personal presence of the Son in the Old Testament. We should also adopt a conscious two-advent hermeneutic, always attending to the ways that the prophets' words testify to the whole work of Christ. Embracing this kind of spiritual sense means that we should always read Scripture with the assumption that Christ is both divine and human and that his economic activity comprises his preexistence, incarnation, birth, life, death, resurrection, ascension, and second coming. Christians living this confession simply cannot read the Old Testament as if the Son has not been revealed.

Like the fathers, we can still focus on method—for example, close readings, catchwords, and intertextual relationships. But only within this theological

84. Origen, *Commentary on Psalms 1–25*, fragment from preface.
85. Farkasfalvy, *Inspiration and Interpretation*, 123.

framework will our methods produce the kinds of readings that guide the faithful toward God. The fathers seam together the personal, prophetic, and partitive senses, bound by a vision of Scripture interpreting Scripture. Contemplating Christ is the objective, and catchwords are the bonds that hold their readings together. Christ is truly the treasure waiting to be found by the spiritual disciple.

This kind of christological interpretation can fail to persuade and edify if interpreters do not embody the virtue taught in the Scriptures. Virtue and the good life are our next subjects, and we now turn to these topics to see how early Christian biblical theology is tied to the good life.

THE GOOD LIFE

Basil of Caesarea was born in 330, seventeen years after the end of the Diocletian persecutions. His family suffered under the weight of Diocletian's brutality, and several of his relatives died for the faith. Basil was torn about his own commitments. He spent his youthful years studying philosophy, first in Caesarea—where he met Gregory of Nazianzus, who would become a lifelong friend—then in Constantinople and Athens. By 355, he was back home teaching rhetoric. He was not terribly impressed with the philosophers. Their vision of life left him wanting, craving something else more fulfilling.

Teaching rhetoric was not satisfying either, and Basil's family and friends had other plans for him. Basil's sister Macrina implored him to leave his life of teaching and commit himself to the church, and eventually she was persuasive. In a letter to the bishop Eustathius of Sebaste, Basil composed a stirring personal account of his conversion. He lamented the wasted years of his old life. "Much time had I spent in vanity, and had wasted nearly all my youth in the vain labour which I underwent in acquiring the wisdom made foolish by God," Basil writes.[1] Then he recounts the joy he found in coming to Christ, comparing his conversion to a person awaking from a deep slumber. "Like a man roused from deep sleep," he writes, "I turned my eyes to the marvellous light of the truth of the Gospel." Cast in light of the revelation of God, the wisdom of the philosophers was unmasked and shown as foolishness.

---

1. All of the quotes in this introductory section are from Basil, *Letter 223*.

Alluding to Paul's words in 1 Corinthians 2:6, Basil asserts, "I perceived the uselessness of the wisdom of the princes of this world." The philosophers offer many different paths and patterns of life that lead to some destination, but only one narrow path leads to true life found in Christ. Broken and contrite before God, Basil joined the church. "I wept many tears over my miserable life," he writes, "and I prayed that guidance might be vouchsafed me to admit me to the doctrines of true religion."

Basil found in Christ something that runs deeper than any philosophical system. Like others before him, he discovered in Scripture the good life—a life not satisfied with the "intimacy with wicked men" but oriented toward beholding God. He discovered a life pursuing sanctification and rightly oriented toward the things of this world, not distracted by the world's cares and concerns or allowing "the soul to be turned by any sympathy to things of earth." With more vigor than that with which he pursued his classical studies, Basil pursued the religious life found in Christ.

The virtuous life became his pursuit. He found special inspiration from those who practiced the disciplined ascetic life, especially those in Egypt, Palestine, Syria, and Mesopotamia. Unlike the philosophers, who often taught one thing and lived another way, these followers of Christ were examples of virtue. "I admired their continence in living, and their endurance in toil," Basil writes. Their self-control and fortitude were exemplary. "I was amazed at their persistency in prayer, and at their triumphing over sleep." They understood that the spiritual life is not found in the satisfaction of material things. They were "subdued by no natural necessity, ever keeping their souls' purpose high and free, in hunger, in thirst, in cold, in nakedness; they never yielded to the body; they were never willing to waste attention on it." These figures inspired him. They put on the virtues, becoming living testimonies to a godly life. They "showed in very deed what it is to sojourn for a while in this life, and what to have one's citizenship and home in heaven."[2] For Basil, the choice was clear: the leisurely life of rhetoric was nothing compared to the good life found in Christian community.

In this chapter, I transition from the general theological assumptions of biblical theology to a specific vision of the human person. To this point, I have discussed the environmental features of early Christian biblical theology: God, the narrative of salvation history, and the person and work of Christ. The previous chapters offered a panoramic view of the early Christian social imaginary; we needed to step into the ancients' world and see things from their vantage point.

2. Basil, *Letter 223*.

The Good Life   123

Now, I turn to the human person. Situated under the care and provision of God and his work in salvation history through the Son and the Spirit are God's creatures. The fathers envision themselves living in this world, and the Scriptures are the prism through which they see life. With God above and the kingdom before them, early Christians lived an interpretive life, a life infused with the virtues characterized by sanctification and holiness, poring over the Scriptures to guide them along the path. Today, discussions of the good life are often relegated to "application," which comes after we have properly mined the text for nuggets of truth. Step one, readers discern the meaning of Scripture, and step two, they apply it to their lives. But for the fathers, something different is going on. They see no divorce between the ontology of the human person and the activity of exegesis. Sanctification and virtue are not just about applying the things discerned through the process of exegesis, but given everything I have argued in the previous chapters, the ancient Christians already believed they were participating in the work of God, which they discovered through Scripture.

Below, I argue first that good biblical theology is intertwined with the fathers' vision of the good life. The pursuit of virtue is indispensable throughout the whole process of interpretation. A cyclical relationship exists here, moving from virtue to virtue, always reading Scripture with the aim to make progress in holiness and godliness. The fathers believe that any good interpreter must come to Scripture with some measure of virtue and a humble heart, willing to sit before the Scriptures and receive their teaching. Interpreters who take this posture will also recognize that they need to mature in virtue, because they have not yet arrived at perfection. Craving to be found in the glorious light of the Son, they pursue virtue and long for beatitude—the beholding of the glory of God—which occurs at the end of the exegete's journey.

Second, I describe how the Scriptures present models and principles for the virtuous life. For Scripture readers, Christ embodies all the virtues, and he is the preeminent example of virtue. The Christian seeks to be conformed to Christ's likeness. Through that vision, the fathers rely principally on several portions of Scripture that tutor the faithful in the wisdom of virtuous living: the Wisdom literature (including Proverbs, Song of Songs, Ecclesiastes, Job) and the Psalms and the accounts of the patriarchs, prophets, and apostles as well as other exemplars in Scripture. Other passages, such as the Sermon on the Mount and Paul's vice lists, come alongside these passages, filling out the vision of the virtue they depict. Like a map for a traveler, these sources work together to provide both the precepts and portraits of the good life. The Wisdom literature, the Psalms, and other New Testament passages offer principles for the Christian life, ways in which the Christian is called to navigate this life in virtue. The lives of certain patriarchs, kings, prophets, apostles, and other leaders, on the other hand, offer living illustrations of the virtuous life, depictions of fellow travelers who have walked the road of God faithfully. For this reason, the Old Testament has been an essential source for theological reflection and growth in conformity to the likeness of Christ. Sometimes, the fathers look to contemporary or near-contemporary people of faith and virtue for inspiration (as Basil does with respect to Christian ascetics in Egypt and elsewhere), but in all cases, these Scripture passages frame the good life.

Biblical Theology and the Spiritual Life

Not surprisingly, the fathers inhabit a whole theological environment, which has shaped how they understand themselves and their spiritual lives. Below, I discuss three key points that structure the ancient interpretive life: first, that the fathers imagine themselves as travelers on a path toward sanctification; second, the essential purpose for reading Scripture is growing in godliness and virtue; and third, that they read Scripture looking for wisdom to guide them on their way.

First is that biblical interpretation is about a journey toward beatitude, toward beholding God. The fathers use many words for this reality, such as *pilgrim*, *sojourner*, or *traveler*, envisioning a destination with striking clarity and passion. They come to Scripture not as static observers but rather as travelers seeking to know how to take the next step or make the next turn. This is one of the most dominant themes in early Christian interpretation. The fathers often use the motif of a journey, speak about the journey in different ways, and refer to its different stages. Scripture in the church serves "as a sacramental guide on the journey of salvation," Hans Boersma writes.[3] Patristic writers recognize that the faithful have received the Spirit of God, who leads them "towards perfection" and prepares them "for incorruption, being little by little accustomed to receive and bear God."[4]

Origen is a good example of this point. Biblical interpretation in Origen's understanding was "an extraordinarily rich practice, as much an intellectual as a spiritual exercise," writes Peter Martens. "It was, in short, a way of life."[5] Origen's stress on the soul's journey toward God saturated his preaching and

3. Boersma, *Scripture as Real Presence*, xii.
4. Irenaeus, *Against Heresies* 5.8.1.
5. Martens, *Origen and Scripture*, 1.

discipleship.[6] He imagined that every believer before him was on a spiritual journey, striving to make progress in godliness. Origen's student Gregory Thaumaturgus (ca. 213–ca. 270) describes Origen's own pursuit of virtue, saying, "I shall not speak of him as a perfect pattern, but as one who vehemently desires to imitate the perfect pattern, and strives after it with zeal and earnestness, even beyond the capacity of men."[7] Origen was a model for his students, an exemplar who strove arduously for the holy life. Speaking of the way he compelled his students, Gregory continues, "He constrained us . . . to practice righteousness on the ground of the personal action of the soul itself, which he persuaded us to study, drawing us off from the officious anxieties of life, and from the turbulence of the forum, and raising us to the nobler vocation of looking into ourselves, and dealing with the things that concern ourselves in truth."[8] Origen set his students on the path of virtue, culling the Scriptures for food to sustain them on their journey.

A key passage in Origen's vision of the good life is the travel narrative of Numbers 33. What is mostly an ordinary account of Israel's travels in the wilderness to the promised land offers a vision of the Christian's journey to God. "Moses wrote down their starting places and their stages by the Word of the Lord," beginning with Rameses and ending on the plains of Moab, awaiting entrance into the promised land (Num. 33:2, 5, 49). These places, Origen writes, were listed so that the people of faith can "read them and see how many starting places and stages lie ahead of us on the journey."[9] After conversion from a pagan life, these stages lead the Christian through the process of sanctification, leading to the promised land or the kingdom of God, where the faithful behold God.[10] For this reason, Origen implores us, "we are making a journey, and the reason we have come into this world is so that we may pass 'from virtue to virtue' [Ps. 84:7], not to remain on the earth for earthly things."[11] Passing "from virtue to virtue," from *dynamis* to *dynamis*, points to progress and growth within a vision of the good life.

The travel narrative in Numbers shows that the journey of sanctification is not easy. The faithful can prepare themselves for this arduous path "by considering the journey that lies ahead," and not allowing the time "to be wasted by laziness and negligence." In this life, there is no easy road, and the stages to the kingdom of God are marked by dangers and toils. Enticements

6. Presley, "Origen of Alexandria," 86.
7. Gregory Thaumaturgus, *Oration and Panegyric Addressed to Origen* 11.
8. Gregory Thaumaturgus, *Oration and Panegyric Addressed to Origen* 11.
9. Origen, *Homilies on Numbers* 27.7.7.
10. Origen, *Homilies on Numbers* 27.5.2.
11. Origen, *Homilies on Numbers* 27.7.7.

and deceptions lie along the path, so we cannot "linger in the vanities of the world," and we indeed "may faint while only halfway there."[12] Before the soul can journey toward perfection, it must dwell "in the wilderness, where, of course, it is trained in the commandments of the Lord and where its faith is tested by temptations."[13]

We are here not to dally or relish earthly things but to incrementally conform to the likeness of Christ. Interpretation is like a road leading up to God, and the road is marked out by virtues.[14] Origen views his congregation as caught in the torrent of a depraved world, with all its vices and sensualities. Whatever the cost and regardless of distractions, the preacher must preach the Word of God for the edification of the people of God. Each time the soul conquers temptation, it makes progress in the good life. When it "conquers one temptation and its faith has been proven by it, from there it goes to another one; and it passes as it were from one stage to another; and then, when it prevails over the things that have happened and endures them faithfully, it moves on to another stage." Step by step, stage by stage, little by little, the faithful make progress in growth and conformity to the likeness of Christ. "And thus, the progress through each of the temptations of life and faith will be said to have stages in which increases in virtues are acquired one by one," Origen continues, "and what is written is fulfilled: 'They will go from virtue to virtue,' until the soul reaches its final end, or rather, the highest degree of the virtues, and it crosses the river of God and receives the promised inheritance."[15] As with Israel's journey, Christians are in the process of journeying toward God, making daily progress in sanctification and seeking the holy life.

Second, the main purpose of the journey—and, consequently, one of the main purposes for reading Scripture—is to pursue the virtues that guide the Christian along the right path. This is a theme I see in the fathers again and again; biblical theology is not simply a method but a way of life. The community does not imagine itself to be perfect, nor does it think perfection is required for good interpretation. Christians will not experience perfection until they behold the glory of God. The Bible repeatedly warns its readers that like infants, they can only handle milk, not solid food, until they mature in their knowledge of God and the Scriptures.[16] A reader should not come to the Scriptures engrossed in sin, but "a reader must have spiritual discipline to control exegesis."[17] They

---

12. Origen, *Homilies on Numbers* 27.7.7.
13. Origen, *Homilies on Numbers* 27.5.2.
14. O'Keefe and Reno, *Sanctified Vision*, 130.
15. Origen, *Homilies on Numbers* 27.5.2.
16. Boersma, *Scripture as Real Presence*, 21.
17. O'Keefe and Reno, *Sanctified Vision*, 128.

The Good Life 127

must seek the spiritual process that recognizes the need to be conformed to the likeness of Christ. Basil writes that after repentance, the faithful person needs "to be cleansed from all defilement of flesh and spirit, so that he might thus become acceptable to God in the good works of holiness."[18] Passages such as Matthew 23:25—"Woe to you, scribes and Pharisees, hypocrites! For you clean the outside of the cup and the plate, but inside they are full of greed and self-indulgence"—and 2 Corinthians 7:1—"Since we have these promises, beloved, let us cleanse ourselves from every defilement of body and spirit, bringing holiness to completion in the fear of God"—are Basil's theological guides.

At every turn, the fathers remind us that virtue envelops the whole process of interpretation. Those who come to Scripture without virtuous eyes aimed at conformity to Christ are already off course and headed to a destination other than God. The fathers read for wisdom to help them on their journey, participating in the cyclical relationship: coming to Scripture with virtue to seek virtue. This cyclical vision celebrates the virtues from beginning to end. At the start, the fathers assume that anyone who reads Scripture rightly will embody these virtues in some measure, as they also actively pursue them.

Interpreting Scripture faithfully is not about applying some simple step-by-step process. The kind of person that reads Scripture matters; the interpreter must be virtuous in all kinds of ways. Take Gregory the Great's (ca. 540–604) summary of the pastoral office. The pastor, he writes, "must, therefore, be a model for everyone. He must be devoted entirely to the example of good living." He explains what this good life looks like, saying that the pastor must be focused on the virtues of the spiritual life. This entails that the pastor is "dead to the passions of the flesh and live[s] a spiritual life" and "should not lust for the possessions of others, but give freely of his own." The pastor should be "quick to forgive through compassion, but never so far removed from righteousness as to forgive indiscriminately"; at the same time, "in his own heart, he must suffer the afflictions of others and likewise rejoice at the fortune of his neighbor, as though the good thing was happening to him."[19] In general, the pastor must be a positive example for others and model the kind of spiritual life that people are called to live through prayer. Those who should not participate in spiritual leadership include those who are wrapped up in vices and sins—those who are unstable in their habits, lacking spiritual discernment, unable to walk the path of righteousness, dominated by the weakness and depravity of the flesh, and lacking the discipline to perform good works.[20]

18. Basil, *On Christian Ethics* 2.2.
19. Gregory the Great, *Book of Pastoral Rule* 10.
20. Gregory the Great, *Book of Pastoral Rule* 11.

Over and over, the fathers plead with the faithful to come to Scripture as virtuous interpreters, looking to grow in godliness. "One of Origen's oft-repeated maxims," Martens tells us, "was that only those who were 'worthy' or 'pure'—that is, only those who have made some moral progress on the itinerary of the Christian faith—could interpret the Scriptures well."[21] Athanasius concurs. In order to study Scripture, he writes, "there is needed a good life and a pure soul and the virtue which is according to Christ." In his thinking, virtue is the path that is laid out before us, and the intellect, as it reasons, must travel along that path. "Without a pure mind and a life modeled on the saints," Athanasius continues, "no one can comprehend the words of the saints." The Old Testament is not some barren wasteland of obscurity; it captures portraits of virtue lived by people of God who have walked before us. We read for wisdom, to see the moral patterns that ought to characterize our lives. Athanasius uses the image of the sun to illustrate the importance of virtue for the interpretive life: "If someone would wish to see the light of the sun, he would certainly wipe and clear his eyes, purifying himself to be almost like that which he desires, so that as the eye thus becomes light it may see the light of the sun." Just as we wipe our eyes in the light of the sun, so do we need to purify our lives if we wish to understand what God has revealed. Anyone who wishes to interpret the Scriptures and "comprehend the mind of the theologians must first wash and cleanse his soul by his manner of life, and approach the saints themselves by the imitation of their works, so that being with them in the conduct of a common life, he may understand also the things revealed to them."[22] Our deceitful hearts cannot avoid the noetic effects of sin, nor can they comprehend the Scriptures without the aid of the Spirit. As Jeremiah teaches, "The heart is deceitful above all things, and desperately sick; who can understand it?" (Jer. 17:9). The point is not to avoid all discussion of virtue or to suspend it until another time but to make it part of the interpretive process.

A chorus of other patristic writers associates virtue and interpretation as well. The second-century apologist Theophilus of Antioch (died ca. 183/185), writing to a pagan interlocutor, argues that true wisdom and understanding are found by "everyone who seeks for the Wisdom of God and is pleasing to him through faith and righteousness and good deeds."[23] In his discussion of

21. Martens, *Origen and Scripture*, 161.
22. Athanasius, *On the Incarnation* 57.
23. Theophilus of Antioch, *Ad Autolycus* 2.38. Theophilus leans on the passage in Hosea that says, "Whoever is wise, let him understand these things; whoever is discerning, let him know them; for the ways of the LORD are right, and the upright walk in them, but transgressors stumble in them" (Hosea 14:9).

interpretation, Hans Boersma shows that Gregory of Nyssa treats virtue as a prerequisite for good reading. Virtue is part of the contents of the Scriptures; the virtuous life is found in Scripture; and at the same time, virtue is the aim of the exegetical project.[24]

Fourth-century bishop Hilary of Poitiers warns his readers that the Scriptures (and the God to whom they point) must be approached with reverence, remembering that "the action of God must not be canvassed by human faculties; the Creator must not be judged by those who are the work of His hands." As biblical interpreters, we must "clothe ourselves in foolishness that we may gain wisdom; not in the foolishness of hazardous conclusions, but in the foolishness of a modest sense of our own infirmity, that so the evidence of God's power may teach us truths to which the arguments of earthly philosophy cannot attain."[25] Through humility and virtue, not arrogance or pride, Christians can learn the wisdom of God. Origen argues that in order "to hear the Scriptures spiritually," the interpreter must "strive with all his effort not to converse with flesh and blood so that he may be worthy of spiritual secrets."[26] Henri de Lubac summarizes Origen's moral requirements for proper exegesis. For Origen, it is "necessary to mortify [the heart's] taste for worldly activities and its attraction for sensible things; it will be necessary to distance itself from 'the life according to flesh and blood, so as to become worthy of receiving the spiritual secrets,' in that way making a place 'for a spiritual desire or love.'"[27] The *sensus carnis* (carnal sense) must decrease, so that the *sensus spiritus* (spiritual sense) increases and the whole person can perceive the Word of God.[28]

Ambrose argues that the philosophers are contradictory and confusing, but the "Scriptures state that nothing is good but what is virtuous, and declare that virtue is blessed in every circumstance, and that it is never enhanced by either corporal or other external good fortune, nor is it weakened by adversity."[29] In a similar way, Augustine describes how we ought to approach the Scriptures. The faithful person submits to the divine Scripture and "reads or hears it piously, deferring to it as of supreme authority." In this way, the Christian "loves being reproved by it, and rejoices that his maladies are not spared until they are healed."[30] Even the obscure passages and apparent contradictions are

---

24. Boersma, *Scripture as Real Presence*, 19.
25. Hilary, *On the Trinity* 3.26.
26. Origen, *Homilies on the Song of Songs* 1.2.
27. De Lubac, *History and Spirit*, 366 (quoting Origen, *Homilies on the Song of Songs* 1.2).
28. De Lubac, *History and Spirit*, 366.
29. Ambrose, *On the Duties of the Clergy* 2.3.8.
30. Augustine, *Sermon on the Mount* 1.11.32.

no deterrent. The Christian continues to pray that he or she may understand them. Summarizing Augustine, Frances Young writes that "the important quality is humility of mind before the text." The Scriptures contain obscurities and paradoxes to "prevent pride and stimulate the intellectual appetite." This is why the interpreter needs the "fear of the Lord, piety, knowledge, strength and resolution, purity of vision, wisdom."[31] All of these virtues are servants that help guide the faithful toward good and right readings of Scripture.

With one accord, the fathers call Christians to come to Scripture with virtue, seeking virtue. Like a continuous feedback loop, the pursuit of virtue guides the whole process. There is no sense in reading Scripture if interpreters have no desire to pursue virtue. We do not merely read Scripture to get knowledge, understand history, or find interesting quotes. We read Scripture to seek virtue. As O'Keefe and Reno argue, "The goal of patristic exegesis was to pass through the narrow opening that led to thoughts that participated in the unspeakable mysteries, and only a person whose vision has been refined by prayer, fasting, and self-control could hope to effect such a passage."[32] The good life and exegesis are intertwined. This is the kind of life evidenced in the Scriptures and the faithful found in its pages.

A virtuous posture means that they come to Scripture recognizing their own inadequacies, so there is an interpretive humility, tempered by a confidence that Scripture provides the virtue to face any situation. They come broken and battered, acknowledging that the Scriptures are medicine given by the Great Physician. One of the most frequent images applied to Scripture in Augustine's writing is God as the divine Physician and the Scriptures as the medicine that heals the people of God.[33] In one place, Augustine writes that "our Lord and God takes care of and heals every ailment of the soul, and so he produced many medicines from the holy scriptures (which you could call the shelves of his pharmacy or drugstore) when the divine readings were being read. It is my ministry to apply these medicines to our wounds."[34] Basil of Caesarea also picks up on this theme and maintains that "all Scripture is inspired by God and is useful, composed by the Spirit for this reason, namely, that we men, each and all of us, as if in a general hospital for souls, may select the remedy for his own condition."[35] John Chrysostom makes a similar argument and explains that the Scriptures are a medicine chest for everything that ails us, saying, "The divine oracles are a treasury of all manner of medicines, so that

31. Young, *Biblical Exegesis*, 275.
32. O'Keefe and Reno, *Sanctified Vision*, 129.
33. Harmless, *Augustine in His Own Words*, 140–45.
34. Augustine, *Sermon 32* 1.
35. Basil, *Exegetic Homilies* 10 (on Ps. 1).

whether it be needful to quench pride, to lull desire to sleep, to tread under foot the love of money, to despise pain, to inspire confidence, to gain patience, from them one may find abundant resource. For what many of those who struggle with long poverty or who are nailed to a grievous disease, will not, when he reads the passage before us, receive much comfort?"[36] Basil argues that the "study of inspired Scripture is the chief way of finding our duty, for in it we find both instruction about conduct and the lives of blessed men, delivered in writing, as some breathing images of godly living, for the imitation of their good works. Hence, in whatever respect each one feels himself deficient, devoting himself to this imitation, he finds as from some dispensary, the due medicine for his ailment."[37]

This virtuous interpretive feedback loop frames their posture toward the exegetical task. The fathers approach Scripture not for mere knowledge or theological propositions but to find wisdom and seek virtue. Stephen Fowl describes both of these processes, arguing that "theological interpretation aids in the cultivation of virtue" and that "virtue aids in the practice of theological interpretation." He calls the former "virtue-through-interpretation" and the latter "virtue-in-interpretation."[38] Cultivating virtue is a cyclical process. The interpretation of Scripture requires virtue, but virtue is also the telos of interpretation.

An Example of Interpretation and the Spiritual Journey

Some patristic writers seam together these views to provide models of sanctification that exemplify the relationship between Scripture and the journey toward holiness. Augustine is a good example. In his thinking, the whole of the Scriptures should be oriented toward the kind of life Christians are called to live. He writes, "It is our duty fully to enjoy the truth which lives unchangeably, and since the triune God takes counsel in this truth for the things which He has made, the soul must be purified that it may have power to perceive that light, and to rest in it when it is perceived." He describes this "purification" as the slow, steady progress toward sanctification, "a kind of journey or voyage to our native land," cultivated through "pure desires and virtuous habits."[39]

Drawing on Isaiah 11:2–3, Augustine marks out seven stages of the spiritual life that cultivate such pure desires and virtuous habits. As he gives it, the passage

---

36. Chrysostom, *Homilies on the Gospel according to St. John* 37.1.
37. Basil, *Letter 2*.
38. Fowl, "Virtue," 837.
39. Augustine, *On Christian Doctrine* 1.10.10.

reads: "And the Spirit of the Lord will rest upon him, the Spirit of wisdom (*sapientiae*) and understanding (*intellectus*), the Spirit of resolve (*consilii*) and fortitude (*fortitudinis*), the Spirit of knowledge (*scientiae*) and piety (*pietatis*). The Spirit of the fear of the Lord (*spiritus timoris Domini*) will fill him."[40] Growth in godliness through the Spirit is the theme that threads these virtues together, though Augustine inverts the order in his commentary on the passage. The spiritual life begins with the fear of the Lord and culminates in wisdom. In other words, the goal of the process is the wisdom of God (Isa. 11:2). To walk wisely in the fear of the Lord is to walk virtuously down the spiritual path.

First, the spiritual life begins with *the fear of the Lord* (working backward through the references in Isa. 11:2–3). Initially, the Spirit of the Lord moves interpreters to perceive their own mortality and their prideful inclinations. Good exegetes "should be led by the fear of God to seek the knowledge of His will, what He commands us to desire and what to avoid," Augustine writes.[41] Like a skilled physician, they should discern their weaknesses and ailments, the areas of their lives still trending toward vices. The fear of God will help keep our mortality before us daily and help us crucify our sin. Desire and self-control are held in tension as the faithful learn to follow the commands of God, living the kind of virtuous life taught in the Wisdom Books and evidenced in the lives of the faithful. But this is only the first step, the initial course in the spiritual life. We have no reason to take another step if we do not begin with the fear of the Lord.

The second stage is *piety*. Piety is pedagogical; it leads readers to understand that the Scriptures are more authoritative than mere rational inquiry. The conviction is that the passions and habits of the reader need to conform to the teachings of the Scriptures. We come not haughtily but humbly, bowing before the sacred words of revelation, that we might, little by little, be conformed to the likeness of Christ. With our hearts "subdued by piety," we do not imagine that we are so ingenious as to have a better vision of the right way to live. "We must rather think and believe that whatever is there written, even though it be hidden, is better and truer than anything we could devise by our own wisdom," Augustine writes.[42] Armed with the fear of the Lord and piety, interpreters are rightly positioned to receive and absorb the teachings of the Scriptures.

The third stage is *knowledge* of the Lord. The knowledge of God in Scripture involves the discernment of the wisdom that leads us to the love of God

40. Augustine, *On Christian Doctrine* 2.7.9–11. See also Augustine, *Letter 171A*.
41. Augustine, *On Christian Doctrine* 2.7.9.
42. Augustine, *On Christian Doctrine* 2.7.9.

The Good Life   133

and neighbor. Every "earnest student of Scripture" longs to love God "for His own sake, and our neighbor for God's sake." The double love command means, Augustine continues, "that God is to be loved with all the heart, and with all the soul, and with all the mind, and one's neighbor as one's self—that is, in such a way that all our love for our neighbor, like all our love for ourselves, should have reference to God [Matt. 22:37–40]." Readers are "entangled in the love of this world"—that is "temporal things," which have drawn them away from the love of God and neighbor.[43] Through the double love command, interpreters come to realize that they are ensnared in conflicting loves, and through fear and piety, they lament their own condition. At this point, reading Scripture is a struggle for love, a conflict that rages within the soul, a fight to reject sin and seek the good life found in the love of God and neighbor.

These three stages bring us to the fourth step, *fortitude*. Here, Augustine points us to the spiritual disciplines of praying and petitioning the Lord, which support the interpreter in their pursuit of virtue. Fortitude is the watchword, as each exegete "hungers and thirsts after righteousness." Their resolute commitment to God, attended through the Spirit, turns them from the "transitory things" of this world—good things, to be sure, but not the lasting and eternal things—and "fixes [their] affection on things eternal, . . . the unchangeable Trinity in unity."[44] The concern is that despair will set in as readers recognize the depth of their conflicting loves and lack of piety— that they will lose the hunger for righteousness and fall back into old habits and sins. But through the Spirit, fortitude strengthens the Christian's resolve to seek God.

After gazing on eternal things and sensing one's own weakness of sight in the fourth step, *resolve*—or the "the counsel of compassion"—sets in. This is the fifth step. It is when Christian interpreters are agitated at their sin, which leads them away from the good life. When they learn to walk in holiness, diligently loving their neighbor—even to the point of loving their enemies—they are ready to progress.[45]

The sixth stage, *understanding*, involves the purification of the eyes and continual dying to the world. In this stage, exegetes see God in proportion to the degree they focus on the things of this world. Christians perceive things, but through a glass darkly; the more they die to this world, the more they will behold the things of God. The light of God becomes clearer and more delightful as exegetes purge their illicit affections, learning to love God with

43. Augustine, *On Christian Doctrine* 2.7.10.
44. Augustine, *On Christian Doctrine* 2.7.10.
45. Augustine, *On Christian Doctrine* 2.7.11.

more and more vigor. Those who find themselves in this stage will be so pure in heart that they "will not step aside from the truth," neither out of a desire to please others nor because of life's struggles.[46]

Finally, the last stage, *wisdom*, ties all the previous stages together, because the fear of the Lord is the beginning of wisdom. Here, in this final stage, the interpreter knows nothing but "peace and tranquility." Wisdom is beholding the glory of God and walking in holiness and faithfulness. This stage captures the progression in holiness that ought to accompany any Bible interpreter, the reader enveloped in the joy and love of knowing God. The more readers attune their lives to Scripture, the more they come to see God.

In the end, Augustine cycles back to the third stage, that of *knowledge*. This is a most crucial step for the Christian exegete. "The most skillful interpreter of the sacred writings," he tells us, "will be he who in the first place has read them all and retained them in his knowledge, if not yet with full understanding."[47] The good exegete knows Scripture—not just a few books or a narrow sliver of Scripture. The whole counsel of the canonical books must be studied diligently and committed to memory as much as possible. A mind soaked in Scripture is crucial for biblical interpretation.

The above discussion shows the weakness of approaches that partition and isolate Scripture. For the fathers, biblical theology is a way of life, a journey that progresses through stages of sanctification. The fathers read the Bible not to find some nice quips or anecdotes but to train themselves and their communities in virtue. They do not imagine themselves to be perfect but recognize that they are making progress toward Christlikeness.

Below, I look at a few key features of Scripture that serve as the docents for the good life, guiding the Christian toward the likeness of Christ.

The Wisdom Literature and Models for the Spiritual Life

As mentioned above, the fathers read Scripture as travelers on a journey toward Christlikeness. Several features of Scripture encourage them along that journey: the example of Christ and his teaching, the Wisdom literature and the Psalms, and personal models of virtue. These features form the framework for any good interpretation. Ironically, modern versions of biblical theology have struggled with the Wisdom literature. In the heyday of the biblical theology movement (mid-twentieth century), Ernest Wright famously commented that in "any outline of biblical theology, the proper place to treat the Wisdom

---

46. Augustine, *On Christian Doctrine* 2.7.11.
47. Augustine, *On Christian Doctrine* 2.8.12.

The Good Life   135

literature is something of a problem."[48] It is easy to see how the Historical Books or the Gospels fit into a larger narrative of salvation history, but modern biblical interpreters have stumbled when they have encountered the strangeness of the Wisdom Books.

Not so for the fathers. Far from ignoring the Wisdom Books, they actually view these works as essential for growth in godliness. These literary pieces are like the prism through which the fathers view the spiritual life, as lived within the story of God's salvation. According to Young, early Christian thinkers arranged "compounded sayings from Psalms, Proverbs and the Gospels into new expressions of the character to be fostered by the Christian." She argues that the fathers were very attentive to "biblical models who exemplified particular virtues or lived a life worth imitating."[49] Biblical scholar Michael Graves agrees. He writes that besides linking texts with the life of Christ, "the most common method used by the Church Fathers for explaining the significance of the Old Testament narratives was to set forth biblical characters as models for Christians to imitate."[50]

First, for the fathers, Christ is the premier example of the virtuous life, both in word and in deed, both in his teachings, such as the Sermon on the Mount, and in his actions. The words of Christ ring with wisdom, and his life embodies all the virtues. The church has always looked to Christ as the embodiment of all virtue, the principal figure to imitate. Any virtue found in the lives of the saints is refracted through him—or, more precisely, is trinitarian and "oriented toward God the supreme good, formed by the life of Christ, and moved toward the good by the indwelling of the Holy Spirit."[51] "Theologically, the person of Jesus—and the Christian understanding of God generally—serves as an important hermeneutical paradigm," Graves writes.[52]

In the opening paragraphs of his work titled *The Instructor*, Clement of Alexandria locates all training in virtue in the Word of God, the Son of God. He is the one who models and exhorts the faithful to be conformed to the likeness of God. Just as those who are sick need a physician, "so also those who are diseased in soul require a pædagogue to cure our maladies; and then a teacher, to train and guide the soul to all requisite knowledge when it is made able to admit the revelation of the Word." The Word "exhorts, then trains, and finally teaches."[53] In his *Confessions*, Augustine, reflecting on John 1:1

48. Wright, *God Who Acts*, 115.
49. Young, *Biblical Exegesis*, 248.
50. Graves, *Inspiration and Interpretation of Scripture*, 32.
51. Wilken, *Spirit of Early Christian Thought*, 278.
52. Graves, *Inspiration and Interpretation of Scripture*, 37.
53. Clement of Alexandria, *Instructor* 1.1.

and contemplating the majesty of Christ, deems Christ "a man of excellent wisdom, to whom no man could be equaled."[54] In Christ are all the riches of wisdom and virtue. Clement of Alexandria argues that Christ is our educator, an instructor who "is like His Father God, whose son He is, sinless, blameless, and with a soul devoid of passion; God in the form of man, stainless, the minister of His Father's will." "He is to us," Clement continues, "a spotless image; to Him we are to try with all our might to assimilate our souls."[55] In all these writers, a system of virtues is communicated through the Scriptures, ultimately pointing to Christ as the example of the spiritual life.

Second, the fathers look to Scripture for wisdom to guide them in their spiritual lives, which exemplify the virtues of Christ. They employ what is called "paraenetic exegesis," which treats Scripture "as the guide to life," as a source of wisdom for moral or existential questions.[56] The Wisdom literature (Job, Song of Songs, Ecclesiastes, Proverbs) and the Psalms are indispensable for this kind of interpretation. In the early church, the Psalms especially— one of the most frequently cited Old Testament books—"lost none of its importance."[57]

Origen explains the importance of the Wisdom Books in his commentary on the Song of Songs. For him, these books reflect "three branches of learning" found among the Greeks: ethics, physics, and enoptics, also known as the moral, natural, and inspective branches of philosophy.[58] The manner of study called "moral," Origen tells us, "inculcates a seemly manner of life and gives a grounding in habits that incline to virtue."[59] "The study called natural," he continues, "is that in which the nature of each single thing is considered; so that nothing in life may be done which is contrary to nature, but everything is assigned to the uses for which the Creator brought it into being." Finally, in the third place, the "inspective is that by which we go beyond things seen and contemplate somewhat of things divine and heavenly, beholding them with the mind alone, for they are beyond the range of bodily sight." He summarizes how the books of Solomon shape the entire intellectual life:

> First, in Proverbs [Solomon] taught the moral science, putting rules for living into the form of short and pithy maxims, as was fitting. Secondly, he covered the science known as natural in Ecclesiastes; in this, by discussing at length the things of nature, and by distinguishing the useless and vain from the profitable

54. Augustine, *Confessions* 7.18.25.
55. Clement of Alexandria, *Instructor* 1.2.
56. Young, *Biblical Exegesis*, 248.
57. Kannengiesser, *Handbook of Patristic Exegesis*, 297.
58. Origen points out that some add logic to this triad.
59. Origen, *Commentary on the Song of Songs*, prologue, 3.

The Good Life   137

and essential, he counsels us to forsake vanity and cultivate things useful and upright. The inspective science likewise he has propounded in this little book that we have now in hand—that is, the Song of Songs.[60]

In this program, Proverbs delineates ethics, or the patterns of living; Ecclesiastes delineates physics, or the patterns of creation and sapiential teaching; and Songs allows readers to contemplate divine things. But Origen views the works of Solomon as the original and preeminent works of wisdom; "all the sages of the Greeks borrowed these ideas from Solomon."[61] The Wisdom literature offered them a telos that transcended all types of learning. All of this might sound odd to the modern ear, but the basic point is that in the early church, the Wisdom literature was the window through which the virtuous life was conceived with rules for living the good life within the narrative of Scripture and under the provision of God.

Other authors reflect on the significance of the Wisdom literature as well. Hippolytus (ca. 170–ca. 235) begins his commentary on Proverbs saying, "Proverbs, therefore, are words of exhortation serviceable for the whole path of life; for to those who seek their way to God, these serve as guides and signs to revive them when wearied with the length of the road."[62] Basil is another good example. He views Scripture as "composed by the Spirit for this reason, namely, that we men each and all of us, as if in a general hospital for souls, may select the remedy for his own condition." He points to Ecclesiastes 10:4—"The remedy will make the greatest sin to cease"—and sees in the Scriptures the remedy for sin. He continues: "Now the prophets teach one thing, historians another, the law something else, and the form of advice found in the proverbs something different still. But the book of Psalms has taken over what is profitable from all."[63] Each portion of Scripture should be read and understood in relation to the spiritual life.[64] I have already observed how Augustine's vision of the spiritual life is framed by the notion that the fear of the Lord is the beginning of wisdom (Ps. 111:10 and Prov. 1:7). Similarly, Origen looks to Proverbs 22:20–21 (LXX)—"Do you portray them threefold in counsel and knowledge, that you might answer words of truth to those who question you?"[65]

Third, the fathers are attuned to the patterns of life in scriptural figures. When we take in the whole of patristic reading, we see them returning again

60. Origen, *Commentary on the Song of Songs*, prologue, 3.
61. Origen, *Commentary on the Song of Songs*, prologue, 3.
62. Hippolytus, *On the Proverbs* 1. See also Basil, *Homilies on the Beginning of Proverbs*.
63. Basil, *Exegetic Homilies* 10.1.
64. Brown, "Saint as Exemplar in Late Antiquity"; Wilken, "Alexandria," 15–30.
65. Origen, *On First Principles* 4.2.4.

and again to the Wisdom literature and the Psalms and to the great examples of faith in the biblical characters. These two points work in tandem. The Wisdom literature and Psalms (or Wisdom sayings drawn from other books) provide content for virtuous living, propositions that guide the daily decisions of life. The figures of the Old Testament, on the other hand, offer living illustrations of wisdom. They put the virtuous life on display. This might be an odd way to read for modern exegetes, who tend to overemphasize the sins of the saints. It is not uncommon to hear sermons or Bible studies stressing their failures and thanking God that he still used sinners such as them. But the fathers have a different emphasis. They do not see these figures as righteous, but they look to them for wisdom in how to walk in faith, not just how to fail. So the early church looked for the ways in which scriptural characters embody Christlike virtues. Its readings did not deny the historicity of these figures or the events with which they are associated; rather, the church recognized that the primary purpose of these figures' lives is to offer a spiritual pedagogy. The genre of *bios* was a common tool for promoting virtue in the ancient world—among both Christians and pagans.[66] "Without examples, without imitation, there can be no human life or civilization, no art or culture, no virtue or holiness," writes Robert Wilken.[67]

We can already see virtue framing exegesis in the New Testament. The earlier discussion of Hebrews 11 and 1 Clement in this book is a good example, as is Paul's injunction in 1 Corinthians 11:1: "Be imitators of me, as I am of Christ." Philip Esler provides a social analysis of 1 Clement that cites several "prototypes" and "antitypes," which typify the positive or negative values and behaviors, or identity descriptors, of a group. Esler points to 1 Clement's use of "examples" (*hypodeigmata*), which signify "a person from the past who has either exhibited an exemplary/prototypical instance of positive behavior or who has suffered from or manifested an exemplary/prototypical instance of negative behavior."[68] Clement of Rome offers models of virtues that Christians should emulate, saying, "Let us be imitators also of those who went about in goatskins and sheepskins, preaching the coming of Christ. We mean Elijah and Elisha, and likewise Ezekiel, the prophets and alongside them those ancient men of renown as well."[69] Together these virtues and the corresponding rejection of vices compose the ethical standards that flow from

---

66. Urbano, *Philosophical Life*; Cox, *Biography in Late Antiquity*.

67. Wilken, *Spirit of Early Christian Thought*, 263.

68. Esler, "Prototypes, Antitypes and Social Identity," 135. For further discussion of the term *hypodeigmata*, see Presley, "Reading Community." The term is also used in a similar way in the New Testament. See John 13:15; Heb. 4:11; 8:5; 9:23; James 5:10; 2 Pet. 2:6.

69. 1 Clement 17.

the teaching of Scripture. The social identity of the Christian community and the activity of the Christian spiritual life ought to embody virtue, as the living testimony of the flourishing found in the Christian life.

In the early church, paraenetic exegesis encouraged the faithful to identify and emulate these models of virtue—what is called mimesis. "*Mimēsis* lay at the heart of apprenticeship," which was commonplace in antiquity; it encouraged the creation of "models out of assumed parallels."[70] When faced with questions of morality and the Christian life, the early church went to Scripture to see, as if in a mirror, the kind of life it was called to live. Mimetic examples provided the "guidelines for the construction of a Christian life." "Like visual art, early Christian discourse presented its audience with a series of images."[71]

Several sustained reflections on Old Testament figures provide good examples of this type of exegesis, such as Ambrose's *On Cain and Abel* and *The Prayer of Job and David* and Gregory the Great's *Morals on the Book of Job*. Another good example of this kind of interpretation is Gregory of Nyssa's *Life of Moses*. In the prologue to his discussion of Moses's life, Gregory describes how he plans to outline Moses's life in the Scriptures and then discern "the spiritual understanding which corresponds to the history in order to obtain suggestions of virtue."[72] He attends to the spiritual understanding of the Scriptures, which assumes a historical account of Moses and is thus tied to the literal sense of Scripture. He first argues that one needs to establish the *historia*, or the history, of the text. Such history comprises the organic, literal sequence of events given in the Scriptures, which offer a basic narrative recounting of the events and an essential interpretive framework. At this stage, he also addresses important grammatical and lexical issues encountered in the passage. Gregory moves beyond the literal sense to discern the spiritual sense, which he calls *theoria*. By discussing virtue and those principles of virtue evident in the life of Moses, Gregory hopes that he will "come to know the perfect life for men."[73] He knows that Christians cannot repeat the events of Moses's life. The point is not repetition. We are not called to be Moses; we are called to be conformed to the likeness of Christ. But through the study of Moses's life, it is possible to see, in part, the evidence of virtue that ought to characterize the godly life. Gregory writes, "Because therefore it has been shown to be impossible to imitate the marvels of these blessed men in these

---

70. Young, *Biblical Exegesis*, 257.

71. Cameron, *Christianity and the Rhetoric of Empire*, 57. See also Cox, *Biography in Late Antiquity*, 134.

72. Gregory of Nyssa, *Life of Moses*, prologue.

73. Gregory of Nyssa, *Life of Moses*, prologue.

exact events, one might substitute a moral teaching for the literal sequence in those things which admit of such an approach."[74]

Other examples include Chrysostom, who uses Abraham's near sacrifice of Isaac in Genesis 22 as an ethical example.[75] The figures of Noah, Abraham, David, the prophets, and the apostles all offer models of the spiritual life. This kind of reading, a reading that discerns the good life, is essential to patristic exegesis. The fathers do not read to pass along information; they read to live, to follow the virtuous path. When Augustine wants to describe piety or the sacred life, he turns to Job. "The true wisdom of man is piety," Augustine writes. "You find this in the book of holy Job. For we read there what wisdom itself has said to man: Behold, the fear of the Lord [*pietas*], that is wisdom."[76]

The Virtues for Reading

Up to this point, I have argued that virtue spans the exegetical process, that Christ embodies all the virtues and is the preeminent example of virtue in practice, and that the Wisdom literature, the Psalms, and the spiritual lives of the faithful offer glimpses of the virtuous life. In this section, I discuss the virtues that should express themselves in the life of the Christian. The Beatitudes in Matthew 5:3–12 and the fruit of the Spirit in Galatians 5:22–23 provide good starting points for this discussion. They complement the Wisdom literature and the Psalms with more descriptions of the patterns of spirituality that radiate from the virtuous believer. All of these passages work together toward Christ's exhortation, "You therefore must be perfect, as your heavenly Father is perfect" (Matt. 5:48).[77]

Perhaps the best way to begin thinking about these virtues and the goal of the good life is to think in terms of the three theological virtues (i.e., faith, hope, and love) and the four cardinal virtues (i.e., prudence, justice, fortitude, and temperance).[78] While these virtues were codified in later tradition, they appear in early Christian writings and provide a simple scheme to frame the conversation. Wilken writes that as early as the second century,

74. Gregory of Nyssa, *Life of Moses*, prologue.

75. Chrysostom, *Homily on Genesis 22*. See also Ambrose, *Jacob and the Happy Life*.

76. Augustine, *Enchiridion on Faith, Hope, and Love* 2. Augustine continues in the same section of this work: "If you ask further what is meant in that place by *pietas*, the Greek calls it more definitely *theosebeia*, that is, the worship of God. The Greeks sometimes call piety *eusebeia*, which signifies right worship, though this, of course, refers specially to the worship of God."

77. See also 2 Cor. 7:1; Heb. 12:14; 1 Pet. 1:13–16; and Gregory of Nyssa, *Homilies on the Beatitudes*.

78. Wilken, *Spirit of Early Christian Thought*, 279–90.

The Good Life   141

Clement of Alexandria cited these virtues to frame the Christian life.[79] These are not the only virtues that the ancients discussed, but they provide a framework for thinking through the fathers' approach to biblical theology.

Early Christians and Greek philosophers defined the virtues differently. For the ancient Greeks, the virtues focused on moderation and, as a result, were relevant only to those privileged enough to attend to moderation. Christians, on the other hand, believed virtue was something for both individuals and the community to pursue. Through his catechesis, Origen sought to persuade his catechumens to become "lovers of virtue."[80] Pursuing virtue is no easy task. Gregory Thaumaturgus understands that. He laments that Origen's catechumens struggle: they "are neither in real possession of any virtue whatsoever, either human or divine, nor have we ever made any near approach to it, but we are still far from it." The virtues are available not to those who merely desire to conjure them up in themselves but only to "one whom God inspires with the power."[81]

Turning to the virtues themselves, first I examine the theological virtues: faith, hope, and love. These three virtues, according to Irenaeus, offer an enduring vision of the spiritual life. "For faith," Irenaeus writes, "which has respect to our Master, endures unchangeably, assuring us that there is but one true God." Love joins faith so "that we should truly love Him for ever, seeing that He alone is our Father." Finally, hope is there with faith and love, so "we hope ever to be receiving more and more from God, and to learn from Him, because He is good, and possesses boundless riches, a kingdom without end, and instruction that can never be exhausted."[82] These three virtues guide us in the present age, leading us humbly to walk in virtue toward God. In the end, Irenaeus notes that love is the greatest of all because apart from love, nothing matters. To possess "knowledge without love toward God is worthless"; so also is the knowledge of the mysteries of God "meaningless and futile" without love. Love, he continues "perfects the perfect man," and "the man who loves God is perfect in this world and in the future."[83] In the end, the love of God guides us to God, conformed us to Christ, prepares us to see the glory of God.

Like Irenaeus, Augustine uses these virtues to frame the spiritual life. In the opening paragraphs of his *Enchiridion*, he argues that "God is to be

79. Wilken, *Spirit of Early Christian Thought*, 279.
80. Gregory Thaumaturgus, *Oration and Panegyric Addressed to Origen* 12.
81. Gregory Thaumaturgus, *Oration and Panegyric Addressed to Origen* 12.
82. Irenaeus, *Against Heresies* 2.27.3.
83. Irenaeus, *Against Heresies* 4.12.2.

worshipped with faith, hope, and love."[84] Then, in the rest of the book, he explains how this worship transpires. He summarizes what this means, saying, "When the mind has been imbued with the first elements of that faith which works by love, it endeavors by purity of life to attain unto sight, where the pure and perfect in heart know that unspeakable beauty, the full vision of which is supreme happiness."[85] These virtues, Augustine argues, provide us the starting place and the goal: "We begin in faith, and are made perfect by sight. This also is the sum of the whole body of doctrine." For Augustine, believers simply cannot read the Bible apart from a conscious affection for God and a love for God and neighbor. "Whoever, then, thinks that he understands the Holy Scriptures, or any part of them, but puts such an interpretation upon them as does not tend to build up this twofold love of God and our neighbor, does not yet understand them as he ought."[86] While the end of exegesis is love, Augustine describes how these things order the spiritual life: "Sight shall displace faith; and hope shall be swallowed up in that perfect bliss to which we shall come: love, on the other hand, shall wax greater when these others fail." Eventually, Augustine argues, faith will become sight, and hope will be realized so that love will remain. "For if we love by faith that which as yet we see not, how much more shall we love it when we begin to see! And if we love by hope that which as yet we have not reached, how much more shall we love it when we reach it!" The love of God, when we see him face-to-face, will satisfy the soul forever.[87]

The vision of the end, enveloping in love, orients all interpretation. "Therefore the apostle says: 'Now abides faith, hope, charity, these three; but the greatest of these is charity,' because, when a man shall have reached the eternal world, while the other two graces will fail, love will remain greater and more assured." These virtues are so essential, Augustine argues, that if a person truly embodies them, he or she no longer needs the Scriptures, except to instruct others. He points to those who live the monastic life and embody biblical virtues without passions and without the Scriptures. While this might press the point too far, it illustrates that the ultimate goal of biblical interpretation is the virtuous life.[88] Reading Scripture is not an end in itself but a guide to beholding God.

Interpreters must keep these virtues steadily before their eyes. Every interpretation is filtered through these virtues. So "if a man fully understands that

84. Augustine, *Enchiridion on Faith, Hope, and Love* 3.
85. Augustine, *Enchiridion on Faith, Hope, and Love* 5.
86. Augustine, *On Christian Doctrine* 1.36.40.
87. Augustine, *On Christian Doctrine* 1.38.42.
88. Augustine, *On Christian Doctrine* 1.39.43.

The Good Life   143

the end of the commandment is charity, out of a pure heart, and of a good conscience, and of faith unfeigned [1 Tim. 1:5], and is bent upon making all his understanding of Scripture to bear upon these three graces," Augustine writes, "he may come to the interpretation of these books with an easy mind." Love orients us toward the right vision of the good life, framing the way that we read Scripture, and setting our sights on the vision of God. As Augustine writes, "Anyone who thinks that he has understood the divine Scriptures or any part of them but cannot by his understanding build up this double love of God and neighbor, has not yet succeeded in understanding them."[89]

Second, the cardinal virtues of prudence, justice, fortitude, and temperance also serve to guide the practice of exegesis. The early fathers use these and other related virtues to explain the good life. Gregory Thaumaturgus reports that Origen, through his own virtue, has inspired in his students "a love at once for the beauty of righteousness the golden face of which in truth was shown to us by him."[90] Gregory describes these virtues as prudence, wisdom, temperance, courage, patience, and piety. Under Origen's tutelage, students have been exhorted to prudence, to know themselves and to train the desires of their innermost self, where "the soul is exercised in beholding itself as in a mirror." Alongside prudence, Origen has emphasized temperance, which "conserve[s] this very prudence which must be in the soul that knows itself," becoming, in a sense, "sound prudence" and fortitude, which sustains the virtues, acting "as a kind of preserver, maintainer, and guardian."[91] Piety is rightly called "the mother of the virtues," because it is "the beginning and the end of all the virtues." Throughout life, "all virtue and wisdom [are] our best conductors and most sagacious priests," and in everything, Gregory follows this advice: "By the pure mind make yourself like to God, that you may draw near to Him, and abide in Him."[92] All the virtues cohere together in Origen's vision of the good life, a life lived on the way toward virtue.

The aim of Scripture study and theological education is, as Gregory explains, "the divine virtues that concern the moral nature." Through words and deeds, Origen has instructed his students in "moral dispositions" and "modes of life." The cultivating of virtue takes time. As with the preparation of a good meal, the students must cultivate and season their lives with virtue as they grow and mature. Their maturity should "preserve them by nursing them in their beginnings, and watching carefully over them until they should reach

89. Augustine, *On Christian Doctrine* 1.88.
90. Gregory Thaumaturgus, *Oration and Panegyric Addressed to Origen* 12.
91. Gregory Thaumaturgus, *Oration and Panegyric Addressed to Origen* 11.
92. Gregory Thaumaturgus, *Oration and Panegyric Addressed to Origen* 12 (slightly modified).

their maturity." Describing this process in more detail, Gregory writes, "The heavenly virtues will ripen in the soul." He then lists and describes the cardinal virtues: "prudence, which first of all is able to judge of those very motions in the mind at once from the things themselves, and by the knowledge which accrues to it of things outside of us, whatever such there may be, both good and evil; and temperance, the power that makes the right selection among these things in their beginnings; and righteousness, which assigns what is just to each; and that virtue which is the conserver of them all—fortitude." Together, each of these—prudence, knowledge, temperance, righteousness, and fortitude—work in harmony and proportion to lead the faithful to maturity in Christ. They must be performed in deeds, not merely in words. For it would be "vain and profitless study, if there was simply the doctrine without the deed; and worthless would that prudence be, which, without doing the things that ought to be done, and without turning men away from those that ought not to be done, should be able merely to furnish the knowledge of these things to those who possessed her."[93]

Another good example is Ambrose. In his work *On the Duties of the Clergy* (modeled after Cicero's *De officiis*), Ambrose works through a series of Old Testament examples of virtue. Joseph "endured the bonds of servitude" and was "wise" and "self-restraining in exercising his power." He did everything in proper order, and he used "opportunities at their season; giving justice to his people by the restraining guidance of his office."[94] Job, too, "in prosperity and adversity, was blameless, patient, pleasing, and acceptable to God."[95] David was "brave in war, patient in time of adversity, peaceful at Jerusalem, in the hour of victory merciful, on committing sin repentant, in his old age foreseeing." Through his life, he "preserved due measure in his actions, and took his opportunities as they came."[96] Reflecting on these examples and others, Ambrose remarks, "What duty connected with the chief virtues was wanting in these men?" These examples are living portraits of the cardinal virtues. "In the first place they showed prudence," he writes, "which is exercised in the search of the truth, and which imparts a desire for full knowledge." After prudence is justice, "which assigns each man his own, does not claim another's, and disregards its own advantage, so as to guard the rights of all." Next is fortitude, "which both in warfare and at home is conspicuous in greatness of mind and distinguishes itself in the strength of the body," and finally temperance, "which preserves the right method and order in all things that we think should either be done or said."[97] Prudence, justice,

93. Gregory Thaumaturgus, *Oration and Panegyric Addressed to Origen* 9.
94. Ambrose, *On the Duties of the Clergy* 24.112.
95. Ambrose, *On the Duties of the Clergy* 24.113.
96. Ambrose, *On the Duties of the Clergy* 24.114.
97. Ambrose, *On the Duties of the Clergy* 24.115.

The Good Life   145

temperance, and fortitude, alongside others, give the faithful a taste of the good life, leading them to the feast that awaits them in the kingdom.

Conclusion

Basil of Caesarea gave up his pursuit of the academic life in preference for something better, the good life found in Christ. This chapter captures something of the personal dimension of biblical theology. Far from espousing some kind of abstract system of biblical unity, the fathers live the story of Scripture. Biblical theology is a progressive journey of the spiritual life, which is a motif that pervades early Christian literature. The fathers argue that anyone who comes to the Scriptures must come humbly, embodying the virtues. Sanctification is not merely the goal of biblical interpretation; it is required for the process. Interpreters are not to be trusted if they do not embrace the call to virtue, if they do not read Scripture as a guide toward their own virtue and that of others. The life of Christ is the supreme example of virtue; he is the exemplar par excellence. In him, we find all the virtues in proper measure and order. The whole purpose of biblical interpretation is to make progress in sanctification, in conformity to the likeness of Christ. Along the way, a few streams of Scripture flow into the river of the spiritual life, the Wisdom literature, the Psalms, and the models of the spiritual life in Scripture. The faithful look to the Wisdom literature and the Psalms for principles of virtue, sayings that help direct them on their virtuous path. Alongside Christ, the lives of the holy men and women of Scripture also serve as models of virtue. Various patriarchs, kings, prophets, and apostles reflect the important virtues of Christ as fellow travelers who have walked the road of God faithfully.

With this piece of the puzzle, the picture of what an ecclesial biblical theology looks like should be becoming clearer. The interpreter of Scripture is not an objective observer but an active participant in the story of Scripture. This is an important realization that the modern church must grapple with. We come to Scripture for the sake of godliness, seeking wisdom and longing to become more like Christ. The Wisdom literature and models of virtue can help us here, but we need to read them with this broader vision of the spiritual life in mind. I pray that we become interpreters who come to the text with virtue, seeking wisdom, praying that we all might grow in godliness, and slowly becoming readers who exemplify virtue.

The next chapter brings this argument home, to the church. The life of the community is where biblical theology truly flourishes.

THE COMMUNITY OF FAITH

Tertullian has been known for his fiery rhetoric. While he was ministering in the late second century, different heretical teachings, especially those of the Gnostics and the Marcionites, percolated throughout his community. He had many issues with their doctrines and practices, but he was particularly bothered that they used the Bible to defend their views. In one place, Tertullian reports that one of their favorite passages was the dominical saying "Seek, and you will find" (Matt. 7:7).[1] For the heretics, this verse offered a hermeneutical license to uncover any fantastical spiritual interpretation. Without the metaphysical constraints of the rule of faith, they could imagine any number of different gods or justify any vices they desired to embrace. Their method relied on, in Tertullian's phrasing, "the rule of reason."[2] Their reason was unfettered, free to twist the Scriptures into any rational system they dreamed up.

Tertullian understood the dominical saying differently. "Seek, and you will find" was not a license but a limit. Christian readers were not free to fabricate just any reading. They had only one thing to seek and find: Christ. Christ is the way, the truth, and the life, and our orientation should be attentive to the way he embodies truth. Tertullian knew that, puffed up by pride and vanity, our rational whims could carry us in all directions. But those in the church

---

1. Tertullian, *Prescription against Heretics* 8.
2. Tertullian, *Prescription against Heretics* 9.

are "bound to believe," Tertullian writes. Faith is their aim. They "seek" in order that they may find Christ, and when they "find" Christ, they believe in him.[3] Tertullian, like many other church fathers, found the pursuit of Christ ultimately freeing; it directed the body and soul toward the right end. True freedom—found in confessing the true Son of God, who has accomplished salvation for his people—rescues the interpreter from the whims of reason.

These two radically different readings, found in the heretics and in Tertullian, were guided by distinct metaphysical commitments. Tertullian understood that good metaphysical commitments are not merely derived from rational reflection; they are handed down in the church's Scriptures. Reading Scripture as about dwelling among the right community positions the reader in a place where the rule of faith is taught and the people of God unite in worship. Other institutions, organizations, religious gatherings, and parachurch ministries may lay claim to the Scriptures, but they do not constitute the church. They merely peer into a window to catch a glimpse of the light refracting through the church's text. Their reading, whatever it may be, is sound only to the degree that it reflects that right reading of Scripture found among the community of faith. "For wheresoever it shall appear that the true Christian religion and faith exist, there will be found the true Scriptures and interpretations and all Christian traditions," Tertullian writes.[4] The apologist defends not only the church's possession of the Scriptures but also the church's interpretation. In the church—and only in the church—is the right exposition of the Scriptures unveiled.

But Tertullian knew that the diversity of the Christian community, even in the ancient world, could problematize his argument. No doubt the same objection is raised today. Still, he found unity in the apostolic testimony. All the churches of Christ spring from the apostles and are, he writes, "proved to be one, in (unbroken) unity, by their peaceful communion, and title of brotherhood, and bond of hospitality—privileges which no other rule directs than the one tradition of the selfsame mystery."[5] The gospel that the apostles preached and embodied, in word and deed, forms the basis of the common communion and unity of the church universal. This is a mysterious thing: the people of God indwelled by the Spirit and united in Christ beyond space and time, gathering in union and communion around the sacred writings of the Old and New Testaments. In these apostolic churches, the apostles' "own authentic writings are read." Whether in Corinth, Philippi, Thessalonica,

3. Tertullian, *Prescription against Heretics* 9.
4. Tertullian, *Prescription against Heretics* 19.
5. Tertullian, *Prescription against Heretics* 20 (slightly modified).

Ephesus, Rome, or throughout Africa, Tertullian continues, the church acknowledges "one Lord God . . . , the Creator of the universe, and Christ Jesus (born) of the Virgin Mary, the Son of God the Creator; and the Resurrection of the flesh." Through this faith, the church unites "the law and the prophets . . . in one volume with the writings of evangelists and apostles," and from these writings, "she drinks in her faith."[6] Doctrine, worship, prayers, and sermons unite in a community chorus, guiding the people in a proper interpretation of the Scriptures. The culture of the church is the fitting and proper home for biblical theology.

Tertullian's argument brings us to the last chapter of this book and to the doorstep of the church. Thus far, we have meandered our way through various dimensions of early Christian biblical interpretation. I have described the rule of faith as the Christian social imaginary that presents God and salvation history in ways that surround and envelop humanity. The people of God are on a joyful, virtue-seeking journey, not distracted by the things of this world but seeking to flourish within it. Their path is not aimless; its goal is to live the divine narrative governed by God's orchestrating hand and layered with his promises. With their eyes fixed on Christ, remembering his first advent and longing for his second, they find themselves living this reality.

But we cannot stop here because biblical theology is also ecclesial. It entails the Christian community gathering around the table of the Scriptures to feast together. Every chapter of this book has been building up to this point; the ecclesial patterning of biblical theology centers the whole life of the community. Previous conceptions of biblical theology have served their purpose, but now the people of God should recover the ecclesial setting as the primary locus for reading Scripture. Besides, as R. R. Reno recognizes, since the 1960s "theology has been [increasingly] driven out of the university and back into the churches."[7] Many universities that teach biblical studies do so without association with a specific Christian tradition. These institutions impart methods, without any theological, moral, or liturgical basis to reinforce good interpretive postures. Other institutions, such as the seminary, voluntary associations, and other parachurch ministries, may support the church or enjoy its Scriptures These institutions do not compose the church, Christ's bride, the centerpiece of his work of redemption.

When Scripture is read within the church, a common metaphysical and liturgical framing shapes the resulting interpretation. The people of God are confessing, worshiping, and praying in unity to the one true God. Here,

6. Tertullian, *Prescription against Heretics* 36.
7. Reno, *End of Interpretation*, 164.

the unified tapestry of the church's biblical theology becomes clearer. "The Universal Church," Irenaeus writes, "through the whole world, has received this tradition from the apostles" ("tradition" in this case refers to the rule of faith or basic apostolic teaching received among the Christ followers).[8] For those who "diligently read the Scriptures in company with . . . presbyters in the Church, among whom is the apostolic doctrine," every word of Scripture will seem consistent.[9] The teaching of the apostles—completed with the metaphysical and ethical assumptions entailed in it—guides the faithful to read Christianly. There is only "one right reading," to borrow a phrase from Mary Ann Donovan's summary of Irenaeus—the reading found in the church.[10]

An ecclesial biblical theology, first of all, entails that catechesis and liturgy are the means by which the church shapes the people of God and forms them in their reading. Biblical theology must be performed and enacted, both within the personal lives of interpreters and within the community at large. The people of God gather, rehearse their stories, and remind themselves that they are on a journey toward the promised land.

Second, I argue that biblical theology entails proclamation; thus, biblical theology and preaching exhibit a necessary correlation. Biblical theology is not about sharing nice quips with students or impressing congregants; it is about proclaiming the true God, who is actively reigning and leading his people toward his appointed end. Participating in the worshiping community is essential for good interpretation; it reinforces the rule of faith confessed at baptism and prepares the faithful for the good life. Together, these points frame the exegetical life, a life that is committed and devoted to following Christ.

Catechesis and Liturgy

In the fathers' ecclesial biblical theology, catechesis and liturgy are two interweaving threads that shape the community with the teachings of Scripture. The culture of the church—its confessional declarations and liturgical rhythms—has been conceived and sustained through the words of Scripture. "The study of Holy Scripture," patristic scholar Manlio Simonetti argues, "was the real foundation of Christian culture in the Church of the earliest centuries."[11] The church took its cues from the Scriptures, and it created a bookish culture that shaped every feature of its identity.

8. Irenaeus, *Against Heresies* 2.9.1.
9. Irenaeus, *Against Heresies* 4.32.1.
10. Donovan, *One Right Reading?*
11. Simonetti, *Biblical Interpretation in the Early Church*, 1.

The Community of Faith   151

First, I describe the catechetical process in the early church and argue that this initial instruction was hermeneutical in nature; it guided the faithful in their reading of Scripture. I do not provide a full account of the catechetical process as it developed in the early church, as much of that narrative is complicated and highly involved; instead, I focus on the general ways in which Scripture was infused in the process. Second, I turn to liturgy and explain how the liturgical life of the community continued to guide the faithful. Once the catechetical process was complete, liturgy picked up where catechesis left off, reinforcing and maturing the Christian in the wisdom of Scripture. The liturgical life of the community created a scriptural culture that guided spiritual rhythms throughout the year, including such features as the regular public reading of Scripture, the institution of the office of the reader, and the role of preaching and the preacher. Of course, baptism and the Eucharist were central to the liturgical experience in the early church, and they often appealed to Scripture as they formed these practices.

Together, these features of the church have shepherded the faithful toward sanctification and beholding the glory of God. Only in the church, where catechesis and liturgy are found, can the faithful be patiently guided toward the right kind of biblical theology. Here, they find their home, which casts a vision of the good life to help them navigate all the thorns and thistles of this world.

Catechesis and Scripture

The fathers observe the close association between hermeneutics and catechesis. As Reno writes, "The church schools us to read Scripture well."[12] *Catechesis* refers to formal instruction in the basics of the Christian faith for those preparing for baptism.[13] It comes from the Greek word *katēcheō*, meaning "to teach." This instruction has often taken the form of theological and moral formation in the basic elements of the church's teaching. Below, I discuss the essential contours of its content, timing, and length.

First, the content of catechesis involves training in doctrine and morality, forging the whole human person, both body and soul, in one continuous journey of discipleship. Like a child riding a bike with two training wheels, the Christian neophyte needed both doctrine and morality to stay in the right direction. Catechesis brings together the discussion of the rule of faith and the spiritual life mentioned in the previous chapters. The rule of faith, which

12. Reno, *End of Interpretation*, 157.
13. Ferguson, "Catechesis, Catechumenate," 223.

I have argued contains the basic theological assumptions of the church and salvation history, must be absorbed into the life of the interpreter. In the early church, new members were catechized, were anointed, and took the Eucharist under the provision and direction of the church.

The doctrinal instruction of the early church was centered on the Bible and brought together all the features of interpretation discussed in the previous chapters. There were differences in the structure and content of catechetical arrangement, but generally, the church agreed that catechesis involved both theological and moral instruction. Origen imagined a two-stage catechumenate process, which he describes in *Contra Celsum*. In the first instance, potential converts are questioned privately until they "seem to devote themselves sufficiently to the intention of living a good life."[14] The earlier stage of instruction focuses on the rudimentary moral demands of the Christian life and on the Law and the Prophets. The later stages communicate doctrinal matters, including the doctrines of the Trinity and the resurrection and then the teaching of the sacraments.[15] Origen concludes his discussion of this topic, saying, "And when those who have been turned towards virtue have made progress, and have shown that they have been purified by the word, and have led as far as they can a better life, then and not before do we invite them to participation in our mysteries. 'For we speak wisdom among them that are perfect.'"[16]

In general, what the catechumen learns is that in order to read Scripture well, they must become a "spiritual disciple." They must have the veil removed so that they can read and become a disciple who diligently follows the Lord. The true spiritual disciple, according to Irenaeus, is one who diligently reads the Bible within the church. He writes, "A spiritual disciple of this sort truly receiving the Spirit of God, who was from the beginning, in all the dispensations of God, present with mankind, and announced things future, revealed things present, and narrated things past—[such a man] does indeed 'judge all men, but is himself judged by no man' [1 Cor. 2:15]."[17] When people turn to Christ, the veil over their hearts is removed (2 Cor. 3:16), so that wherever the Lord is there is freedom to read and perceive his glory. So now, "we all, with unveiled face, beholding the glory of the Lord, are being transformed into the same image from one degree of glory to another" (2 Cor. 3:18).

The church did not always agree about doctrinal claims, though it held to the basic contours of the rule of faith as a theological guide for its confession.

14. Origen, *Contra Celsum* 3.51.
15. Ferguson, *Baptism in the Early Church*, 420–21.
16. Origen, *Contra Celsum* 3.59.
17. Irenaeus, *Against Heresies* 4.33.1.

Take Origen's reflections, for example. Even in the third century, Origen realized that not all Christians agree about every theological and moral point. So he laid down a tiered framework that traced the fundamental assumptions embedded within apostolic teaching. "Many . . . of those who profess to believe in Christ differ from each other, not only in small and trifling matters, but also on subjects of the highest importance," he writes. Among these subjects, he includes the church's doctrine of God and Christ and "the holy virtues." Given such differences, Origen lays down "an unmistakable rule regarding each one of these, and then to pass to the investigation of other points." This "rule" is Origen's rule of faith, which is a consistent summary of "the teaching of the Church" that is "transmitted in orderly succession from the apostles, and remaining in the Churches to the present day." This rule alone "is to be accepted as truth which differs in no respect from ecclesiastical and apostolic tradition."[18]

When catechesis integrates the theological and the moral visions of the faith, it forges a whole culture of exegesis. Through catechesis the "Scripture absorbs the theologian, rather than the theologian and his ideas absorbing the text."[19] It casts a vision of a narrative that moves from creation to new creation and envelops God's people amid God's work. These catechetical practices reinforce the essential social imaginary of the church. New members are now committed to a different conception of reality, a distinctly Christian vision of life with a whole new set of political and social entailments. They cannot view themselves in the way they viewed themselves before, nor can they hold the same set of assumptions they held before. They are able to cast a vision of the good life and the hope of beholding God face to face.

Second, alongside content, the length of catechesis in the ancient world also tells us something about its importance. The fathers knew that if the early church was going to survive in a world filled with competing religions and religious claims, the church had to do a better job of training new converts. The early Christian text *On the Apostolic Tradition* provides a brief window into this process. It never describes the contents of catechesis in detail, but it clearly suggests that it involved doctrinal and moral teaching from the Scriptures.[20] In the next century, Cyril of Jerusalem composed his catechetical lectures, which worked through the Nicene Creed point by point to give careful instruction in the faith. Many other early Christian preachers delivered sermons on the

---

18. Origen, *On First Principles* 1.pf.2.
19. Reno, *End of Interpretation*, 68.
20. See Hippolytus, *On the Apostolic Tradition* 17, 20–21, 35, 42.

essential contours of Christian belief, including Gregory of Nyssa (*Catechetical Discourse*) and John Chrysostom (*Baptismal Instructions*).

Irenaeus also implies a longer catechesis, especially for his fellow Romans, who have to process competing metaphysical claims. He compares the story of Philip and the Ethiopian eunuch with Paul's mission to the gentiles and, citing Paul's words in 1 Corinthians 15:10 (that he "worked harder than any of [the other apostles]"), argues that the evangelization of the gentiles was more difficult than that of the Jews, since gentiles had fewer shared theological assumptions than the Jews did.[21] Evangelizing gentiles meant that they had to be persuaded first to move from polytheism to monotheism, from the "superstition of idols" to the worship of "one God, the Creator of heaven and earth, and the Framer of the whole creation."[22] They had to be convinced that only one God exists, "far above all rule and authority and power and dominion, and above every name that is named" (Eph. 1:21). Persuasion in these doctrines was not instantaneous. They had to simmer for a bit. Irenaeus does not give the timing, but certainly the process of discipleship was rather involved.

On the Apostolic Tradition provides a timeline for catechesis: the normal length in pre-Constantinian churches was three years.[23] While the text gives a temporal guideline, it also insists that the catechumen who is "earnest" and "perseveres well" can be admitted into the church before that guideline is met. The length of catechesis evolved over time too. After the age of Constantine (ca. 272–337), as the church became more institutionalized, catechesis was shortened and often tied to the Lenten season.

Liturgy and Scripture

Once the catechesis process is complete and a new believer joins the church, liturgy picks up where catechesis leaves off, continuing to reinforce good Scripture reading through regular worship and participation in the ordinances or sacraments. Liturgy, or worship, can be understood on different levels. The word *liturgy* derives from the Greek lexeme *leitourgia*, which is linked with temple sacrifices and means "public service" (Luke 1:23). The term has been used throughout church history to designate "the church's official (or unofficial) public and corporate ritual of worship, including the Eucharist (or communion), baptism and other sacred acts."[24] Put simply, it refers to the

---

21. Irenaeus, *Against Heresies* 4.23–24.
22. Irenaeus, *Against Heresies* 4.23.2.
23. Hippolytus, *On the Apostolic Tradition* 17.
24. Grenz, Guretzki, and Nordling, *Pocket Dictionary of Theological Terms*, 73.

regular activity of the church's worship, in which the church guides believers to imbibe Christian virtue. The habits of worship, infused with the mores of the ecclesial culture, tutor the people of God in the right reading of Scripture. Liturgy can take different forms, including the liturgical calendar, weekly worship services, and daily prayer. Each of these forms has its own history. Here, I want to highlight two levels of the liturgical shaping of the church: the regular worship of the church, including the liturgical calendar, and the regular public reading of Scripture. In the next section, I will discuss the kinds of personal habits that the early church cultivated for the sake of reading Scripture well.

Cultivating regular liturgical practices is an essential way the church has developed readers who embody the teachings of Scripture. With respect to the liturgical calendar, the people of God have been patiently trained to think about time in theological ways. Time, Ephraim Radner tells us, "must be completely congruent with the loving will of God, with its origins, means, and ends."[25] With weekly services and daily prayer, the liturgical calendar captures time and orients lives toward Christ's return. Worship is the regular encounter with God, who is the Author and Creator of all things, and that encounter is an expression of God's love. What and how we pray will shape our beliefs and practices. As Reno writes, "The mind of a person whose thoughts are formed by the church's doctrine and whose sensibilities are governed by the church's liturgies will be attuned to Scripture's most powerful and consequential meanings."[26]

First, the development of liturgy in the early church was complex and varied. In various ways, the Scriptures were tethered to the life of the community, creating a scriptural culture. There is a long tradition of the development of daily prayer and sacred days of worship in the early church. Prayer was the way people inhabited time within the unfolding of salvation history. For example, praying at least three times per day was "a widespread, if not universal, custom in the early church."[27] Some encourage prayer in the morning, at noon, and at night, while others followed the pattern of praying at the third, sixth, and ninth hours.[28] The Didache encourages the faithful to pray the Lord's Prayer three times per day, not praying "like the hypocrites," but "as the Lord commanded in his gospel."[29] Similar instructions are found in *On The Apostolic Tradition*, though prayer is combined with instruction in the word. "Every faithful man and woman, when they have risen from sleep

25. Radner, *Time and the Word*, 88–89.
26. Reno, *End of Interpretation*, 157.
27. Bradshaw, *Search for the Origins of Christian Worship*, 176.
28. *On The Apostolic Tradition*, 41.
29. Didache 8.

in the morning, before they touch any work at all, should wash their hands and pray to God, and so go to work," the text reads. "But if instruction in the word of God takes place, each one should choose to go to that place, reckoning in his heart that it is God whom he hears in the one who instructs. For he who prays in the church will be able to pass by the wickedness of the day."[30] No substitute existed for cultivating the habits of regular prayer and instruction in the word.

From the earliest years, Sunday was set aside as a day for worship, though Christians quickly designated other days too, often in accordance with the cycle of Scripture reading, as they began ordering time around the vision of salvation history. The emergence of liturgical time in the early church was an extension of their doctrine of God and narrative of salvation history; it brought their whole world into accordance with a "structure of history" that reveals God and God's work of redemption and calls human beings into God's service.[31]

Take the Sabbath, for example. "But we all hold this common gathering on Sunday, since it is the first day, on which God transforming darkness and matter made the Universe, and Jesus Christ our Savior on the same day rose from the dead," writes Justin Martyr.[32] He uses biblical and theological reasons to explain Sunday worship: it signifies the first day of the week when God began creating, which also coordinates with the day Christ rose from the dead. So from the beginning of creation to the new creation wrought in Christ, Sabbath worship signaled a renewed commitment to live within the story of salvation history. Tertullian also advocated for honoring the Sabbath, encouraging the faithful to refrain from "every attitude and practice of duty on the day of the Lord's resurrection, even putting off business in case we give opportunity to the devil."[33] The emphasis on Sabbath rest supports the biblical and theological arguments mentioned above (Gen. 2:2; Exod. 20:8–11; Deut. 5:12–15).

Other sacred days emerged as the church continued to grow and worship. The ascension of Constantine in the fourth century allowed the Christian community to solidify and institutionalize many of these practices. Easter, Pentecost, Christmas, Epiphany, and Lent were all formulated to bring the whole calendar year into accordance with the gospel. One of the earliest controversies in the church was the dating of Easter, known as the Quartodecimanism (meaning "fourteenth day") controversary. Eastern churches still

---

30. *On the Apostolic Tradition*, 41.
31. McGowan, *Ancient Christian Worship*, 218.
32. Justin Martyr, *First Apology* 67.
33. Tertullian, *On Prayer* 23.2.

The Community of Faith 157

followed the Jewish calendar and celebrated Easter on the fourteenth day of Nisan rather than the designated Sunday, as it was celebrated in Western churches. Irenaeus wrote to Victor, the bishop of Rome, compelling him to keep peace and allow the diversity of worship practices. "This diversity existing among those that observe it, is not a matter that has just sprung up in our times, but long ago among those before us," Irenaeus writes, signaling that these differences in Easter observances were ancient practices, emerging from different communities. But Irenaeus does not stop there. He appeals for peace and even suggests that the disagreement about different practices "establishes the unanimity in faith."[34] The churches remain unified in their confession, even if their practices diverge in certain ways. But all these practices, these developments in liturgical time, signaled "a new cultural formation," one that was working to bring time and history itself into accordance with the church's social imaginary.[35]

Through their reading of Scripture, the people of God have followed different daily rhythms. The whole liturgical life of the church is oriented toward the right reading of Scripture and cultivating people who imbibe the Bible. "We enter as a community of Christians with shared practices, such as worshiping the triune God and celebrating baptism and the Lord's Supper. These practices and commitments will—and should—influence our interpretation of Scripture. They make us 'biased,' but in a good way—a way by which the Spirit brings the word of God to fruition in our lives," Todd Billings writes.[36] Liturgy is based on the church's integration of Scripture. Whenever we experience Scripture in worship—whenever it is read, heard, prayed, preached, and lived—we are reminded of the glory of God. The true church is where, according to Irenaeus, there is the "lawful and diligent exposition in harmony with the Scriptures."[37] This textual culture sanctifies all members of the community, as it guides them and prepares them for the virtuous life. "For where the Church is, there is the Spirit of God; and where the Spirit of God is, there is the Church, and every kind of grace; but the Spirit is truth," Irenaeus writes. Those who reject the church "do not partake of Him." They "dig for themselves broken cisterns out of earthly trenches, and drink putrid water out of the mire, fleeing from the faith of the Church lest they be convicted; and rejecting the Spirit, that they may not be instructed."[38] Through liturgy,

34. Eusebius, *Ecclesiastical History* 5.24. Irenaeus's letter to Victor is preserved in Eusebius's *Ecclesiastical History*.

35. McGowan, *Ancient Christian Worship*, 259.

36. Billings, *Word of God*, 9.

37. Irenaeus, *Against Heresies* 4.33.13.

38. Irenaeus, *Against Heresies* 3.14.1.

158   Biblical Theology in the Life of the Early Church

the community of faith imbibes the Scriptures, drinks from its fertile waters, and feasts on its truths.

Second, communal reading was essential to worship and the corporate life. The public reading of Scripture was the normal way Scripture was received and imbibed. Even in the New Testament, the apostolic writers exhort Christians to read Scripture publicly. For example, 1 Timothy 4:13 reads, "Until I come, devote yourself to the public reading of Scripture, to exhortation, to teaching." Colossians 4:16 states that the faithful should read and exchange letters, saying, "And when this letter has been read among you, have it also read in the church of the Laodiceans; and see that you also read the letter from Laodicea." Finally, 1 Thessalonians 5:27 suggests that the letter has been read aloud to the community: "I put you under oath before the Lord to have this letter read to all the brothers."

The second-century apologist Justin Martyr gives a good summary of public Scripture reading in the early church: "And on the day called Sunday, all who live in cities or in the country gather together to one place, and the memoirs of the apostles or the writings of the prophets are read, as long as time permits; then, when the reader has ceased, the president verbally instructs, and exhorts to the imitation of these good things."[39] We do not know how much Scripture was read, but the saying "as long as time permits" indicates that the reading was not short. Justin shows us that from the earliest days of the church, the reading of Scripture had a communal and performative sense. The practice of reading from both the Old and New Testaments—or, in Justin's words, "the memoirs of the apostles" and "the writings of the prophets"—developed quickly. As this practice developed, early Christians likely followed the *lectio continua*, or reading Scripture sequentially over a period of time, and their reading reflected the emerging liturgical calendar.[40] Both developments proved important for shaping a Christian identity. The community of faith read the stories, heard the work of God, and responded together. Verbal instruction guided the whole community of faith in conformity to the likeness of Christ. The whole community participated in exegesis.

To support the reading community, early churches cultivated "congregational libraries," which were collections of texts for liturgical purposes. Theologians such as Tertullian or Origen almost certainly had their own collections of texts. The first explicit references to church libraries appear in accounts from the Great Persecution under Diocletian (ca. 303–13). After an edict was issued in 303 against the possession of Christian texts, there were

39. Justin, *First Apology* 67.
40. Gamble, *Books and Readers*, 217.

The Community of Faith 159

several attempts to confiscate and destroy the Scriptures.[41] These acts assume that many communities and individuals must have been gathering texts together before then. Origen disposed of his pagan texts and acquired Christian texts for research and teaching.[42] *Acts of the Scillitan Martyrs* records an interchange between a Christian named Speratus and the Roman governor Saturninus, who questions him about the books he is carrying. "What do you have in your satchel?" asks Saturninus. "Books and letters of Paul, a righteous man," replies Speratus.[43] The early Christian sermon 2 Clement records a very similar phrase, referring to "the books and the apostles."[44] Both of these phrases seem to indicate the possession of prophetic and apostolic collections for personal study and research. These personal libraries were often the seeds of church libraries, which served the life and ministry of the church. Origen donated his library to the church in Caesarea. Augustine did something similar with the church in Hippo.[45] Such libraries suggest that the church adopted a bookish culture and that it crafted its doctrine and liturgical life through them.

Early Christians relied on the Scriptures for their life and practice. While many of them were probably illiterate, they were nonetheless engrossed in Scripture. "Texts were read aloud in worship, interpreted in preaching and catechesis, cited in apologetical debates, deployed in intramural theological disputes, and perused for personal edification," writes Gamble.[46] Early Christian culture was a textual culture; Christians read their lives through the sacred texts. Liturgists and preachers needed Bibles for regular public worship. Origen, for example, "improvised his sermons in Caesarea with an annotated Bible in his hand."[47] The presence of Scripture in worship was a visible testimony to its authority in the life of the community. Within this culture, the church was nourished in the Scriptures and was taught to live faithfully and to read Scripture in continuity with the church's faith.

Another sign of the importance of Scripture reading was the cultivation of the office of the reader. The reader was one of the minor orders of the clergy, mentioned by several church fathers.[48] In *Epistle 32*, Cyprian of Carthage (ca. 210–58) explains that he has ordained Aurelius the Confessor as

41. Gamble, *Books and Readers*, 145.
42. Eusebius, *Ecclesiastical History* 6.3.
43. *Acts of the Scillitan Martyrs* 12.
44. 2 Clement 14.2.
45. Gamble, *Books and Readers*, 174.
46. Gamble, *Books and Readers*, 141.
47. Markschies, *Christian Theology and Its Institutions*, 273.
48. Tertullian, *Prescription against Heretics* 41; Hippolytus, *On the Apostolic Tradition* 1.12; Eusebius, *Ecclesiastical History* 6.43.11; *Constitutions of the Holy Apostles* 8.22; *Didascalia apostolorum* 2.28.

a reader. Aurelius is apparently young, but Cyprian describes his virtue and faithfulness in the face of suffering and persecution and recommends him to the office of the reader: "I judged it well, that he should begin with the office of reading; because nothing is more suitable for the voice which has confessed the Lord in a glorious utterance, than to sound Him forth in the solemn repetition of the divine lessons."[49] Cyprian seams together the virtue of the reader with the virtue of the Scriptures. The Scriptures are the guide to the good life; the one reading Scripture publicly must strive to be a living testimony of this life. In another letter, Cyprian affirms the importance of a reader named Celerinus: "There is nothing in which a confessor can do more good to the brethren than that, while the reading of the Gospel is heard from his lips, every one who hears should imitate the faith of the reader."[50] Cyprian continues to explain why certain readers have been selected: "Know, then, that these for the present are appointed readers, because it was fitting that the candle should be placed in a candlestick, whence it may give light to all, and that their glorious countenance should be established in a higher place, where, beheld by all the surrounding brotherhood, they may give an incitement of glory to the beholders."[51]

Other early Christian writings affirm this same reality—that readers should exude the virtues of Scripture. *The Apostolic Church Order* reads, "For the reader, one should be appointed after he has been carefully proved: no babbler, nor drunkard, nor jester, of good morals, submissive, of benevolent intentions, first in the assembly at the meetings on the Lord's Day, of plain utterance, skillful in exposition, mindful that he functions in the place of the evangelist."[52] Of course, readers have to be literate, but more is involved. They have to embody the virtue of Scripture; after all, they do stand "in the place of the Evangelist." In the early church, other aesthetic features communicated the solemnity of the book being read as well. The reader would likely have been elevated and stationed in front of the congregation.[53] The raised platform, also called a bema or ambo, would have allowed the reader to be heard clearly, but it also conveyed a sense of authority and holiness. The style of reading probably resembled a song-like chant; that would have also highlighted the importance of the text.[54] The emphasis on books and reading in Christian worship involves "the construction of a different culture (or

49. Cyprian, *Epistle 32* 2.
50. Cyprian, *Epistle 33* 4.
51. Cyprian, *Epistle 33* 5.
52. *Apostolic Church Order* 3.
53. Gamble, *Books and Readers*, 224.
54. Gamble, *Books and Readers*, 225.

The Community of Faith   161

cultures) of reading,"[55] a culture that celebrated the Scriptures and looked to them to formulate their beliefs and practices.

Finally, we know that the Bible was read privately and woven into an active spiritual life. The German historian of early Christianity Adolf von Harnack once detailed the personal reading habits of the early church with many examples.[56] He shows that the church was a bookish community, with Christians—at least those who could afford texts—studying privately, outside liturgical settings, often with their family members and others. From the very beginning, the church was a bookish culture. It inherited the Hebrew Scriptures, which were read regularly in the synagogue, and began reading and circulating Christian texts early on (Col. 4:16; 1 Thess. 5:27). Clement of Alexandria exhorts his readers to regular prayer and Scripture readings, suggesting that the Christian's "whole life is a holy festival." "His sacrifices are prayers, and praises and readings in the Scripture before meals, and psalms and hymns during meals and before bed, and prayers also during the night."[57] Tertullian assumes that married couples would read the Scriptures together.[58] Many other references in the early church assume that copies of the Scriptures were available for reading, either by those outside the church, or members of the congregation. It was a textual culture that gathered around the Scriptures where "Bible reading forms an ideal part of the Christian life."[59]

In the early church, engagement with Scripture outside the regular worship gatherings was also coupled with a personal devotional life that guided Christians on their journey. This is a theme I have touched on several times, but here I simply want to stress that a liturgical life guided the ancients' daily decisions. "The devout Christians of the early church were expected to take Paul's injunction 'pray without ceasing' (1 Thess. 5:17) seriously."[60] As mentioned earlier, as early as the second century Christians were observing weekly fasts and daily prayers in accordance with the teachings of Scripture.[61] They aimed to create a liturgical life bathed in prayer. In his treatise on prayer, Origen assumes "the whole life of a saint as one great continuous prayer."[62] In one illustrative passage, Clement of Alexandria imagines what this might look like for the Christian life. He argues that Christians do not merely revere Christ on one day or another; rather, they revere him "continually in [their]

---

55. McGowan, *Ancient Christian Worship*, 93.
56. Harnack, *Bible Reading in the Early Church*.
57. Clement of Alexandria, *Stromata* 7.7.
58. Tertullian, *To His Wife*, 2.6.
59. Harnack, *Bible Reading in the Early Church*, 55.
60. Bradshaw, *Daily Prayer in the Early Church*, 47.
61. Didache 8.
62. Origen, *On Prayer* 7.

162   Biblical Theology in the Life of the Early Church

whole life, and in every way." Clement continues: "The [Christian] in every place, even if he be alone by himself, and wherever he has any of those who have exercised the like faith, honours God, that is, acknowledges his gratitude for the knowledge of the way to live. . . . Holding festival, then, in our whole life, persuaded that God is altogether on every side present, we cultivate our fields, praising; we sail the sea, hymning; in all the rest of our conversation we conduct ourselves according to rule."[63] After the time of Constantine, prayer became more formalized and institutionalized, as seen in the rise of the daily morning and evening prayers.

Much more can be said about the liturgical shaping of the ancient Christian life, but what we have already discussed, I think, is enough to point to the kind of ecclesial biblical theology that guided the church. Catechesis and liturgy were the ongoing activities of the church that patiently guided believers and kept them on the right path. The telos of interpretation was communion. What Fowl writes about the church today can be written about the ancient church as well: reading Scripture calls the church into an "ongoing struggle to live and worship faithfully before the triune God in ways that bring them into ever deeper communion with God and others."[64] The spiritual life is personal, and the church greatly emphasizes personal growth on the journey, but such growth does not occur apart from one's participation in the life of the community. Stanley Hauerwas argues that the Scriptures do not merely concern themselves with identifying God; they speak to the reality of who we are to become. The Scriptures should not merely shape our communal identity but should also shape our virtue and character. The church, in the words of Hauerwas, is called to be "a community of character."[65] This ecclesial biblical theology defined the community and gave it the rhythms and patterns that taught it to live out the text.

Preaching and the Preacher

Given that biblical theology has shaped the church's catechesis and liturgy, the goal of biblical theology is also closely aligned with preaching. "There are two things necessary to the treatment of the Scriptures," Augustine writes, "a way of discovering those things which are to be understood, and a way of teaching what we have learned."[66] Like two hands working together, interpretation and

63. Clement of Alexandria, *Stromata* 7.7.
64. Fowl, *Engaging Scripture*, 7.
65. Hauerwas, *Community of Character*.
66. Augustine, *On Christian Doctrine* 1.1.1.

The Community of Faith 163

teaching are necessary and coordinate. The fathers cannot conceive of the act of biblical interpretation apart from edification and exhortation. But this means that the preacher or Bible teacher must embody all the previous points discussed. The Bible teacher must embrace an ecclesial biblical theology, coming to Scripture with a Christian metaphysic expressed in the church's rule of faith that confesses the one, true God, Creator of all things. The Bible teacher must embrace all the assumptions that flow from this confession: Scripture is God's self-revelation, and every interpretation and proclamation must be worthy of God. The Christian preacher must let Scripture interpret Scripture, a true hermeneutic of coherence, because Scripture is internally consistent. The preacher must walk in humility, knowing that they are handing the very words of God and need God's Spirit to comprehend the revelation given to the prophets and apostles. These assumptions help the Bible teacher imagine the world through the Christian social imaginary, perceiving the lives of their community as participating in the narrative of Scripture, and, in that narrative, seeing the person and work of Christ bind all things together. The preacher, who strives to embody the virtues of Christ, beckons the people of God down the road of salvation, pointing them to the waters of Scripture to drink in the good life. In Scripture they all see how to live virtuously, like so many others before them, as children of God walking the path of righteousness in this life.

With all these things in place, the preacher must, in the words of Paul, communicate Scripture "for teaching, for reproof, for correction, and for training in righteousness, that the man of God may be complete, equipped for every good work" (2 Tim. 3:16–17). In other words, the role of the Bible teacher falls into a few general categories that I describe as edification, apologetics, and evangelism.

Below, I discuss each of these features and explain how preaching is the final proclamation of an ecclesial biblical theology. The purpose of the worship service, as I have argued above, is to patiently guide the faithful toward sanctification. Now, I argue that the application of biblical theology takes on two discernible features in the life of the preacher. First, the preacher must strive to embody the virtues of the faith, leading the people in godliness and serving as a spiritual guide, pointing the faithful to the truth of the text. Second, the preacher should serve as both an apologist, defending the faith against any charges, and an evangelist, persuading others to come and follow Christ. Together, these roles help the people of God encounter the truth of Scripture and guide them in their incremental growth in godliness.

Beginning with the first point, the fathers believe that preachers should embody the pursuit of virtue as they point the people of God toward

164   Biblical Theology in the Life of the Early Church

sanctification. The Word of God should be proclaimed by those enmeshed in the Christian life. "Those who are ready to toil in the most excellent pursuits," writes Clement of Alexandria, "will not desist from the search after truth, till they get the demonstration from the Scriptures themselves." Once the Christian has "received the Gospel, even in the very hour in which he has come to the knowledge of salvation, not turn back, like Lot's wife, as is said; and let him not go back either to his former life, which adheres to the things of sense, or to heresies."[67] We can also observe this point in the writings of Origen. Most studies of Origen focus on his discussions of allegory or typology or other features of his exegetical method, but they miss the forest for the trees. Origen certainly offers unusual interpretations, but his general vision of biblical interpretation assumes a "sweeping and integrative vision of scriptural exegesis as a way of life."[68] The spiritual vision of the church means that every sermon delivered from the Word of God is aimed at shaping and building a Christian culture embodied in the church. A good sermon should convict and encourage and direct sinners back to the way of life lived within the scriptural narrative. Only among the community of faith is "the preaching of the Church . . . everywhere consistent, and continues in an even course, and receives testimony from the prophets, the apostles, and all the disciples."[69]

Not only should preachers embody virtues, but the wisdom and eloquence of the Scriptures are at their disposal to lead the people. "All those powers and beauties of eloquence which they make their boast, are to be found in the sacred writings which God in His goodness has provided to mould our characters," Augustine writes.[70] The wise words of Scripture, eloquently written to persuades and delight, led the Christian away from the wickedness of the world. Eloquence shapes the way preachers communicate the text, but Augustine also recognizes that not every teacher possesses the gifts of rhetoric. "For one who wishes to speak wisely, therefore, even though he cannot speak eloquently," Augustine continues, "it is above all necessary to remember the words of Scripture." The Scriptures are eloquent even when the teacher is not, so the preacher should lean on the Scriptures. "The poorer he sees himself to be in his own speech, the more he should make use of Scripture so that what he says in his own words he may support with the words of Scripture," Augustine adds.[71] The feelings of inadequacy are not regarding the grammatical or syntactical analysis, but regarding the way the interpretation leads

---

67. Clement of Alexandria, *Stromata* 6.16.
68. Martens, *Origen and Scripture*, 6.
69. Irenaeus, *Against Heresies* 3.14.1.
70. Augustine, *On Christian Doctrine* 4.6.10.
71. Augustine, *On Christian Doctrine* 4.5.8.

The Community of Faith   165

to godliness, which is why James exhorts the church that "not many of you should aspire to be teachers, my brothers, for you know that we who teach will be judged with greater strictness" (James 3:1). Today, I hope that Bible teachers feel this sense of trepidation before the Word of God. I hope many, like Augustine, "treat the scripture of God as the face of God," and "melt in front of it," knowing that their calling is to lead their people in godliness.[72] Or as Chrysostom wonders about preachers even in his day, "How is it that they do not shudder when they measure themselves with so great a man as this [Paul]?"[73]

The proclamation of the Word of God works to strengthen the faith of believers who are progressing in their salvation. The faithful are journeying toward beatitude, and the preaching of the Word offers the daily bread to encourage them on their journey. "Perfection of teaching," the great "golden-mouthed" preacher Chrysostom writes, is "when the teachers both by what they do, and by what they say as well, bring their disciples to that blessed state of life which Christ appointed for them."[74] Preaching reminds the faithful of their confession and helps them make incremental steps toward conformity to the likeness of Christ. "Holy Scripture is the Word of God that resides in the Lord's hands as he continues to guide and instruct his people," write R. B. Jamieson and Tyler Wittman, "so that we may worship him in spirit and in truth."[75] The ascended Christ is reigning now and guiding his church, through the Spirit, in all truth. The whole aim of Scripture's interpretation is realizing the virtue of the good life in the present age.

Second, the preacher must act as an apologist and an evangelist, helping the people of God navigate the dangers that lie along their path. Part of guiding the people of faith along the path of virtue is helping them avoid the pitfalls of heresy or immorality; this begins with Christian leaders living in harmony with the instruction they offer. There is "no sound faith if the life [of the teacher] is corrupt," writes Chrysostom.[76] He argues that when a teacher fails, the people of God are apt to blame the doctrine of the church and lose faith. Augustine makes a similar argument: "Whatever may be the majesty of the style, the life of the speaker will count for more in securing the hearer's compliance."[77] The hypocrites may instruct others, but they cannot instruct themselves. Augustine highlights the Pauline saying "Whether in pretense or

72. Augustine, *Sermon 22* 7.
73. Chrysostom, *On the Priesthood* 4.6.
74. Chrysostom, *On the Priesthood* 4.8.
75. Jamieson and Wittman, *Biblical Reasoning*, 47.
76. Chrysostom, *On the Priesthood* 4.9.
77. Augustine, *On Christian Doctrine* 4.27.59.

in truth, Christ is proclaimed" (Phil. 1:18), which he understands as meaning that truth is preached but not preached in truth. Thus, some may do well by preaching truth, which may instruct and persuade, "but they would do good to very many more if they lived as they preach." If the people of God see Christian leaders living contrary to their instruction, they will follow suit. How many times have preachers and Bible teachers failed in the modern age, causing people, both inside and outside the church, to stumble? There are those looking to justify their own sinful behavior who will use Scripture to do so, but interpreting Scripture calls the faithful to live in light of its teaching. Those who strive to live evil lives will reject the truth and turn to their own ways. They will "cease to listen with submission to a man who does not listen to himself, and in despising the preacher they learn to despise the word that is preached."[78]

On the other hand, heresies and divergent philosophies arise that need to be addressed. The Christian teacher must decipher the pitfalls and dangers of their culture and help the people of God weave their way through these dangers. Perhaps a good example is Origen's first homily on Luke. Speaking of the different Gnostic Gospels, Origen describes how "many have tried" to write Gospels about Christ, but Matthew, Mark, Luke, and John did not just "try"; they were filled with the Holy Spirit when they wrote.[79] Augustine gives us another example. In his view, the duty of the Christian preacher is to be "the interpreter and teacher of Holy Scripture, the defender of the true faith and the opponent of error." The interpreter, Augustine continues, is called "both to teach what is right and to refute what is wrong, and in the performance of this task to conciliate the hostile, to rouse the careless, and to tell the ignorant both what is occurring at present and what is probable in the future." The demands of the situation call the interpreter to respond accordingly and to aim their interpretation toward an appropriate end. The style of teaching is shaped, for Augustine, "in whatever way the case requires."[80] In other words, the instruction focuses on aiding the people's progress in spiritual growth. If they need edification, entreaties, exhortations, or upbraidings, the preacher should direct the faithful toward the kind of spiritual growth that will help them. Throughout all such spiritual guidance, wisdom is the ordering principle. The preacher should be "one who can argue and speak with wisdom, if not with eloquence, and with profit to his hearers, even though he profit them less than he would if he could speak with eloquence too."[81] The culture of the

78. Augustine, *On Christian Doctrine* 4.27.60.
79. Origen, *Homilies on Luke* 1.1.
80. Augustine, *On Christian Doctrine* 4.4.6.
81. Augustine, *On Christian Doctrine* 4.5.7.

The Community of Faith   167

church seeks to embody biblical virtues as the people live and engage the world around them. Those who join the community and relish the Scriptures create a culture of interpretation that forms and fashions the people of God. In this way, the Scriptures' meaning is "at home in all cultures and nationalities."[82]

All these features of the textual community point to the uniqueness and sacredness with which the early Christians treated the Scriptures. The Scriptures were the community's text. The elements of the worship service were used to teach and lead believers to live and confess the gospel. The liturgy, including preaching, Scripture reading, and prayer, was oriented toward the Scriptures and the virtuous life. The Scriptures were not like any other book. They were treated as sacred, and they were upheld for their vision of the good life. They were read, prayed, and honored. The Scriptures were read publicly and privately. They were revered in worship, and those who read the Scriptures embodied the virtues espoused in them. Grasping this point allows us to begin to understand patristic exegesis. Interpretation in the early church was not just an issue of applying a method but also an issue of forming an interpretive culture that promoted the kind of virtuous life championed in the Scriptures. The whole point was to involve the community in the reading of Scripture, a community set apart and distinct.

Conclusion

Tertullian knew that just reading the Bible was not enough. The right community matters. Good biblical theology occurs only where the rule of faith and the liturgical life of the church guide the people. The fathers point us to an ecclesial biblical theology that subsumes the whole life of the community of faith. Biblical interpretation and the liturgical patterns of the community are closely connected. Good biblical theology is not complete until it is imparted to others in ways that teach, delight, and persuade. Those who follow the example of the fathers and capture the kind of biblical theology that they employ will experience a different kind of spiritual life. Biblical theology is not just studied but performed and enacted, both within the personal lives of interpreters and within the culture of the community.

This last chapter completes the call for an ecclesial biblical theology. We need to recover a thick ecclesiology that is infused with catechesis and liturgy, training the faithful to read Scripture well. Biblical theology must be performed in our churches and among our people, patiently guiding them toward godliness and love for God and neighbor.

82. Billings, *Word of God*, 122.

CONCLUSION

I began this book with a story of my visit to the Church of Saint-Germain-des-Prés. Walking through that church, I discovered a contrast that testifies to the struggle of biblical theology. Sitting in the nave, I was surrounded by the visible testimony of frescoes depicting the glorious story of Christ, the crowning point of the story of salvation history. Yet, in the same building, just a stone's throw away sits Descartes's grave. One church building housing two contrasting legacies with two very different intellectual trajectories. The story of Christ and the church and the story of the modern world after Descartes have left us with competing conceptions of reality and competing visions of life that have struggled even to the present day.

The opening story of another book, Michael Legaspi's *The Death of Scripture and the Rise of Biblical Studies*, illustrates the results of these competing visions. Over the years, I have ruminated over this illustration—and my experience in Saint-Germain-des-Prés—many times. Legaspi recounts two contrasting scenes related to biblical interpretation.[1] The first is the liturgy of John Chrysostom during an Eastern Orthodox service. The community of faith gathers in a hallowed sanctuary. The rich ornamentation dazzles the senses. An ambience of solemnity and peace hangs over the gathering. Each moment of the service is carefully crafted, much of it derived from reflection on the Scriptures.

At a key moment in the liturgy, a priest appears carrying a gold-plated book: the Book of the Gospels. When he appears, everyone stands in reverence for the Holy Writ. In this liturgical act the Word is read to them. This context stresses a reverent posture and a communal receptivity toward the

---

1. Legaspi, *Death of Scripture*, vii–viii.

Word. The words of the priest reinforce the holiness of the book: "Wisdom! Let us attend!" he proclaims. In this service—like so many other services in various Christian traditions—"the faithful see the Bible in procession, hear it in song, and venerate its holiness and authority with signs of loyalty and submission."[2] The Bible is read and preached—the Word of God proclaimed. They imbibe this teaching and accept it as sacred and authoritative.

While Legaspi chooses an Orthodox service, I could make the same basic point with the worship service of almost any Christian denomination or tradition, at least one where the Bible is revered, read, preached, confessed, and applied. It lives at the heart of the Christian community, guiding their faith and practice. The best Christian churches embody what I have described as an ecclesial biblical theology in the preceding pages. In the worship services, the people of God, called to embrace the teaching of the Scriptures, receive guidance for their spiritual lives. They imagine themselves as part of the grand narrative of God's work of redemption, trending toward the telos of the kingdom of God.

The second scene Legaspi depicts takes place in a university seminar room. The Bible is sprawled out before a gathering of academics. In this setting, people are seated, not standing, and the Bible—or should I say Bibles?—is laid out before them in different translations and editions, like creatures pinned down on a dissection table. Scattered among these translations is an assortment of other writings: clusters of notes, commentaries, dictionaries, and other background sources. The atmosphere is congenial, but also solemn and scholarly. In this place, heads are not humbly bowed to receive the Word of God but stoically bowed over the books and armed with a critical eye. It is an erudite gathering, unpolluted by anything sacrosanct. There is no prayer, no song, no preface to the study of the Scriptures—only the posture of serious investigation. There are, of course, academic contexts infused with liturgical and devotional practices where the Christian spiritual life can thrive, but, ever since the rise of modernity following Descartes, this second scene is all too familiar.

This vivid illustration captures two extremes, two drastically different approaches to the Bible in the modern world. They reflect the contrast between what Legaspi terms "the *scriptural* Bible and the *academic* Bible."[3] Prior to the rise of the Enlightenment, "for over a millennium, Western Christians read and revered the Christian Bible as Scripture, as an authoritative anthology of unified, authoritative writings belonging to the Church." The church had its

2. Legaspi, *Death of Scripture*, vii.
3. Legaspi, *Death of Scripture*, viii (emphasis original).

Scriptures. The Scriptures were absorbed, and they shaped the community and the social environment surrounding the church. The "scriptural Bible," Legaspi tells us, "was not simply the foundation of the Church's academic theology; it also furnished its moral universe, framed its philosophic inquiries, and fitted out its liturgies." The Bible furnished the social imaginary for the Christian community, which in turn shaped the culture. The Bible, Legaspi, continues, "provided the materials for thought, expression, and action, becoming what Northrop Frye famously called the 'great code' of Western civilization. As the book at the center of Western Christendom, the Bible functioned scripturally."[4] The foundation of Western civilization is the Scripture that was received into the community of the church, which imbibed them and, in turn, transformed the world through them.

But the Bible's relationship to culture evolved throughout the centuries, and the people of God did not always agree over the best interpretation, nor did they always apply Scripture in virtuous ways. But now the direction of interpretation is changing. Slowly over the past few centuries, "Scripture died a quiet death."[5] The teachings of Scripture no longer provide the unifying norms or mores that shape our cultural institutions; the vacuum left by the evaporating church has been filled with a host of other competing mores derived from other personal preferences and tastes. Scripture is no longer the culture-shaping text that it once was.

This book is, in part, a response to these developments. It has been written in the hope of recovering biblical theology as it was reflected in the earliest centuries of the church. The work of biblical theology within the past century has represented a step in the right direction, but it needs to go further. The preeminent biblical theologian Brevard Childs, I think, anticipated this move. One of his last publications returned to the history of biblical interpretation for inspiration.[6] The study of Scripture, or even the narrower discipline of biblical theology, lives within the walls of academic institutions, which toss about intellectual systems with no direct engagement with the spiritual lives or liturgical gatherings of the people of faith. The study of the Bible in many institutions is now trying to flourish in a kind of half light, a secular eventide hosted for students and professors, not a gathering of the people of God. Older academic institutions, particularly those founded for religious purposes, still try to value the Scriptures, but things are changing. In recent years, more academic institutions are hemorrhaging students and facing all

---

4. Legaspi, *Death of Scripture*, 3.
5. Legaspi, *Death of Scripture*, 3.
6. Childs, *Struggle to Understand Isaiah*. See also Radner, *Time and the Word*, 2–3.

kinds of pressures, and such challenges have profound consequences for both the academy and the church. We need a new vision of biblical theology to lead us through the institutional transformations that lie ahead, and I think the biblical theology lived in the early Christian community can help guide the church toward the kind of cultural engagement and institutional transformation that will help the people of God flourish. This vision of the intersection between the Bible and the spiritual life can prepare the people of God to thrive in a secular world that is often set against them.

Looking back to the earliest Christian theologians, we can see that the vision of biblical theology in the early church was ecclesial. These theologians knew implicitly that they needed to come to Scripture with Christian assumptions, because Scripture must be interpreted in relation to some other reality. For the fathers, it was their confession (or what they called the rule of faith) that stood at odds with their inherited cultural assumptions—pagan philosophical assumptions that proliferated through the Roman world. They did not read the Bible through the lens of culture; they read the culture through the lens of the Bible. They cultivated a vision of life that shaped their culture— not the other way around. The fathers knew that the real difference between ancient Christian and pagan approaches to the Bible lay in the competing views of reality that they assumed, what Charles Taylor calls a "social imaginary." The early church's social imaginary was thoroughly theological and commensurate with their rule of faith. It is not possible to understand the methods of exegesis in the patristic period without understanding the theological assumptions informing those methods, assumptions infused within an ecclesial culture of interpretation that united the biblical texts in a drama of salvation under the guidance of God.

Biblical theology today needs to focus on community and culture, recovering what I call an *ecclesial biblical theology*. The proper context for biblical theology, I contend, is not canon or historical context or even salvation history; it is the Christian community formed through the intertwining threads of confession and liturgy. These features of an ecclesial biblical theology work together in a symbiotic unity to form Christians in sound doctrine and morality.

What this means is that the goal of biblical theology is to behold the glory of God. We are all on a journey toward God, desiring above all else to see God. This reality entails three essential features: Scripture, the rule of faith, and liturgy. The Scriptures are the object of reflection, while the rule of faith and liturgy come alongside and guide the interpreter toward a right understanding of the nature and work of God. Positioned safely within this trio, the biblical theologian is free to enjoy the blessings of biblical interpretation.

Conclusion 173

We have no need to worry about those who reject this symbiosis, those who think Christian interpretation is silly. Let them read as their foolish reason and desire lead them. But in the church, we read differently. The Scriptures sustain us; they are our food for the journey of life, leading to the kingdom of God.

With this ecclesial culture in mind, I began this book by laying the framework for an ecclesial biblical theology as it was envisioned in the early church. I started with first principles, the nature of God and God's relationship with the world. For some, this may seem backward. But the fathers believe all interpretation must be done with the right metaphysic. What we think about God has a bearing on our readings of Scripture. Some might construe this point as an attempt to "read one's theology into Scripture," but the fathers view it the other way around. They know that everyone approaches Scripture with some philosophical or theological assumptions; the question is, Are we approaching with the right theological assumptions?

From Irenaeus to Augustine, the rule of faith distills the Christian metaphysic, the essential contours of the church's faith; it is received through baptism. The rule held in tension the economic and immanent descriptions of God. It had both a narratival sense, highlighting the salvation-historical plain on which the biblical theologian lived, and a dogmatic sense, portraying the nature of God, who has orchestrated the events of salvation history. Exegesis cannot exist apart from some conception of God, so when we read the Bible, we need to see God in and through the Bible.

For sound biblical theology, the implications are simple; every interpreter must be asked the most basic question: Do you believe in God? We really have no need to discuss other features of interpretation until we get this question right. God is the source and the aim of all biblical reflection, and we must have our ship directed toward the right port to see our way safely home.

Having established this theological framework, I drew from Augustine and others and explained a basic Christian vision of semiotics. The nature and work of God compose the framework for understanding the nature of sign and referent, or *signs* and *things*. The signs of Scripture ultimately point to the one true *Thing*—God. This gives a general framework for the importance of the spiritual sense, which develops in the person and work of Christ.

I also discussed some of the hermeneutical principles that logically flow from the metaphysic assumed in the rule of faith. Such principles include the notions that Scripture is God's self-revelation and that all interpretation must be worthy of God. These two notions work together, as the interpreter reads Scripture and contemplates how any interpretation must conceive of God as God is revealed. In addition to these first two assumptions, the interpreter must assume that Scripture is internally self-referential and consistent. All

Scripture is from God and reveals God truly and consistently. Another assumption related to the interpreter is that biblical theology requires divine assistance. The interpreter is not an individual actor but indwelled by the Spirit of God and given spiritual discernment. Once baptized and admitted into the community of faith, the Christian is a citizen of the heavenly kingdom, and all subsequent interpretation should lead the Christian and the community toward a greater love for God and others. The liturgical setting reinforces these things regularly, as it guides readers toward God.

Transitioning from God to creation, as the first point of the rule of faith does, ecclesial biblical theology assumes that Scripture depicts a narrative of salvation history. Many modern discussions of biblical theology begin with this narrative. But without the theological assumptions discussed above, the narrative of Scripture makes little sense. The rule of faith frames this narrative through a series of theological points, from creation to the resurrection of the dead and the life of the world to come. These events reflect an ideal narrative that embraces the people of God. The faithful participate in a story of salvation and are able to perceive the beauty of this drama. This narrative is tantamount to the literal sense and forms the narrative substructure, containing the spiritual sense. Many other narratives filter in and through this scriptural narrative. The fathers often frame this narrative in a variety of ways, including thematic or covenantal connections that reinforce its narrative substructure, while at the same time showing the continuity of different themes, which also reinforces the unity of Scripture.

When the narrative is lived under the direction of God, Christ is the centerpiece of an ecclesial biblical theology. Understanding Christ (in continuity with the divine referent in the signs of Scripture) composes the spiritual sense, which relates to the nature and work of God mentioned earlier, only with more specificity. The second point of the rule of faith, which discusses the person and work of Christ, also helps frame the spiritual sense.

To discern the spiritual sense, the Christian exegete should adopt a way of reading that explains how the Scriptures point to Christ. I described three ways of reading that I termed *personal*, *prophetic*, and *partitive* strategies. The personal perspective necessitates that we attend to the personal activities of Christ in Scripture, including his appearances, theophanies, and dialogues (or prosopological conversations). The prophetic perspective examines how each aspect of Christ's ministry fulfills prophecy. Included here are his birth, life, death, resurrection, ascension, and second coming. This prophetic sense assumes what I call a "two-advent" approach to prophecy; the exegete must carefully discern whether passages apply to Christ's first or second coming. Finally, the partitive perspective assumes that the two natures of Christ—his divine and human natures—concur in one person, which is known as the hypostatic union. Assuming this union, interpreters also assume something called the *communicatio idiomatum*, or the "communication of idioms," when they read Scripture. This "communication" assumes that Scripture applies a variety of divine and human attributes to the person of Christ; accordingly, any interpretation must assume that Christ possesses the completeness of both natures regardless of the attribute ascribed. In all these ways, we can see the complexity of the spiritual sense and of Scripture's teaching about Christ. These interpretive perspectives reinforce the metaphysical framing that guides our interpretation and, therefore, the ecclesial culture that flows from our readings.

Assuming all these features of ecclesial biblical theology, I then turned to the human person and the spiritual life. I discussed the basic assumption of the spiritual journey toward beatitude, which orients all Christians. When interpreters open the Bible, they are traveling somewhere or trying to grow in some way. The church has been very concerned to remind the people of God that they are journeying toward sanctification. Only when interpreters find themselves within the story of God, traveling toward beatitude, will they find the true meaning of the text and enjoy the true vision of life with God. The fathers do not go to the Bible to find application; they go to the Bible to see what kind of people they are called to be—people infused with virtue and character.

I argued that a cyclical relationship exists between virtue and the hermeneutical process. Virtue is not merely the application of exegesis; it is required for every engagement with the text. Interpreters approach the text embodying the virtues and then read in conformity with them. They aim to grow, little by little, in their encounter with Scripture. They also look to Scripture for examples of the spiritual life—one of the most important features of biblical theology. Christ is the preeminent example and the standard for all others. The patriarchs, kings, prophets, and apostles, fellow travelers on the journey of the spiritual life, are also important for their reflection. For this reason, the Old Testament is an essential source for theological reflection and growth in conformity to the likeness of Christ. The fathers recognize that there is no biblical theology, no discussion of the Scripture whatsoever, without a discussion of the good life. Together, these points frame the exegetical life, a life devoted to following Christ. This vision of the good life is a key piece of biblical theology. We construct not unified readings of Scripture that are external to us but rather narratives that we live. We are living God's story. God is calling us to follow him and embrace the virtuous life.

Finally, I brought all these things together in the life of the church. In this discussion, we saw the threefold structure of an ecclesial biblical theology (i.e., Scripture, the rule of faith, and the liturgical life) come together. Ecclesial biblical theology assumes a vibrant, living community of faith, a community that actively reads and imbibes the Scriptures. The church is the proper and ultimate setting for biblical theology. All things come together in the church, the central and preeminent institution. Catechesis, liturgy, and preaching are the means by which the church shapes the people of God from beginning to end. The worshiping community gathers to rehearse its stories and to encourage one another on the journey toward the kingdom of God. Biblical theology is not merely about structures of biblical unity; rather, it is also about living the narrative and proclaiming it to others. The goal of exegesis is edification, love of God, and love of neighbor, and preachers should guide their churches toward that end. This is the living and active ministry of the church as it forms a community and shapes the culture. This vision of biblical theology will help sustain the church through the cultural transformation swirling around it. The Scriptures will be our guide, and the church will lean on them.

The fathers encourage us to consider an ecclesial biblical theology that imagines Scripture as the church's text—the living community reading it, praying it, worshiping with it, and revering it. Scripture is the authoritative, life-giving Word of God for the people of God. We have no need to worry about the academic Bible; it will cease to exist, and when it is gone, the worshiping community will be left gathered around the Scriptures, fostering a culture imbued with the love of God and neighbor.

I believe that if we embrace the best of patristic biblical interpretation, we can finally emerge out of the world created by Descartes and others and return to worship in the nave of Saint-Germain-des-Prés. There, we behold the story of Scripture and find ourselves in it.

ABBREVIATIONS

ANF   *Ante-Nicene Fathers*. Edited by Alexander Roberts and James Donaldson. 10 vols. Reprint, Peabody, MA: Hendrickson, 1994.

NPNF[1]   *Nicene and Post-Nicene Fathers*. Series 1. Edited by Philip Schaff. 14 vols. Reprint, Peabody, MA: Hendrickson, 1994.

NPNF[2]   *Nicene and Post-Nicene Fathers*. Series 2. Edited by Philip Schaff and Henry Wace. 14 vols. Reprint, Peabody, MA: Hendrickson, 1994.

BIBLIOGRAPHY

Primary Sources

Acts of the Scillitan Martyrs. Translated by Bryan M. Litfin. In *Early Christian Martyr Stories: An Evangelical Introduction with New Translations*, by Bryan M. Litfin, 87–90. Grand Rapids: Baker Academic, 2014.

Ambrose. *Exposition of Psalm 118 (119)*. Translated by J. E. Tweed. In *NPNF*[2], vol. 8.

———. *Jacob and the Happy Life*. In *Seven Exegetical Works*, translated by Michael P. McHugh, 117–86. Fathers of the Church 65. Washington, DC: Catholic University of America Press, 1972.

———. *On the Duties of the Clergy*. Translated by H. de Romestin, E. de Romestin, and H. T. F. Duckworth. In *NPNF*[2], vol. 10.

The Apostolic Church Order: The Greek Text Edited and Translated with an Introduction and Notes. Edited by Alistair C. Stewart. Rev. ed. Early Christian Studies 10. Norwest, Australia: Sydney College of Divinity, 2021.

Aquinas, Thomas. *The Power of God*. Translated by Richard J. Regan. Oxford: Oxford University Press, 2012.

Aristotle. *Metaphysics, Books I–IX*. Translated by Hugh Tredennick. Loeb Classical Library 271. Cambridge, MA: Harvard University Press, 1933.

Athanasius. *Against the Heathen*. Translated by Archibald Robertson. In *NPNF*[2], vol. 4.

———. *Four Discourses against the Arians*. Translated by John Henry Newman and Archibald Robertson. In *NPNF*[2], vol. 4.

———. *On the Incarnation*. Translated by John Behr. Popular Patristics Series 44a. Yonkers, NY: St Vladimir's Seminary Press, 2011.

Augustine. *Against Two Letters of the Pelagians*. Translated by Peter Holmes and Robert Ernest Wallis. Revised by Benjamin B. Warfield. In *NPNF*[1], vol. 5.

———. *Catholic and Manichean Ways of Life*. Translated by Donald A. Gallagher and Idella J. Gallagher. Washington, DC: Catholic University of America Press, 1966.

———. *The City of God against the Pagans*. Edited and translated by R. W. Dyson. Cambridge Texts in the History of Political Thought. Cambridge: Cambridge University Press, 1998.

———. *Confessions*. Translated by Henry Chadwick. Oxford: Oxford University Press, 1991.

———. *The Enchiridion on Faith, Hope, and Love*. Translated by Henry Paolucci. Washington, DC: Regnery Gateway, 1961.

———. *Exposition of the Psalms, 99–120*. Translated by Maria Boulding. Edited by Boniface Ramsey. Works of Saint Augustine. Hyde Park, NY: New City, 2003.

———. *The First Catechetical Instruction*. Translated by Joseph P. Christopher. Ancient Christian Writers 2. Mahwah, NJ: Paulist Press, 1946.

———. *Letter 82*. Translated by Roland Teske. In *Letters 1–99*. Edited by John E. Rotelle. Works of Saint Augustine. Hyde Park, NY: New City, 2001.

———. *Letter 148*. Translated by Roland Teske. In *Letters 100–155*. Edited by Boniface Ramsey. Works of Saint Augustine. Hyde Park, NY: New City, 2003.

———. *Letter 171A*. Translated by Roland Teske. In *Letters 156–210*. Edited by Boniface Ramsey. Works of Saint Augustine. Hyde Park, NY: New City, 2001.

———. *The Literal Meaning of Genesis*. Translated by John Hammond Taylor. 2 vols. Ancient Christian Writers 41–42. Pine Beach, NJ: Newman, 1982.

———. *On Christian Doctrine*. Translated by D. W. Robertson Jr. Upper Saddle River, NJ: Prentice Hall, 1958.

———. *On the Creed: A Sermon to Catechumens*. Translated by H. Browne. In *NPNF²*, vol. 3.

———. *On the Merits and Forgiveness of Sins, and on the Baptism of Infants*. Translated by Peter Holmes and Robert Ernest Wallis. Revised by Benjamin B. Warfield. In *NPNF¹*, vol. 5.

———. *On the Proceedings of Pelagius*. Translated by Peter Holmes and Robert Ernest Wallis. Revised by Benjamin B. Warfield. In *NPNF¹*, vol. 5.

———. *On the Profit of Believing*. Translated by C. L. Cornish. In *NPNF¹*, vol. 3.

———. *Reply to Faustus the Manichaean*. Translated by Richard Stothert and Albert H. Newman. In *NPNF¹*, vol. 4.

———. *Sermon on the Mount*. Translated by William Findlay. In *NPNF¹*, vol. 6.

———. *Sermon 22*. In *Sermons 20–50 on the Old Testament*, translated by Edmund Hill, edited by John E. Rotelle. Works of Saint Augustine. Brooklyn, NY: New City, 1990.

———. *Sermon 32*. In *Sermons 20–50 on the Old Testament*, translated by Edmund Hill, edited by John E. Rotelle. Works of Saint Augustine. Brooklyn, NY: New City, 1990.

Bibliography

———. *A Treatise on the Spirit and the Letter*. Translated by Peter Holmes and Robert Ernest Wallis. Revised by Benjamin B. Warfield. In *NPNF*[1], vol. 5.

———. *The Trinity*. Translated by Stephen McKenna. Fathers of the Church 45. Washington, DC: Catholic University of America Press, 1963.

Basil of Caesarea. *Against Eunomius*. Translated by Mark Delcogliano and Andrew Radde-Gallwitz. Fathers of the Church 122. Washington, DC: Catholic University of America Press, 2011.

———. *Exegetic Homilies*. Translated by Agnes Clare Way. Fathers of the Church 46. Washington, DC: Catholic University of America Press, 1963.

———. *Hexameron*. Translated and edited by Philip Schaff and Henry Wace. In *NPNF*[2], vol. 8.

———. *Letter 2*. Translated by Blomfield Jackson. In *NPNF*[2], vol. 8.

———. *Letter 189*. Translated by Blomfield Jackson. In *NPNF*[2], vol. 8.

———. *Letter 223*. Translated by Blomfield Jackson. In *NPNF*[2], vol. 8.

———. *Letter 283*. Translated by Blomfield Jackson. In *NPNF*[2], vol. 8.

———. *On Christian Ethics*. Translated by Jacob N. Van Sickle. Popular Patristics Series 51. Yonkers, NY: St Vladimir's Seminary Press, 2014.

Chrysostom, John. *Baptismal Instructions*. Translated by Paul W. Harkins. Westminster, MD: Newman, 1962.

———. *Homilies on First Corinthians*. Translated by Talbot W. Chambers. In *NPNF*[1], vol. 12.

———. *Homilies on Genesis 1–17*. Translated by Robert C. Hill. Fathers of the Church 74. Washington, DC: Catholic University of America Press, 1986.

———. *Homilies on Second Corinthians*. Translated by Talbot W. Chambers. In *NPNF*[1], vol. 12.

———. *Homilies on the Gospel according to St. John*. Translated by Charles Marriott. In *NPNF*[1], vol. 14.

———. *Homily on Genesis 22*. Translated by Robert C. Hill. In *Homilies on Genesis 18–45*. Washington, DC: Catholic University of America Press, 1990.

———. *On the Priesthood*. Translated by W. R. W. Stephens. In *NPNF*[1], vol. 9.

Clement of Alexandria. *Exhortation to the Heathen*. Translated by William Wilson. In *ANF*, vol. 2.

———. *The Instructor*. Translated by William Wilson. In *ANF*, vol. 2.

———. *St. Basil's Address to Young Men, on How They Might Derive Benefit from Greek Literature*. In *Letters 249–368, on Greek Literature*, translated by Roy J. Deferrari and Martin R. P. McGuire. Loeb Classical Library 270. Cambridge, MA: Harvard University Press, 1934.

———. *The Stromata, or Miscellanies*. Translated by William Wilson. In *ANF*, vol. 2.

Clement of Rome. 1 Clement. In *The Apostolic Fathers in English*, translated and edited by Michael W. Holmes, 36–72. Grand Rapids: Baker Academic, 2006.

Constitutions of the Holy Apostles. Translated by James Donaldson. In *ANF*, vol. 7.

Cyprian of Carthage. *Epistle 32*. Translated by Robert Ernest Wallis. In *ANF*, vol. 5.

———. *Epistle 33*. Translated by Robert Ernest Wallis. In *ANF*, vol. 5.

Cyril of Alexandria. *Letter 17*. In *Letters 1–50*, translated by John I. McEnerney. Fathers of the Church 76. Washington, DC: Catholic University of America Press, 1985.

———. *On the Unity of Christ*. Translated by John Anthony McGuckin. Popular Patristics Series 13. Crestwood, NY: St Vladimir's Seminary Press, 2015.

Cyril of Jerusalem. *Catechetical Lectures*. Translated by Edwin Hamilton Gifford. In *NPNF²*, vol. 7.

Definition of Chalcedon. In *Creeds of the Churches: A Reader in Christian Doctrine from the Bible to the Present*, edited by John H. Leith, 34–36. Louisville: John Knox, 1963.

Didache. In *The Apostolic Fathers in English*, translated and edited by Michael W. Holmes, 163–71. Grand Rapids: Baker Academic, 2006.

Eusebius. *Ecclesiastical History*. Translated by C. F. Cruse. Peabody, MA: Hendrickson, 1998.

Gregory of Nazianzus. *On Baptism*. Translated by Charles Gordon Browne and James Edward Swallow. In *NPNF²*, vol. 7.

———. *Theological Orations*. In *On God and Christ: The Five Theological Orations and Two Letters to Cledonius*, translated by Frederick Williams and Lionel Wickham. Popular Patristics Series 23. Crestwood, NY: St Vladimir's Seminary Press, 2002.

Gregory of Nyssa. *Against Eunomius*. Translated by William Moore and Henry Austin Wilson. In *NPNF²*, vol. 5.

———. *Catechetical Discourse: A Handbook for Catechists*. Translated by Ignatius Green. Popular Patristics 60. Crestwood, NY: St Vladimir's Seminary Press, 2020.

———. *Homilies on the Beatitudes*. Translated by Stuart George Hall. Edited by Alberto Viciano and Hubertus R. Drobner. Leiden: Brill, 2000.

———. *The Life of Moses*. Translated by Abraham J. Malherbe and Everett Ferguson. New York: Paulist Press, 1978.

———. *On the Holy Trinity*. Translated by William Moore and Henry Austin Wilson. In *NPNF²*, vol. 5.

———. *On the Soul and the Resurrection*. Translated by Catharine Roth. Popular Patristics Series 12. Crestwood, NY: St Vladimir's Seminary Press, 1993.

Gregory Thaumaturgus. *Oration and Panegyric Addressed to Origen*. Translated by S. D. F. Salmond. In *ANF*, vol. 6.

Gregory the Great. *The Book of Pastoral Rule*. Translated by George E. Demacopoulos. Popular Patristics Series 34. Crestwood, NY: St Vladimir's Seminary Press, 2007.

Hilary of Poitiers. *On the Trinity*. Translated by E. W. Watson and L. Pullan. In *NPNF²*, vol. 9.

Hippolytus. *On the Apostolic Tradition*. Translated by Alistair Stewart-Sykes. Popular Patristics Series 22. Crestwood, NY: St Vladimir's Seminary Press, 2001.

———. *On the Proverbs*. Translated by S. D. F. Salmond. In *ANF*, vol. 5.

———. *Treatise on Christ and the Antichrist*. Translated by J. H. MacMahon. In *ANF*, vol. 5.

Irenaeus. *Against the Heresies, Book 1*. Translated by Dominic J. Unger and John J. Dillion. Ancient Christian Writers 55. New York: Newman, 1992.

———. *Against the Heresies, Book 2*. Translated by Dominic J. Unger and John J. Dillion. Ancient Christian Writers 65. New York: Newman, 2012.

———. *Against the Heresies, Book 3*. Translated by Dominic J. Unger and Irenaeus M. C. Steenberg. Ancient Christian Writers 64. New York: Newman, 2012.

———. *Against the Heresies, Books 4 and 5*. Translated by Dominic J. Unger and Scott D. Moringiello. Ancient Christian Writers 72. New York: Newman, 2024.

———. *On the Apostolic Preaching*. Translated by John Behr. Popular Patristics Series 17. Crestwood, NY: St Vladimir's Seminary Press, 1997.

Jerome. *Letter 53*. Translated by W. H. Fremantle, G. Lewis, and W. G. Martley. In *NPNF²*, vol. 6.

Justin Martyr. *Dialogue with Trypho*. Translated by Thomas B. Falls, revised by Thomas P. Halton and edited by Michael Slusser. Washington D.C.: Catholic University of America Press, 2003.

———. *The First Apology*. In *The First and Second Apologies*, translated by Leslie William Barnard. Ancient Christian Writers 56. New York: Paulist Press, 1997.

The Muratorian Fragment. In *The Canon of the New Testament: Its Origin, Development, and Significance*, translated by Bruce M. Metzger, 305–7. Oxford: Clarendon, 1987.

Novatian. *On the Trinity*. Translated by Robert Ernest Wallis. In *ANF*, vol. 5.

Origen. *Commentary on Psalms 1–25, Fragment from Preface*. In *Origen*, translated by Joseph W. Trigg, 69–72. Early Church Fathers. New York: Routledge, 1998.

———. *Commentary on the Song of Songs*. Translated by R. P. Lawson. Ancient Christian Writers 26. New York: Newman, 1957.

———. *Contra Celsum*. Translated by Henry Chadwick. Cambridge: Cambridge University Press, 1953.

———. *Homilies on Genesis*. In *Homilies on Genesis and Exodus*, translated by Ronald E. Heine. Fathers of the Church 71. Washington, DC: Catholic University of America Press, 1982.

184 Bibliography

———. *Homilies on Luke*. Translated by Joseph T. Lienhard. Fathers of the Church 94. Washington, DC: Catholic University of America Press, 1996.

———. *Homilies on Numbers*. Translated by Thomas P. Scheck. Edited by Christopher A. Hall. Ancient Christian Texts. Downers Grove, IL: IVP Academic, 2009.

———. *Homilies on the Song of Songs*. In *The Song of Songs: Commentary and Homilies*, translated by R. P. Lawson. Ancient Christian Writers 26. Westminster, MD: Newman, 1957.

———. *On First Principles: A Reader's Edition*. Edited and translated by John Behr. Oxford Early Christian Texts. Oxford: Oxford University Press, 2017.

———. *On Prayer*. In *An Exhortation to Martyrdom, Prayer, and Selected Works*, translated by John J. O'Meara. Ancient Christian Writers 19. Westminster, MD: Newman, 1954.

2 Clement. In *The Apostolic Fathers in English*, translated and edited by Michael W. Holmes, 77–86. Grand Rapids: Baker Academic, 2006.

Tertullian. *Against Marcion*. Translated by Peter Holmes. In *ANF*, vol. 3.

———. *Against Praxeas*. Translated by Peter Holmes. In *ANF*, vol. 3.

———. *Apology*. Translated by S. Thelwall. In *ANF*, vol. 3.

———. *Concerning the Veiling of Virgins*. Translated by S. Thelwall. In *ANF*, vol. 4.

———. *On Monogamy*. Translated by S. Thelwall. In *ANF*, vol. 4.

———. *On the Resurrection of the Flesh*. Translated by Peter Holmes. In *ANF*, vol. 3.

———. *Prescription against Heretics*. Translated by Peter Holmes. In *ANF*, vol. 3.

———. *To His Wife*. Translated by S. Thelwall. In *ANF*, vol. 4.

Tertullian, Cyprian, and Origen. *On the Lord's Prayer*. Translated by Alistair Stewart-Sykes. Popular Patristics Series 29. Yonkers, NY: St Vladimir's Seminary Press, 2004.

Theophilus of Antioch. *Ad Autolycus*. Translated by Robert M. Grant. Oxford: Clarendon, 1970.

Secondary Sources

Andresen, Carl. "Zur Entstehung und Geschichte des trinitarischen Personbegriffes." *Zeitschrift für die neutestamentliche Wissenschaft* 52 (1961): 1–39.

Andrews, James A. *Hermeneutics and the Church: In Dialogue with Augustine*. Notre Dame, IN: University of Notre Dame Press, 2012.

Auerbach, Erich, *Mimesis: The Representation of Reality in Western Literature*. Princeton: Princeton University Press, 1968.

Bartholomew, Craig G. "Biblical Theology." In *Dictionary for Theological Interpretation of the Bible*, edited by Kevin J. Vanhoozer, 84–90. Grand Rapids: Baker Academic, 2005.

Bibliography

Bartholomew, Craig G., and Michael W. Goheen. *The Drama of Scripture: Finding Our Place in the Biblical Story*. Grand Rapids: Baker Academic, 2004.

Bartholomew, Craig G., and Heath A. Thomas, eds. *A Manifesto for Theological Interpretation*. Grand Rapids: Baker Academic, 2016.

Bauckham, Richard. "Reading Scripture as a Coherent Story." In *The Art of Reading Scripture*, edited by Ellen F. Davis and Richard B. Hays, 38–53. Grand Rapids: Eerdmans, 2003.

Bebbington, David W. *Patterns in History: A Christian Perspective on Historical Thought*. 4th ed. Waco: Baylor University Press, 2018.

Behr, John. *Irenaeus of Lyons: Identifying Christianity*. Christian Theology in Context. Oxford: Oxford University Press, 2015.

———. *The Nicene Faith: True God of True God*, vol. 2, part 1 of *The Formation of Christian Theology*. Crestwood, NY: St Vladimir's Seminary Press, 2004.

Bellah, Robert N., Richard Madsen, William M. Sullivan, Ann Swidler, and Steven M. Tipton, eds. *Habits of the Heart: Individualism and Commitment in American Life*. New York: Harper & Row, 1985.

Billings, J. Todd. *The Word of God for the People of God: An Entryway to the Theological Interpretation of Scripture*. Grand Rapids: Eerdmans, 2010.

Blowers, Paul. "The Regula Fidei and the Narrative Character of Early Christian Faith." *Pro Ecclesia* 6, no. 2 (1997): 199–228.

Boersma, Hans. *Scripture as Real Presence: Sacramental Exegesis in the Early Church*. Grand Rapids: Baker Academic, 2017.

Bradshaw, Paul F. *Daily Prayer in the Early Church: A Study of the Origin and Early Development of the Divine Office*. London: SPCK, 1981.

———. *The Search for the Origins of Christian Worship: Sources and Methods for the Study of Early Liturgy*. 2nd ed. Oxford: Oxford University Press, 2002.

Breisach, Ernst. *Historiography: Ancient, Medieval, and Modern*. 3rd ed. Chicago: University of Chicago Press, 2007.

Brown, Peter. "The Saint as Exemplar in Late Antiquity." In *Saints and Virtues*, edited by John Stratton Hawley, 3–14. Berkeley: University of California Press, 1987.

Cameron, Averil. *Christianity and the Rhetoric of Empire: The Development of Christian Discourse*. Berkeley: University of California Press, 1994.

Carter, Craig A. *Interpreting Scripture with the Great Tradition: Recovering the Genius of Premodern Exegesis*. Grand Rapids: Baker Academic, 2018.

Childs, Brevard S. *Biblical Theology of the Old and New Testaments: Theological Reflection on the Christian Bible*. Minneapolis: Fortress, 2011.

———. *The Struggle to Understand Isaiah as Christian Scripture*. Grand Rapids: Eerdmans, 2004.

Clark, Elizabeth A. *Reading Renunciation: Asceticism and Scripture in Early Christianity*. Princeton: Princeton University Press, 1999.

Cochrane, Charles Norris. *Christianity and Classical Culture: A Study of Thought and Action from Augustus to Augustine*. Carmel, IN: Liberty Fund, 2003. First published in 1940.

Cox, Patricia. *Biography in Late Antiquity: A Quest for the Holy Man*. Berkeley: University of California Press, 1983.

Daley, Brian E. "Is Patristic Exegesis Still Usable? Some Reflections on Early Christian Interpretation of the Psalms." In *The Art of Reading Scripture*, edited by Ellen F. Davis and Richard B. Hays, 69–88. Grand Rapids: Eerdmans, 2003.

de Lubac, Henri. *History and Spirit: The Understanding of Scripture according to Origen*. Translated by Anne Englund Nash. San Francisco: Ignatius, 2007.

———. *Medieval Exegesis: The Four Senses of Scripture*. Vol. 1. Translated by Mark Sebanc. Ressourcement: Retrieval and Renewal in Catholic Thought. Grand Rapids: Eerdmans, 1998.

Donovan, Mary Ann. *One Right Reading? A Guide to Irenaeus*. Collegeville, MN: Liturgical Press, 1997.

Duncan, J. Ligon, III. "The Covenant Idea in Irenaeus of Lyons: An Introduction and Survey." In *Confessing Our Hope: Essays in Honor of Morton Howison Smith on His Eightieth Birthday*, edited by Joseph A. Pipa Jr. and C. N. Willborn, 31–55. Taylors, SC: Southern Presbyterian Press, 2004.

Esler, Philip F. "Prototypes, Antitypes and Social Identity in First Clement: Outlining a New Interpretative Model." *Annali di Storia dell'Esegesi* 24 no. 1 (2007): 125–46.

Farkasfalvy, Denis. *Inspiration and Interpretation: A Theological Introduction to Sacred Scripture*. Washington, DC: Catholic University of America Press, 2010.

Ferguson, Everett. *Baptism in the Early Church: History, Theology, and Liturgy in the First Five Centuries*. Grand Rapids: Eerdmans, 2013.

———. "Catechesis, Catechumenate." In *Encyclopedia of Early Christianity*, edited by Everett Ferguson, 223–25. 2nd ed. New York: Routledge, 1999.

———. "The Covenant Idea in the Second Century." In *The Early Church at Work and Worship*, vol. 1, *Ministry, Ordination, Covenant, and Canon*, 173–200. Eugene, OR: Cascade Books, 2013.

Fowl, Stephen E. *Engaging Scripture: A Model for Theological Interpretation*. 1998. Reprint, Eugene, OR: Wipf & Stock, 2008.

———. "Virtue." In *Dictionary for Theological Interpretation of the Bible*, edited by Kevin J. Vanhoozer, 837–39. Grand Rapids: Baker Academic, 2005.

Frei, Hans W. *The Eclipse of Biblical Narrative: A Study in Eighteenth and Nineteenth Century Hermeneutics*. New Haven: Yale University Press, 1974.

Gabler, Johann Philipp. "An Oration on the Proper Distinction between Biblical and Dogmatic Theology and the Specific Objectives of Each." In *Old Testament Theology: Flowering and Future*, edited by Ben C. Ollenburger, 498–506. Sources for Biblical and Theological Study 1. Winona Lake, IN: Eisenbrauns, 2004.

Bibliography

Gadamer, Hans-Georg. *Truth and Method*. Translation revised by Joel Weinsheimer and Donald G. Marshall. Rev. ed. New York: Bloomsbury Academic, 2004.

Gamble, Harry Y. *Books and Readers in the Early Church: A History of Early Christian Texts*. New Haven: Yale University Press, 1997.

Genette, Gérard. *Narrative Discourse: An Essay in Method*. Ithaca, NY: Cornell University Press, 1980.

Graham, Susan L. "Irenaeus and the Covenants: 'Immortal Diamond.'" In *Studia Patristica*, vol. 40, *Papers Presented at the Fourteenth International Conference on Patristic Studies, Held in Oxford 2003*, edited by F. Young, M. Edwards, and P. Parvis, 393–98. Leuven: Peeters, 2006.

Grant, Robert. *Irenaeus of Lyons*. Early Church Fathers. New York: Routledge, 1996.

Graves, Michael. *The Inspiration and Interpretation of Scripture: What the Early Church Can Teach Us*. Grand Rapids: Eerdmans, 2014.

Grenz, Stanley J., David Guretzki, and Cherith Fee Nordling. *Pocket Dictionary of Theological Terms*. Downers Grove, IL: InterVarsity, 1999.

Hägglund, Bengt. "Die Bedeutung der 'regula fidei' als Grundlage theologischer Aussagen." *Studia Theologica* 12, no. 1 (1958): 1–44.

Hagner, Donald. *The Use of the Old and New Testaments in Clement of Rome*. Novum Testamentum Supplements 34. Leiden: Brill, 1973.

Harmless, William, ed. *Augustine in His Own Words*. Washington, DC: Catholic University of America Press, 2010.

Harnack, Adolf von. *Bible Reading in the Early Church*. Translated by J. R. Wilkinson. London: Williams & Norgate, 1912.

Hartog, Paul. "The 'Rule of Faith' and Patristic Biblical Exegesis." *Trinity Journal* 28, no. 1 (2007): 65–86.

Hauerwas, Stanley. *A Community of Character: Toward a Constructive Christian Social Ethic*. Notre Dame, IN: University of Notre Dame Press, 1991.

Holmes, Christopher R. J. *A Theology of the Christian Life: Imitating and Participating in God*. Grand Rapids: Baker Academic, 2021.

Hood, Jason B., and Matthew Y. Emerson. "Summaries of Israel's Story: Reviewing a Compositional Category." *Currents in Biblical Research* 11, no. 3 (2013): 328–48.

Jamieson, R. B., and Tyler R. Wittman. *Biblical Reasoning: Christological and Trinitarian Rules for Exegesis*. Grand Rapids: Baker Academic, 2022.

Jefford, Clayton N. *Reading the Apostolic Fathers: A Student's Introduction*. 2nd ed. Grand Rapids: Baker Academic, 2012.

Jowett, Benjamin. "On the Interpretation of Scripture." In *Essays and Reviews*, by Frederick Temple, Rowland Williams, Baden Powell, Henry Bristow Wilson, C. W. Goodwin, Mark Pattison, and Benjamin Jowett, 399–527. 10th ed. London: Longman, Green, Longman, and Roberts, 1862.

Kannengiesser, Charles. *Handbook of Patristic Exegesis: The Bible in Ancient Christianity*. Leiden: Brill, 2006.

Kelly, J. N. D. *Early Christian Doctrines*. Rev. ed. New York: HarperOne, 1978.

Klink, Edward W., III, and Darian R. Lockett. *Understanding Biblical Theology: A Comparison of Theory and Practice*. Grand Rapids: Zondervan Academic, 2012.

Kugel, James L. *Traditions of the Bible: A Guide to the Bible as It Was at the Start of the Common Era*. Cambridge, MA: Harvard University Press, 1999.

Legaspi, Michael C. *The Death of Scripture and the Rise of Biblical Studies*. Oxford Studies in Historical Theology. Oxford: Oxford University Press, 2011.

Levering, Matthew. *Participatory Biblical Exegesis: A Theology of Biblical Interpretation*. Notre Dame, IN: University of Notre Dame Press, 2008.

Lewis, C. S. Preface to *On the Incarnation*, by Saint Athanasius, 9–15. Translated by John Behr. Popular Patristics Series 44a. Yonkers, NY: St Vladimir's Seminary Press, 2011.

———. "They Asked for a Paper." In *Is Theology Poetry?*, 150–65. London: Geoffrey Bles, 1962.

Lindbeck, George A. *The Nature of Doctrine: Religion and Theology in a Postliberal Age*. Louisville: Westminster John Knox, 1984.

———. "The Story-Shaped Church: Critical Exegesis and Theological Interpretation." In *The Theological Interpretation of Scripture: Classic and Contemporary Readings*, edited by Stephen E. Fowl, 39–52. Malden, MA: Blackwell, 1997.

Lyotard, Jean-François. *The Postmodern Condition: A Report on Knowledge*. Translated by Geoff Bennington and Brian Massumi. Theory and History of Literature 10. Manchester: Manchester University Press, 1984.

MacDonald, Nathan. "Israel and the Old Testament Story in Irenaeus' Presentation of the Rule of Faith." *Journal of Theological Interpretation* 3, no. 2 (2009): 281–98.

MacIntyre, Alasdair. *After Virtue: A Study in Moral Theory*. 2nd ed. Notre Dame, IL: University of Notre Dame Press, 1984.

Markschies, Christoph. *Christian Theology and Its Institutions in the Early Roman Empire: Prolegomena to a History of Early Christian Theology*. Translated by Wayne Coppins. Baylor–Mohr Siebeck Studies in Early Christianity. Waco: Baylor University Press, 2015.

Martens, Peter W. *Origen and Scripture: The Contours of the Exegetical Life*. Oxford Early Christian Studies. Oxford: Oxford University Press, 2012.

———. "Revisiting the Allegory/Typology Distinction: The Case of Origen." *Journal of Early Christian Studies* 16, no. 3 (2008): 283–317.

McGowan, Andrew B. *Ancient Christian Worship: Early Church Practices in Social, Historical, and Theological Perspective*. Grand Rapids: Baker Academic, 2014.

McGuckin, John A. *St. Cyril of Alexandria and the Christological Controversy: Its History, Theology, and Texts*. New York: Brill, 1994.

Bibliography

O'Donovan, Oliver. *The Desire of the Nations: Rediscovering the Roots of Political Theology.* Cambridge: Cambridge University Press, 1996.

O'Keefe, John J., and R. R. Reno. *Sanctified Vision: An Introduction to Early Christian Interpretation of the Bible.* Baltimore: Johns Hopkins University Press, 2005.

Pelikan, Jaroslav. *The Emergence of the Catholic Tradition (100–600).* Vol. 1 of *The Christian Tradition: A History of the Development of Doctrine.* Chicago: University of Chicago Press, 1971.

Presley, Stephen O. "Biblical Theology and the Unity of Scripture in Irenaeus of Lyons." *Criswell Theological Review* 16, no. 2 (2019): 25–48.

———. *Cultural Sanctification: Engaging the World like the Early Church.* Grand Rapids: Eerdmans, 2024.

———. *The Intertextual Reception of Genesis 1–3 in Irenaeus of Lyons.* Bible in Ancient Christianity 8. Leiden: Brill, 2015.

———. "Origen of Alexandria: Preaching as Edification." In *A Legacy of Preaching,* vol. 1, *Apostles to the Revivalists,* edited by Benjamin K. Forrest, Kevin L. King, Bill Curtis, and Dwayne Milioni, 81–94. Grand Rapids: Zondervan, 2018.

———. "Reading Community: Election, Salvation History, and Christian Identity in 1 Clement." In *"The Teaching of These Words": Intertextuality, Social Identity, and Early Christianity; Essays in Honor of Clayton N. Jefford,* edited by Jonathan A. Draper, Shawn Wilhite, and Nancy Pardee, 251–68. Bible in Ancient Christianity 16. Leiden: Brill, 2024.

Radner, Ephraim. *Time and the Word: Figural Reading of the Christian Scriptures.* Grand Rapids: Eerdmans, 2016.

Reno, R. R. *The End of Interpretation: Reclaiming the Priority of Ecclesial Exegesis.* Grand Rapids: Baker Academic, 2022.

Roberts, Vaughan. *God's Big Picture: Tracing the Storyline of the Bible.* Downers Grove, IL: InterVarsity: 2003.

Rowe, C. Kavin. "Biblical Pressure and Trinitarian Hermeneutics." *Pro Ecclesia* 11, no. 3 (2002): 295–312.

Sanders, Fred. *The Triune God.* New Studies in Dogmatics. Grand Rapids: Zondervan Academic, 2016.

Simonetti, Manlio. *Biblical Interpretation in the Early Church: An Historical Introduction to Patristic Exegesis.* New York: T&T Clark, 1994.

Slusser, Michael. "The Exegetical Roots of Trinitarian Theology." *Theological Studies* 49, no. 3 (1988): 461–76.

Smith, James K. A. *Desiring the Kingdom: Worship, Worldview, and Cultural Formation.* Cultural Liturgies 1. Grand Rapids: Baker Academic, 2009.

Smith, Steven D. *Pagans and Christians in the City: Culture Wars from the Tiber to the Potomac.* Grand Rapids: Eerdmans, 2018.

Stewart-Sykes, Alistair, trans. *Tertullian, Cyprian, and Origen on the Lord's Prayer*. Popular Patristics Series 29. Crestwood, NY: St Vladimir's Seminary Press, 2004.

Swain, Scott R. *The Trinity and the Bible: On Theological Interpretation*. Bellingham, WA: Lexham Academic, 2021.

Taylor, Charles. *A Secular Age*. Cambridge, MA: Belknap Press of Harvard University Press, 2007.

———. *Sources of the Self: The Making of the Modern Identity*. Cambridge, MA: Harvard University Press, 1989.

Trueman, Carl R. *The Rise and Triumph of the Modern Self: Cultural Amnesia, Expressive Individualism, and the Road to Sexual Revolution*. Wheaton, IL: Crossway, 2020.

Urbano, Arthur P. *The Philosophical Life: Biography and the Crafting of Intellectual Identity in Late Antiquity*. Patristic Monograph Series 21. Washington, DC: Catholic University of America Press, 2013.

Watkin, Christopher. *Biblical Critical Theory: How the Bible's Unfolding Story Makes Sense of Modern Life and Culture*. Grand Rapids: Zondervan Academic, 2022.

Wilken, Robert Louis. "Alexandria: A School for Training in Virtue." In *Schools of Thought in the Christian Tradition*, edited by Patrick Henry, 15–30. Philadelphia: Fortress, 1984.

———. *The Spirit of Early Christian Thought: Seeking the Face of God*. New Haven: Yale University Press, 2005.

Williams, Rowan. "Language, Reality, and Desire." *Journal of Literature and Theology* 3, no. 2 (1989): 138–50.

Wright, G. Ernest. *God Who Acts: Biblical Theology as Recital*. London: SCM, 1952.

Yarchin, William. *History of Biblical Interpretation: A Reader*. Grand Rapids: Baker Academic, 2011.

Yeago, David S. "The New Testament and the Nicene Dogma: A Contribution to the Recovery of Theological Exegesis." *Pro Ecclesia* 3, no. 2 (1994): 152–64.

Young, Frances M. *The Art of Performance: Towards a Theology of Holy Scripture*. London: Darton, Longman & Todd, 1990.

———. *Biblical Exegesis and the Formation of Christian Culture*. 1997. Reprint, Peabody, MA: Hendrickson, 2002.

Zimmermann, Jens. *Incarnational Humanism: A Philosophy of Culture for the Church in the World*. Strategic Initiatives in Evangelical Theology. Downers Grove, IL: IVP Academic, 2012.

INDEX OF AUTHORS

Andresen, Carl, 102n26
Andrews, James A., 22n25, 45nn34–35, 61n119
Auerbach, Erich, 71

Bakhtin, Mikhail, 116
Bartholomew, Craig G., 4, 68, 90
Bauckham, Richard, 72
Bebbington, David W., 71nn19–20
Behr, John, 50n56, 111
Bellah, Robert N., 3n1
Billings, J. Todd, 17n8, 20n20, 26, 51n62, 90, 157, 167n82
Blowers, Paul, 25n33, 80
Boersma, Hans, 8n11, 18n12, 19, 71, 124, 126n16, 129
Bradshaw, Paul E., 155n27, 161n60
Breisach, Ernst, 71, 72n24
Brown, Peter, 137n64

Cameron, Averil, 139n71
Carter, Craig A., 19
Childs, Brevard S., 4, 70, 171
Clark, Elizabeth A., 98–99, 115n72, 116–17
Cochrane, Charles Norris, 9n16
Cox, Patricia, 138n66, 139n71

Daley, Brian E., 52, 72
de Lubac, Henri, 40, 54n81, 57, 91n95, 96n7, 97n8, 106n38, 129
Donovan, Mary Ann, 150
Duncan, J. Ligon, III, 85n69

Emerson, Matthew Y., 72n28
Esler, Philip F., 138

Farkasafalvy, Denis, 99, 118
Ferguson, Everett, 152n15
Fowl, Stephen E., 131, 162
Frei, Hans W., 4–5, 69, 73, 74, 75
Frye, Northrop, 171

Gabler, Johann Philipp, 4
Gamble, Harry Y., 158n40, 159, 160nn53–54
Genette, Gérard, 74
Goheen, Michael W., 68, 90
Graham, Susan L., 85n69, 86
Graves, Michael, 52n71, 53n74, 80n52, 135
Grenz, Stanley J., 154n24
Guretzki, David, 154n24

Hägglund, Bengt, 24n28
Hagner, Donald, 85n65
Harmless, William, 130n33
Harnack, Adolf von, 161
Hauerwas, Stanley, 162
Holmes, Christopher R., 46n40
Hood, Jason B., 72n28

Jamieson, R. B., 16n4, 17n7, 38n7, 110n61, 112, 165
Jefford, Clayton, 84n60
Jowett, Benjamin, 51

Kannengiesser, Charles, 136n56
Kelly, J. N. D., 21–22, 25
Klink, Edward W., III, 5
Kristeva, Julia, 116
Kugel, James L., 50n56, 51n64, 53n75

Legaspi, Michael C., 5n7, 9n15, 169–71
Levering, Matthew, 24
Lewis, C. S., 10, 59
Lindbeck, George A., 73
Lockett, Darian R., 5
Lyotard, Jean-François, 70

MacIntyre, Alasdair, 70, 79
Markschies, Christoph, 159n47
Martens, Peter W., 90n92, 98, 124, 164n68
McGowan, 156n31, 157n35, 161n55
McGuckin, John, 91, 101–2

Nordling, Cherith Fee, 154n24

O'Donovan, Oliver, 68n12
O'Keefe, John J., 38n9, 39nn12–13, 40n15, 44n29, 51, 73, 97, 98n13, 115n73, 126n14, 126n17, 130

Pelikan, Jaroslav, 6–7
Presley, Stephen O., 53n76, 84n60, 85n69, 125n6, 138n68

Radner, Ephraim, 155
Reno, R. R., 8n11, 25, 38n9, 39nn12–13, 40n15, 44n29, 51, 73, 97, 98n13, 115n73, 126n14, 126n17, 130, 149, 151, 153n19, 155
Roberts, Vaughan, 68
Rowe, C. Kavin, 38, 39n14, 54

Sanders, Fred, 8–9
Simonetti, Manlio, 150
Slusser, Michael, 101n21
Smith, James K. A., 17n6, 19n15, 28
Smith, Steven D., 9n17
Swain, Scott R., 19

Taylor, Charles, ix, 8, 9, 18, 19, 39, 172
Trueman, Carl R., 3n1

Urbano, Arthur P., 138n66

Vos, Geerhardus, 70

Watkin, Christoper, 3n1
Wilken, Robert Louis, 19n14, 22, 61n122, 135n51, 137n64, 138, 140–42
Williams, Rowan, 44n30
Wittman, Tyler, 16n4, 17n7, 38n7, 110n61, 112, 165
Wright, G. Ernest, 134–35

Yarchin, William, 38
Yeago, David S., 39n14, 117
Young, Frances M., 8n12, 18n11, 25n34, 43, 46n43, 55n85, 116, 130, 135, 136n56, 139n70

Zimmermann, Jens, 59

INDEX OF SCRIPTURE AND OTHER ANCIENT WRITINGS

Old Testament

Genesis

1:1 19n14, 104
2:2 156
11:1–8 2
12:1–2 88
12:1–3 87
14:18 2
15:5 87
22 140
37:23–28 2

Exodus

3:14–15 19n14
12:29 52
20:8–11 156

Numbers

24:17 2
33 125
33:2 125
33:5 125
33:49 125

Deuteronomy

5:12–15 156

Joshua

24:15 21

2 Samuel

7:12 87

2 Kings

2:11 2

Psalms

2:7 100, 104
14:1 27
19:6 51
47:2 16
68:2 51
84:7 125
105:4 20
106:6–46 72
107:9 17
110 103
110:1 43, 104
111:10 137
128 xi
131:11 87
146:5 16

Proverbs

1:7 137
8:22 27
22:20–21 137

Isaiah

7:14 107, 108
11:2 132
11:2–3 131, 132
26:19 109
45:1 104
45:5 19n14, 66
53:1–2 104

Jeremiah

17:9 128
22:22 44
31 87

Ezekiel

37:12–14 109

Daniel

6:10–12 31
7:9–10 81n55
7:13–14 81n55

Hosea

11:1 2
14:9 128n23

Zechariah

11:17 44

New Testament

Matthew

1 83
1:21 100
2:1–2 2
2:15 2
3:17 100
5:3–12 140
5:48 140
7:7 147
12:38–41 2
16:15 32
16:16 100
17:5 100
22:37–40 45, 133
22:41–45 43
23:25 127
26:29 110
26:47–50 2
28:18–20 2
28:19 25, 26

Mark

1:1 100

Luke

1:23 154
3 83
22:19–20 2
24:51 2

193

John

1:1 104, 135
1:1–2 100
1:12 23
1:14 100
4:24 52
5:26 100
10:11 43
13:13 100
13:15 138n68
20:29 57n95

Acts

2:36 100
2:38–42 29
3:22–23 2
7:2–53 72
8:36–39 29
17:24 20
17:24–25 19n14

Romans

1:20 49
5:12–17 2
8:30 16n4
12:11 51
13:9–10 45n34
13:13–14 16

1 Corinthians

1:21 49
2:2 96
2:6 122
2:7 96
2:12–13 96
2:13 40
2:14 39, 44
2:14–15 39
2:15 152
2:16 60, 96
8:1 62n125
8:6 113
10:1–2 2
11:1 138
13:12 16
15:10 154

2 Corinthians

3:16 152
3:18 152
7:1 127, 140n77

Galatians

3:26–27 2
4:22 88
5:22–23 140

Ephesians

1:21 154

Philippians

1:18 166
2:5 60
2:15 87
3:21 16n4

Colossians

1:17 3
4:16 158, 161

1 Thessalonians

5:17 31, 161
5:27 158, 161

1 Timothy

1:5 45n34, 143
4:13 158

2 Timothy

2:4 7
3:16–17 163

Hebrews

1:1–5 100
4:11 138n68
8:5 138n68
9:23 138n68
11 138
11–12 83
11:17–19 2
11:39–40 3, 83
12:14 140n77
13:20 44

James

3:1 165
5:10 138n68

1 Peter

1:13–16 140n77
2:9 10
5:4 44

2 Peter

2:6 138n68

Aristotle

Metaphysics

4.1 19n13

Early Christian Literature

Acts of the Scillitan Martyrs

12 159n43

Ambrose

Exposition of Psalm 118 (119)

8.59 56n92

On the Duties of the Clergy

2.3.8 129n29
24.105–15 84n61
24.112 144n94
24.113 144n95
24.114 144n96
24.115 144n97

Apostolic Church Order

3 160n52

Athanasius

Against the Heathen

1.1 58n99
3.45 58n105, 59n106

Four Discourses against the Arians

2.18.32 27n42

On the Incarnation

57 128n22

Augustine

Against Two Letters

3.6–11 88n83

City of God

11.1 61n121
15.2 88n83
15.2 88n84
16.16 88, 88nn85–86
16.27 89nn88–89
17 89
17.8 89n90
17.9–10 89n91
22.30 17n9

Confessions

1.1.1 16n5
7.18.25 136n54
8.12.28 16nn1–2
8.12.29 16n3

Enchiridion on Faith, Hope, and Love

2 140n76
3 142n84
5 142n85

Exposition of the Psalms

105.36 53n80

First Catechetical Instruction

3.5 77n46, 78n47
3.6 77n45
4.8 45n34, 78n48
6.10 79n50
7.11 78n49

Letter 82

3 61n120

Index of Scripture and Other Ancient Writings

Letter 148
in toto 59n108

Letter 171A
in toto 132n40

Literal Meaning of Genesis
2.5 42n24

On Christian Doctrine
1.1.1 162n66
1.4.4 44n31, 45n32, 49n55
1.5.5 46n38
1.5.5–1.21.19 25n34
1.6 43n26
1.7.7 45n33
1.10.10 49n52, 49n54, 55n86, 131n39
1.11.11–1.15.14 106n41
1.12.11 49n53
1.22.21 45nn36–37, 46n39
1.26.27 45n36, 46n39
1.36.40 142n86
1.38.42 142n87
1.39.43 142n88
1.88 143n89
2.7.9 52n70, 132nn41–42
2.7.9–11 132n40
2.7.10 133nn43–44
2.7.11 133nn45–46
2.8.12 134n47
2.9.14 115n76
4.4.6 166n80
4.5.7 166n81
4.5.8 164n71
4.6.10 164n70
4.27.59 165n77
4.27.60 166n78

On the Creed
1.1 31n54

On the Merits and Forgiveness of Sins
3.7 54n84

On the Proceedings of Pelagius
13–15 88n83

On the Profit of Believing
5 41n22, 42n23

Reply to Faustus the Manichaean
11.5 61n121

Sermon 22
7 51n60, 165n72

Sermon 32
1 130n34

Sermon on the Mount
1.11.32 129n30

Treatise on the Spirit
34–42 88n83
41 89n87

Trinity
1 32n61
1.3.5 20n19
13.2.5 23n27

Basil

Address to Young Men
1 62n124

Against Eunomius
2.23–24 52n68

Exegetic Homilies
10 (on Ps. 1) 130n35
10.1 137n63

Hexameron
1.4 20n21

Letter 2
in toto 131n37

Letter 189
3 58n104

Letter 223
in toto 121n1, 122n2

Letter 283
in toto 56n89

On Christian Ethics
2.2 127n1

Chrysostom

Homilies on First Corinthians
1.23 60n117

Homilies on Genesis 1–17
3.1 115n75

Homilies on Second Corinthians
13 60n116

Homilies on the Gospel according to St. John
37.1 131n36
59.2 50n59

Homily on Genesis 22
33 140n75

On the Priesthood
4.6 165n72
4.8 165n73
4.9 165n76

Clement of Alexandria

Exhortation to the Heathen
9 50n58

Instructor
1.1 135n53
1.2 136n55

Stromata
1 117n83
2.2 57nn94–95
4.25 20n20
6.15 51n66
6.16 164n67
7.7 161n57, 162n63
7.16 51n65, 53n77, 59n107

Clement of Rome

1 Clement
3 84
4 84n62
4–7 84
5 84n63
6 84n64
7 85n65
9–12 85n65
17 138n69
17–18 85n65
45.2–3 50n57

Constitutions of the Holy Apostles

8.22 159n48

Cyprian

Epistle 32
2 160n49

Epistle 33
4 160n50
5 160n51

Index of Scripture and Other Ancient Writings

Cyril of Alexandria

Letter 17
8 113n66
9 112n63
13 112n64
anathema 4 113n66

On the Unity of Christ
133 113n65

Cyril of Jerusalem

Catechetical Lectures
pro.6 56n88
4.17 60n114
5.12 26n35
9.13 58n100
16.4 53n78

Didache
8 31n57, 155n29, 161n61

Didascalia apostolorum
2.28 159n48

Eusebius

Ecclesiastical History
1.2 80n54, 81n55
2.1 108n48
5.24 157n34
6.3 159n42
6.43.11 159n48

Gregory of Nazianzus

On Baptism
4 30nn51–52

Theological Orations
29.19 113n67
29.20 114nn69–70

Gregory of Nyssa

Against Eunomius
1.23 60n118

Catechetical Discourse
24.5–7 52n68

Life of Moses
prologue 139nn72–73, 140n74
2 35n1
2.23 36n4, 37n5
2.24 36n2
2.25 36n3
2.26 37n6
2.91 52n73

On the Holy Trinity
327 58n103

On the Soul and the Resurrection
3 58n101

Gregory Thaumaturgus

Oration and Panegyric Addressed to Origen
2 141nn80–81
9 144n93
11 125nn7–8, 143n91
12 143n90, 143n92

Gregory the Great

Book of Pastoral Rule
10 127n19
11 127n20

Hilary of Poitiers

On the Trinity
1.18 27nn40–41, 46n41
3.26 129n25

Hippolytus

On the Apostolic Tradition
1.12 159n48
17 153n20, 154n23
20–21 153n20
21 29nn48–49, 30n50, 31n56
35 153n20
41 155n28, 156n30
42 153n20

On the Proverbs
1 137n62

Treatise on Christ and the Antichrist
44 110n59

Irenaeus

Against Heresies
1 66n6
1.1.1 65n1
1.2.1 67n8
1.2.4 67n9
1.5.4 66n2, 66n7
1.5.6 66n3
1.6.1 66n4
1.6.2 66n5
1.8.1 47, 47n49, 48nn50–51, 100n20
1.9.4 28n46
1.10.1 25n34
1.22.1 25n34
2.9.1 150n8
2.10.1 47nn45–46
2.10.2 47n44
2.25.1–2 67n10
2.26.1 62n125
2.27.1 59n112, 115n74
2.27.2 59n110, 62n125
2.27.3 141n82
2.28.3 54n83, 62nn125–26
3.3.3 67n11, 82n57
3.4.2 25n34, 87n57
3.6.1 47n47

3.10.3–5 86n71
3.11.8 86nn71–72
3.12.3–15 86n71
3.14.1 157n38, 164n69
3.15.3 87n57
3.16.6 87n57
3.17.2 86n71
4.1–19 86n70
4.4.2 86n71
4.6.4 56n90
4.9.1 86n70
4.9.1–3 86n71
4.11.3 86n71
4.12.2 141n83
4.12.3 86n71
4.15.2 86n71
4.16.1–5 86n71
4.17.1–5 86n71
4.20.5 30n53, 56n91, 109n50
4.20–35 86n70
4.21.3 107n43
4.23.2 154n22
4.23–24 154n21
4.24.1–3 86n71
4.26.1 104n33, 109n51, 110n55
4.28.2 86n71
4.32.1 150n9
4.32.1–2 86n71
4.33.1 152n17
4.33.13 157n37
4.33.14 86n71
4.34.2–4 86n71
4.36.6 86n71
4.36–41 86n70
5.2.3 110n54
5.8.1 124n4
5.9.4 86n71
5.15.1 109n52
5.34.1 86n71
5.36.3 110n53

On the Apostolic Preaching
3 24nn29–30
6 100n19
9–32 82n56
10 87n58
22–24 86n71

Index of Scripture and Other Ancient Writings

30 82n59, 86n74
31–42 86
35 87nn77–78
36 87n79
37 87n80
42–86 103
43 104n32
49 104n29
52 104n31
52–86 107n42
53 107n44
66 108n45, 108n47
86 108n46
89–90 87
90 86n71, 87n81
91 87n82

Jerome

Letter 53
10 58n101

Justin

*Dialogue
with Trypho*
7 56n93, 60n113
31 110n57
49 110n56
126 102n23

First Apology
11 110n58
31 106n36
36 103nn27–28
67 156n32, 158n39

Muratorian
Fragment

20–22 105n35
23–26 105n34

Novatian

On the Trinity
9 25n34

Origen

*Commentary
of Psalms 1–25*
fragment from pref-
ace 118n84

*Commentary
on the Song of
Songs*
prologue 136n59,
137nn60–61

Contra Celsum
1.2 60n115
1.56 106n37
2.27 94n3
2.28 94n4
3.47 56n90
3.51 152n14
3.59 152n16
6.1 93n1
7.7 94n5
7.11 94n2, 95n6
7.42 56n90

*Homilies
on Genesis*
9.1 57nn97–98

Homilies on Luke
1.1 166n79
3.1 55n87

*Homilies
on Numbers*
9.7.5 46n42

27.5.2 125n10,
126n13, 126n15
27.7.7 125n9,
125n11, 126n12

*Homilies on the
Song of Songs*
1.2 129n26

On First Principles
1.pf.2 153n18
1.pf.4 79n51, 102n34,
106n40
1.pf.4–10 25n34
1.pf.8 42n25
2.7.2 40n20
4.2.4 76n40, 137n65
4.2.5 76n40
4.2.6 76n41
4.2.7 40n20
4.2.8 76n42, 97n9
4.2.8–9 52n67
4.2.9 40nn18–19,
52n72, 76n43,
97n10
91 108n49

On Prayer
3.1 85n66
3.2 85n67
7 31nn58–59, 161n62

2 Clement

14.2 159n44

Tertullian

Against Marcion
3.7 110n59

Against Praxeas
2 25nn34–35, 106n39
11 104n30
20 53n79

Apology
21 110n59

*Concerning the
Veiling of Virgins*
1.3 25n34

On Monogamy
11 53n79

On Prayer
23.2 156n33

*On the Resurrec-
tion of the Flesh*
21 54n84

*Prescription
against Heretics*
8 147n1
9 147n2, 148n3
13.1–6 25n34
19 148n4
20 148n5
36 149n6
41 159n48

To His Wife
2.6 161n58

Theophilus
of Antioch

Ad Autolycus
2.38 128n23

INDEX OF SUBJECTS

Abraham, 140
Abrahamic covenant, 86, 87, 88
academic study of Scripture, 7, 170
Acts of the Scillitan Martyrs, 159
Adamic covenant, 86, 87
Aeon, 65
aetiology, 41
Alexandria, catechetical school in, 61
allegorical interpretation, 42, 95
allegorical-typology distinction, 97–99
allegory, 12, 41, 55, 96–97, 98
Ambrose, 15, 56, 84n61, 129, 139, 140n75, 144
anagogical sense, 42
analogy, 41
anthropomorphisms, 52
antitypes and prototypes, 138
Apostles' Creed, 31
Apostolic Church Order, 160
apostolic testimony, 148, 150, 153
Aquinas, Thomas, 41, 42
Arianism, 20
Arians, 27
Aristotle, 18–19
Athanasius, 27, 57–59, 128
atheism, 20
Augustine, 10, 20n19, 41–46, 53, 54, 55n86, 56, 59, 106, 162
    on authority of Scripture, 60–61, 129
    church library of, 159
    covenantal narrative of, 87–89
    on intense familiarity with the text, 115
    on Job, 140
    on narrative of Scripture, 77–79
    on preaching, 164–65, 166

on purity of the mind, 49
on rule of faith, 31, 100, 101, 173
on Scripture as medicine, 130
on Scripture as very face of God, 51
on semiotics, 43, 116, 173
on stages of sanctification, 131–34
on telos of biblical interpretation, 15–17, 32
on theological virtues, 141–43
on two senses of faith, 23
on virtuous life of Christ, 135–36
Aurelius the Confessor, 159–60

baptism, 28–29, 30, 31, 151
Basil of Caesarea, 20, 35, 52, 56, 58, 61–62, 121–22, 124, 127, 130–31, 137nn62–63, 145
beatific vision. *See* beholding the glory of God
Beatitudes, 140
beholding the glory of God, 12, 16–17, 37, 45, 46, 49, 124, 134, 172, 175
biblical interpretation
    and faith, 24
    fixation on method, 17, 32
    as journey toward beatitude, 124
    and metaphysics, 18–21
    methodological diversity in, 5–6
    as participating in the narrative of Scripture, 77
    and pursuit of virtue, 123, 127–31, 145
    requires divine assistance, 55–58
    and sanctification, 145
    as stepping into the world of the text, 90, 115
    worthy of God, 38, 50, 51–52, 55, 63, 101, 163, 173
biblical studies, atomizes Scripture, 92
biblical theology

199

200 Index of Subjects

in the church, 150
and preaching, 150
premodern vision of, 3
and the spiritual life, 124–31
and vision of the good life, 123
See also ecclesial biblical theology
burning bush, 36–37, 62

cardinal virtues, 140, 143–45
catchwords, in narratives of Scripture, 84
catechesis, 21, 33, 141, 150–54, 162, 167, 176
  forges a culture of exegesis, 153
  involves doctrinal and moral teaching, 153
  and narrative of Scripture, 77–79
Celsus, 40, 93, 106, 118
chant, 160
character, 135, 162, 175
Christendom, 9
Christian social imaginary, 49, 163. *See also*
  early Christian social imaginary
Christian view of history, 71–72
Christlikeness, 126–27, 134, 145, 175
Christological interpretation, 90–91, 114–19
Christological prophecy and fulfillment,
  104–10
Chrysostom, John, 50, 60, 115, 130, 140, 154,
  165
church
  arena for reading the Bible, 13
  as bookish community, 161
  as bride of Christ, 149
  as community of character, 162
  liturgical life of, 151
  proper setting for biblical theology, 148–49,
    176
Church of Saint-Germain-des-Prés, 1–4, 14,
  169, 176
Cicero, 144
circumcision, 88, 89
city image, 89–90
cleansing, 49
Clement of Alexandria, 20n20, 50, 51, 53, 57,
  59, 117–18, 135, 136, 141, 161, 164
Clement of Rome, 50, 83–84, 85n65, 138
communal reading, 157–60
communicatio idiomatum, 100, 111, 175
congregational libraries, 158–59
Constantine, 154, 156
Constitutions of the Holy Apostles, 29n47
consummation, 76
corporeal and spiritual things, 55
counsel of compassion, 133

covenantal narrative of Scripture, 55, 83, 85–89
covenants, 70
creation, 11, 25, 76
creation, incarnation, redemption, and consummation metanarrative, 76
critical biblical scholars, 92
cultural engagement, ix
cultural liturgies, 28
Cyprian, 31n60, 159–60
Cyril of Alexandria, 112–13
Cyril of Jerusalem, 25–26, 53, 55–56, 58, 60,
  153

daily prayer, 155, 161
daily study of Scripture, 57
David, 144
Davidic covenant, 86, 87, 89
deductive exegesis, 26
Definition of Chalcedon, 111
deism, 20, 21
Demiurge, 66
Descartes, René, 3–4, 14, 169, 170
devotional life, 31
Didache, 31, 155, 161n61
Diocletian persecution, 121, 158
divine attributes, 24–25
divine Author, 41
divine processions and missions, 24
dying to the world, 133

early Christian social imaginary, 8–9, 122, 171,
  172
earthly city, 88–89
Easter, dating of, 156–57
ecclesial biblical theology, x, 7, 10, 13, 150,
  170, 172
Ecclesiastes, 136–37
edification, 176
Enlightenment philosophy, 69–70
enoptics, 136
eschatological sense, 99
ethics, 136
Eucharist, 29–30, 151
Eusebius, 80–81, 108, 157n34, 159n42, 159n48
exegesis, and knowledge, 134
exemplars of virtue in Scripture, 123
expressive individualism, 3

faith, 141
  and biblical interpretation, 24
  and biblical theology, 32
  and reason, 62

Index of Subjects

faithfulness, 134
fasting, 31, 161
fear of the Lord, 130, 132, 140
fides qua creditur, 22–23
fides quae creditur, 22–23
figural readings, 41, 42, 91, 98. *See also* allegory
Flandrin, Hippolyte, 1–3
fortitude, 132, 133, 143–45
fourfold method of interpretation, 41–42
French Revolution, 1
fruit of the Spirit, 140

genealogies of Jesus, 83
general revelation, 62
glory of God. *See* beholding the glory of God
Gnostics, 22, 26, 46–48, 65–67, 91, 104, 109–10, 147
God
  ad intra and ad extra, 54
  attributes, 24–25
  beauty of, 45
  as divine Author, 41
  as divine Physician, 130
  nature of, 11
  ontology of, 98
  processions and missions, 24
  relationship with the world, 11
  work within divine economy, 98
"God-fittingness" of interpretation, 52
godliness, 124, 128, 132, 145
"gods" in Scripture, 47
good life. *See* virtue
Greek philosophy, 57, 60, 93, 136, 141
Gregory of Nazianzus, 30, 113–14, 121
Gregory of Nyssa, 35–37, 46, 52, 58, 60, 73–74, 129, 139–40, 154
Gregory Thaumaturgus, 61n123, 125, 141, 143–44
Gregory the Great, 127, 139

heart, deceitfulness of, 128
Heavenly City, 88–89
heresies, heretics, 46, 147–48, 166
hermeneutical methods, 17
hermeneutic of piety, 52
Hilary of Poitiers, 27, 46, 129
Hippolytus, 29–30, 31, 110n59, 137, 153n20, 154n23, 159n48
historia, 13. *See also* literal sense
history, 41
holiness, 123, 134
Holy Spirit

illumines biblical interpretation, 40, 55–58
inspiration of Scripture, 103
intended spiritual sense to be difficult to ascertain, 42
reveals secret and hidden wisdom, 96
Homer, 71
homeward journey, 49–50
homo liturgicus, 16–17
human author, 103
humans, created for God, 16–17
humility, in biblical interpretation, 129, 145
hypostatic union, 100, 111

idiom, 111–12
illumination, 30, 56–57, 62
imitation of saints in the Scriptures, 128, 131, 138, 158
immanent frame, 39
incarnation, 76, 112
intensive reading, 115
interpretation. *See* biblical interpretation
intertextuality, 11, 68, 82–83, 91, 98, 115, 116–17
Irenaeus, 21n23, 22, 24, 26, 28n46, 30, 46–48, 54, 56, 59n110, 59n112, 62, 65–67, 91, 100, 124n4, 150, 152, 157, 164n69
  covenantal narrative of, 85–87
  on fulfillment of prophecy in life of Christ, 107–8
  on meditation on Scripture, 115
  prosopological exegesis, 103–4
  on rule of faith, 100, 173
  on salvation history, 81–82
  on second coming of Christ, 109–10
  on theological virtues, 141

jealousy, as thematic narrative, 84
Jerome, 58
Jesus Christ
  brings about unity of Scripture, 96–97
  center of ecclesial biblical theology, 174
  first advent of, 107–9
  genealogies of, 83
  and the Old Testament, 2
  person and work of, 95
  as premier example of the virtuous life, 135, 140, 145
  resurrection of, 25
  second advent of, 109–10
  as true Davidic King, 87
  two natures of, 100, 101, 111–13, 174
  work of, 25

Job, 140, 144
Joseph, 144
journey motif, 124
judgments, and concepts, 117
justice, 143–45
Justin Martyr, 56, 60, 102, 103, 105–6, 110, 156, 158

kingdom of God, 25, 77
knowledge, 132–33

lectio continua, 158
life of Christ, 13
literal sense, 11, 40–41, 42, 67–69, 73, 75, 90–91, 95, 96, 139
liturgical calendar, 155
liturgical time, 156
liturgy, 10, 18, 167, 172, 176
  of John Chrysostom, 169–70
  reinforces faith, 30
  reinforces rule of faith, 33
  and Scripture, 28–32, 154–60
Lord's Prayer, 31
love, 141–43
  as end of exegesis, 44–46, 48
  for God and neighbor, 46, 78, 133, 176
  as purpose of biblical narrative, 78
  of this world, 133
lovers of virtue, 141

Macrina, 35, 58, 121
Manicheans, 15
Marcion, 22
Marcionites, 147
marital imagery, 26
meditation, 114
memorization, 114
metanarratives, as oppressive, 70
metaphysics, and biblical interpretation, 18–21, 98, 116
mimesis, 139
mind of Christ, 60, 96
modern biblical theology, struggles with Wisdom literature, 134–35
modern exegesis, without rule of faith, 21
modernity, 170
Monarchianism, 20
Monica, 15
Mosaic covenant, 86, 89
mosaic image (Irenaeus), 48

Moses
  life of, 139
  narrative of, 71
  as paradigm for true spiritual life, 36–37
Muratorian Fragment, 105
music imagery, 116

narration, 74
narrative of salvation history, 11, 67–69, 95, 173
  as Christologically conceived, 90–91
  in the early church, 71–73
  loss of, 69–70
  as multilayered, 82–91
  See also literal sense
new covenant, 87, 88
Nicene Creed, 35, 153
Noah, 140
Numbers, 125–26

Old Testament
  illustrations of wisdom in, 138–40
  relationship to the New Testament, 5
On the Apostolic Tradition (Hippolytus), 29–30, 31, 153, 154, 155–56
"one right reading," 150
Origen, 31, 40–41, 42n25, 46, 51–52, 55, 57, 90, 102, 106, 108, 117–18, 161, 164, 166
  on biblical interpretation as a spiritual exercise, 124–26, 128, 129
  on catechesis, 61, 141, 152–53
  Contra Celsum, 56n90, 60n115, 93–95
  misunderstandings of his exegesis, 98
  on narrative of Scripture, 76, 79–80, 82
  on prayer, 85
  on rule of faith, 101
  on virtues, 143
  on Wisdom Books, 136–37

paganism, ix
pagan literature, 60–61
pantheism, 20, 21
parables, 54
paraenetic exegesis, 136, 139
participating in the narrative of Scripture, 75, 77, 82, 91
partitive reading, 99, 100–101, 111–14, 174
partitive strategy, 12
pastoral office, 127
patient endurance, as thematic narrative, 84–85
Paul
  on Mars Hill, 20
  vice lists, 123

Index of Subjects

Paulinus, bishop of Rome, 58
person, 101
personal, 12
personal reading, 99, 100–104, 174
phenomenology, 39
Philo, 35
philosophy, study of, 61. *See also* Greek philosophy
physics, 136
piety, 132
pilgrim, 124
Plato, 60, 93
polytheism, 20, 21
postmodern hermeneutics, 5, 20–21
postmodernism, 70–71, 77, 92
Praxeas, 22
prayer, 31, 85
preaching, 162–67, 176
premodern interpretation of Scripture, 7, 74
pride, 130, 147
proclamation, 150
prophecy, and figural reading, 91
prophetic fulfillment, 55
prophetic reading, 12, 42, 99–101, 104–10, 174
prophets, life of, 94
prosopological exegesis, 102–3, 174
prototypes and antitypes, 138
Proverbs, 136–37
prudence, 143–45
Psalms, 13, 123, 134, 136, 137, 138, 140, 145
purification, 49, 131, 133
Pythagoras, 60

quadriga, 42
Quartodecimanism controversy, 156–57

reader (office), 159, 160
reading Scripture
  and growing in godliness, 124
  as pursuit of virtue, 126
redemption, 76
resolve, 132, 133
resurrection, 109–10, 152
rule of faith, 10, 17–18, 37, 44–45, 47, 172, 173–74
  as dogmatic summary, 24–27
  as fluid and fixed, 22
  frames reality, 18, 38
  metaphysical restraints of, 147
  narrative character, 24–27, 80
  and personal, prophetic, and partitive readings, 100–101

  as social imaginary, 21
  theological assumptions of, 26–27
rule of love, 44–45, 47
rule of reason, 147

Sabbath, 88, 156
sacraments, 152, 153
sanctification, 123, 163–64
  and biblical interpretation, 145
  journey toward, 124, 125–26, 174
  stages, 131
scriptural narrative, 73–75, 76
Scripture
  as all-encompassing worldview, 77
  authority, 58–62
  and catechesis, 151–54
  coherence, 53
  as community's text, 167
  cultivated vision of life, 172
  as eloquent, 164
  exactness, 116
  exerts pressure on readers, 54
  as God's self-revelation, 38, 50–51
  as guide to life, 136
  as highest source of authority, 50
  historical diversity, 5
  inspiration, 103
  internally consistent, 53–54, 173–74
  interprets Scripture, 38, 50, 53–55, 115, 117–18, 163
  and liturgy, 154–60
  metaphysic embedded in, 27
  private reading, 161, 167
  provides models and principles for the virtuous life, 123
  public reading, 151, 155, 158, 167
  reading fearfully, 52
  requires divine assistance to interpret, 50
  reveals spiritual things, 63
  as revelation, 44
  and rule of faith, 18–21
  and spiritual life, 32
  superiority over pagan literature, 60–61
  theological unity, 5
  totalizing discourse, 72
  unity, 7–8, 96–97
Scripture's hypothesis, 21n24
Second Ecumenical Council (Constantinople), 35
secularism, ix
semiotics, 37, 43, 116, 173
sensus carnis, 129

sensus spiritus, 129. *See also* spiritual sense
Sermon on the Mount, 123, 135
shepherd, as sign, 43–44
shopping mall, as cultural liturgy, 28
signs (*signa*) and things (*res*), 37, 43, 46, 116, 173
Sinai, Mount, 89
social imaginary, ix, 8, 18, 19, 172
sojourner, 124
Solomon, 89
Son, as Second Person of the Trinity, 99–100, 102
Song of Songs, 136–37
Son of God, 101–4
Sophia, 66
spiritual disciple, 152
spiritual perception, 94–95
spiritual sense, 12, 37, 38–42, 63, 95–98, 173–75
   text and referent, 42–46
   transcends the literal, 96
spirit of the world, 96
story, 70, 74
sun imagery, 128

teleological sense, 98
telos, of biblical interpretation, 17
temperance, 143–45
Tertullian, 22, 31n60, 53, 54, 102, 106, 110n59, 147–49, 156, 159n48, 161, 167
   prosopological exegesis, 103–4
   on rule of faith, 101

thematic narrative, 83–85
theological interpretation of Scripture, 5
theological metaphysics, 19
theological virtues, 140–42
Theophilus of Antioch, 128
theoria, 139. *See also* spiritual sense
Thomas Aquinas, 41, 42
transitory things, 126, 133
traveler, 124
Trinity, 9, 19, 152
tritheism, 20
tropological, 42, 98, 99
two-advent hermeneutic, 12, 100, 105–10, 174
typological reading, 42, 95
typology, 12, 55, 91, 96–97, 98

understanding, 132, 133–34
use (*uti*) and enjoyment (*fui*), 44–45

Valens, Emperor, 35
Valentinians, 65
virtue, 12, 13, 119, 121–31, 175

wedding vows, 23
whole counsel of God, 134
wisdom, 132, 134
Wisdom literature, 13, 123, 134, 136–38, 140, 145
worldview, 19
worship. *See* liturgy